CALIFORNIA
REAL ESTATE
SALES EXAM

CALIFORNIA REAL ESTATE SALES EXAM

Second Edition

LEARNINGEXPRESS®

NEW YORK

Library of Congress Cataloging-in-Publication Data:
California real estate sales exam.— 2nd ed.
    p. cm.
  ISBN 1-57685-513-9
     1. Real estate agents—Licenses—California—Examinations, questions, etc.
2. Real estate business—Licenses—California—Examinations, questions, etc.
HD278.C35 2004
333.33'09794—dc22

                                         2004001214

Printed in the United States of America

9 8 7 6 5 4 3 2 1

Second Edition

ISBN 1-57685-513-9

For more information or to place an order, contact LearningExpress at:
  55 Broadway
  8th Floor
  New York, NY 10006

Or visit us at:
  www.learnatest.com

About the Contributors ▶

Allan Nuttall is currently active in the real estate industry handling mortgages and selling properties for the past fourteen years. He is also in charge of the Real Estate Department for a community college, Skyline College, located in the peninsula area of San Francisco.

Craig Luna has been an adjunct faculty member at Long Beach City and Glendale Community Colleges for the last five years. He has been employed with the City of Los Angeles since 1987, and is currently the Director of Real Estate for the Los Angeles Department of Water and Power. Craig is a licensed real estate broker and holds a B.S. and Masters degree in Business Administration.

Robert Rooks' career in real estate began in sales in 1976. Since 1991, he has owned and operated Robert Rooks & Associates, a full service brokerage and management firm. He is a long-time member of the California Association of Realtors, National Association of Realtors, and the California Real Estate Educators Association (CREEA). In addition to being an elected CREEA board member, he continues his role as both real estate broker and educator.

Sherry Shindler Price has been a California Community College real estate instructor since 1986. She has also used her extensive knowledge to write test questions for state licensing examinations in Nevada, Wisconsin, Minnesota, Maryland, and Iowa. Sherry has also authored *California Real Estate Principles, Escrow Principles and Practices,* and *Real Estate Finance,* and written numerous continuing education courses for private real estate schools.

Robert Abelson, Ph.D. is a California Certified General Real Estate Appraiser and has been in real estate appraisal practice for over ten years. He is a member of the California Real Estate Educators Association (CREEA) and the El Camino College Real Estate Advisory Committee. He is co-revision author of the California Community

Colleges' *Real Estate Appraisal Instructor and Student Study Guides* and has served as a review editor for other real estate publishers.

Edwin Estes, J.D. has been a REALTOR® for nineteen years. He holds the designations of Graduate, REALTORS Institute (GRI), Senior Real Estate Specialist (SRES), and Certified Commercial Investment Member (CCIM). He is a Master Instructor for the California Association of REALTORS, has taught for National University School of Law, University of Phoenix, and Palomar College. Currently, he is the Director of Training for One Source Realty GMAC in San Diego, California.

Harry Mason is an educational consultant, real estate instructor, and public school teacher. He earned a B.A. from the University of Arizona, and did his graduate work at Chapman University. He is State Certified in Technology Education and Real Estate.

Chris Grover holds a Bachelor's degree in Finance and a Masters degree in Business Administration. He has been a licensed salesperson since 1972, and a licensed broker since 1975. Currently, he is Department Chairman of Business Real Estate at Victor Valley College and has taught real estate courses in real estate principles, practices, finance, marketing, economics, and property management.

Contents

CALIFORNIA
REAL ESTATE
SALES EXAM

1 ▶ The California Real Estate Sales Exam

CHAPTER SUMMARY

A career in real estate sales can be challenging, rewarding, and profitable. California's explosive growth in population and economic wealth make real estate a dynamic field. Licensed, knowledgeable, and qualified salespeople are in high demand. This is great news for you, since you have already decided that you want to get your real estate sales license.

NOW YOU NEED to pass the salesperson exam. But becoming a licensed salesperson in California requires more than simply passing the exam. There are many other steps you must complete (before and after the exam) in order to arrive at your ultimate goal—receiving your real estate salesperson license. This chapter will guide you through these steps, including: the prerequisites; the exam application process; the exam content and format; and the sales license application process.

This chapter also serves as a guide for using this book effectively. LearningExpress wants you to succeed, so use this book to maximize your preparation for your upcoming exam.

▶ Who Needs to Take the California Real Estate Salesperson Exam?

Each month thousands of people take the California Real Estate Salesperson Exam. Anyone wishing to make official, licensed real estate transactions in California must have a valid California Real Estate Salesperson License and be employed by a broker licensed by the State of California. You will need to take this exam if:

- you are applying for an original license
- your previous California Salesperson License has been expired for at least two years
  OR
- your suspended conditional license has expired due to noncompletion of required courses

The State of California does not have reciprocity with any other state, meaning California does not honor out-of-state real estate licenses.

Note: You may obtain your salesperson license without being employed by a licensed broker; however, you may not legally perform licensed transactions during that time.

▶ Eligibility Requirements

The Department of Real Estate (DRE) requires that all examinees and licensees meet the following minimum requirements:

- **Age**—You must be at least 18 years old.
- **Legal Presence**—You must be a citizen of the United States or be a lawfully admitted alien. *You do not need to be a California resident to have a California Salesperson License.*
- **Honesty**—You must be completely honest and truthful. Failure to include complete and accurate information may be grounds for denial of your application. Convictions of felony or morally questionable crimes may also be cause for denial and must be included on your application. Please see the "Help Avoid Denial of Your License Application" and the "Application Eligibility Information" sections on the DRE website (www.dre.ca.gov).
- **Education**—You must meet the DRE's education requirements, described later in this chapter.
- **No experience is required.**

Important Contact Information

If you have Internet access, the DRE prefers that you consult their user-friendly website for information: www.dre.ca.gov.

If you do not have Internet access, or if you are unable to get your question(s) answered on the website, please contact:

Examination Questions
DRE Examinations Office
P.O. Box 187001
Sacramento, CA 95818-7001
Phone: 916-227-0900
Fax: 916-227-0925

Licensing Questions
DRE Salesperson Inquiries & Licensing Information
P.O. Box 187003
Sacramento, CA 95818-7003
Phone: 916-227-0931
Fax: 916-227-0925

▶ Education Requirements

Before you even apply for the exam, you must have completed a three semester-unit or four quarter-unit, college-level course in Real Estate Principles. **The DRE requires that you provide evidence (i.e. official transcripts) of successful completion of the Real Estate Principles course when submitting your exam application.**

Either with your exam application or your license application you must include transcripts for *two additional* three semester-unit or four quarter-unit college-level courses in: Real Estate Practice and one of the following courses:

- Real Estate Appraisal
- Property Management
- Real Estate Finance
- Real Estate Economics
- Legal Aspects of Real Estate
- Real Estate Office Administration
- General Accounting
- Business Law
- Escrows
- Mortgage Loan Brokering and Lending
- Computer Applications in Real Estate

Should you require more time to complete these two courses, you may take an additional 18 months after applying for your license to fulfill the requirement, in which case you will only be granted a conditional license.

All three of the required courses must be completed through accredited colleges or universities, or through DRE-approved private course sponsors. Fortunately, many colleges and universities in California have recognized the demand for these courses. Approved courses are offered at most community colleges, University of California campuses, and California State University campuses.

All questions regarding courses taken at foreign institutions, private vocational real estate schools outside of California, or correspondence schools, should be directed to the DRE Examinations Office.

Exemptions

1. If you have graduated from any law school recognized by the California State Bar, or if you are a member of the bar in any state in the United States, you may qualify for exemption from the above education requirements.
2. If you have completed the eight required college-level courses needed for the broker exam, you may also be exempt.

Consult the DRE's website for more information regarding exemptions.

Examination Fees

Original Exam Fee: $25
First Rescheduling Fee: $10
Subsequent Rescheduling Fee: $25
Reexamination Fee: $25
Note: All fees are non-refundable.

▶ Applying for the Exam

After obtaining your *California Salesperson Examination Application* (Form RE 400A) from the DRE website or requesting it by phone, you are ready to begin the application. Fill it out completely and honestly, otherwise you may experience long delays, or worse—rejection. You will have the opportunity to request a schedule date, however, the DRE cannot guarantee your request. The schedule of upcoming exam dates is available on the DRE website. The DRE schedules exams for the first available date on or after the date you requested. So, it is generally a good idea to be prepared for the exam before submitting your application, or at least select a date that is far enough in advance to allow you adequate time to study.

Exams are given in the following cities:

- Fresno
- Los Angeles
- Oakland
- Sacramento
- San Diego

Exams are generally given at many different locations within each city. Exam locations and dates vary, due to changes in demand, availability, and other factors. The DRE will schedule your exam in the city you request, but will not accept any requests for a specific test site within that city.

Along with your completed exam application, include:

- official transcripts for your completed Real Estate Principles course. If available, you should also include the transcripts for the other two courses at this time.
- a check or money order payable to the Department of Real Estate in the amount of $25 (See procedures for credit card payments below.) Never mail cash.
- a letter describing your disability and request at this time, if you require special accommodations for a disability.
- a *Consent to Service of Process* (Form RE 234, available online), if you are an out-of-state applicant.

Mail your completed application and accompanying materials to:

Department of Real Estate
Examination Section
P.O. Box 187001
Sacramento, CA 95818-7001

Any changes to your application (e.g. a name change, a new address) must be submitted to the DRE in writing.

Allow six to seven weeks to receive your *Examination Schedule Notice*—this will inform you of your scheduled exam date, time, and location. You will also need to present your *Examination Schedule Notice* when you arrive at the exam. You can obtain this information online or by using a touchtone phone on the DRE's interactive voice response system at 916-227-0900.

Once your application is filed, you have up to two years to pass the exam. There is no limit to the number of times that you can take the exam during that time. However, a reexamination fee of $25 applies each time. If you have not successfully completed the exam within the given time frame, you will have to repeat both the application and exam process.

Paying by Credit Card

Credit card payments will **not** be accepted by phone for first-time exam scheduling. You may pay by credit card via fax or mail. Download a credit card payment form from the DRE website or call the Examinations Office to request one by phone.

▶ Exam Content

You will have three hours and fifteen minutes to complete your examination. The exam is multiple-choice, and your answers will be submitted on a Scantron answer sheet.

The law requires that examinees demonstrate adequate reading and writing skills in the English language and the ability to perform basic real estate math computations. Furthermore, examinees must have proficient knowledge of: real estate principles; the responsibilities and obligations of licensed salespersons; and the legal provisions, effects, and consequences of real estate transactions.

The exam covers seven major real estate subject areas:

1. Property Ownership and Land Use Controls and Regulations (approximately 18% of exam)
- Classes of Property
- Property Characteristics
- Encumbrances
- Types of Ownership

- Descriptions of Property
- Government Rights in Land
- Public Controls
- Environmental Hazards and Regulations
- Private Controls
- Water Rights
- Special Categories of Land

2. Laws of Agency (approximately 12% of exam)

- Law, Definition and Nature of Agency Relationships, Types of Agencies, and Agents
- Creation of Agency and Agency Agreements
- Responsibilities of Agent to Seller/Buyer as Principal
- Disclosure of Agency
- Disclosure of Acting as Principal or Other Interest
- Termination of Agency
- Commission and Fees

3. Valuation and Market Analysis (approximately 12% of exam)

- Value
- Methods of Estimating Value

4. Financing (approximately 13% of exam)

- General Concepts
- Types of Loans
- Sources of Financing
- How to Deal with Lenders
- Government Programs
- Mortgages/Deeds of Trust/Notes
- Financing/Credit Laws
- Loan Brokerage

5. Transfer of Property (approximately 9% of exam)

- Title Insurance
- Deeds
- Escrow
- Reports
- Tax Aspects
- Special Processes

6. Practice of Real Estate and Mandated Disclosures (approximately 24% of exam)

- Trust Account Management

- Fair Housing Laws
- Truth in Advertising
- Record Keeping Requirements
- Agent Supervision
- Permitted Activities of Unlicensed Sales Assistants
- DRE Jurisdiction and Disciplinary Actions
- Licensing, Continuing Education Requirements, and Procedures
- California Real Estate Recovery Fund
- General Ethics
- Technology
- Property Management/Landlord-Tenant Rights
- Commercial/Industrial/Income Properties
- Specialty Areas
- Transfer Disclosure Statement
- Natural Hazard Disclosure Statements
- Material Facts Affecting Property Value
- Need for Inspection and Obtaining/Verifying Information

7. Contracts (approximately 12% of exam)
- General
- Listing Agreements
- Buyer Broker Agreements
- Offers/Purchase Contracts
- Counteroffers/Multiple Counteroffers
- Leases
- Agreements
- Promissory Notes/Securities

Note: The above list was composed by the DRE and should be viewed as a general guide, not as comprehensive list of exactly what will be covered on the test. In other words, some of these areas may not be covered on the test, while there may be questions on the test that were not mentioned in the above list.

Number of Questions

You may be wondering, "Just how many questions are on the exam?" Unfortunately, that is something we cannot answer for you. The DRE does not reveal the exact number of test questions that will be on the salesperson exam. Regardless of the number of questions on your exam, you must get a minimum of 70% of those questions correct to pass the exam.

► Real Estate Math

If you are worried about the math that will be covered on the exam, relax. The math problems on the exam will not be terribly complex, and they will *all* relate to real estate, so you may have already tackled problems like these in your real estate courses. Plus, LearningExpress understands that math can intimidate many people, especially on exams, so Chapter 5 in this book is devoted to reviewing real estate math to help you brush up on math skills.

Also, you will not be expected to figure out these problems entirely in your head. You will be provided with scratch paper at the exam, and you are allowed to bring a calculator with you. Remember to take the problem step-by-step, reading it carefully and using your scratch paper to set up the problem before you start punching in numbers.

Calculators

The calculator you bring to the exam must be a pocket-sized, silent, battery-operated, electronic calculator with no printing capability or alphabetic keyboard. It is a good idea to bring a calculator that you are already familiar with using and make sure you have extra batteries.

► Exam Day

Try to get a good night's sleep the night before the exam, and allow plenty of time in the morning to get to your exam location, especially if you are unfamiliar with the area. Allow plenty of time to get there early (at least 30 minutes before your exam) in order to sign in, present your identification and *Examination Schedule Notice*, and get yourself settled.

You must bring:
1. a valid picture I.D. (such as a driver's license or passport) and your *Examination Schedule Notice*
2. a calculator (see the calculator specifications on page 8, or double-check on the DRE website)

You will be provided with:
1. a Scantron answer sheet
2. a #2 pencil
3. scratch paper

There will be a designated area for placing cell phones/pagers (which must be turned off), purses, bags, books, food, and other prohibited items. You may not bring your children or anyone else with you into the exam room. You may keep bottled water at your desk.

Using a Scantron

At one time or another during high school, college, or your real estate courses, you have probably taken a multiple-choice test on a Scantron answer sheet. If not, don't worry. Instructions on how to use a Scantron sheet will be described to you at the exam.

Rescheduling an Exam

To reschedule your exam, fill out and return your *Examination Schedule Notice* or an *Examination Change Application* (Form RE 415A) with the appropriate fee ($10 for the first time and $25 for each subsequent time you reschedule) to the DRE Examinations Office. Credit card payments are accepted by fax, mail, or (unlike with your original exam application) you can submit credit card payments by phone at 916-227-0900.

Exam Results

All examinees must correctly answer 70% or more of the questions to pass the exam. You will only be notified of your exact score and number of questions you answer correctly if you do **not** pass the exam. Your results will be mailed to you on an *Examination Result Notice* within approximately five working days following your exam. Results are also usually available online or by touchtone phone on the interactive voice response system at 916-227-0900 after five business days.

When you pass your exam, you will be notified by mail and receive an *Application for Salesperson License*. You will also be sent the appropriate fingerprinting forms or cards. Upon passing the exam, you will have one year to apply for your license and submit your fingerprints. Remember, you will not be given your score or the number of questions that you answered correctly.

If you do not receive a passing score, you will be given the opportunity to apply for reexamination. Remember, you can take the exam as many times as needed within the two-year time frame after your original application was processed. If you do not pass, you will be notified of your exact score and the number of questions you answered correctly.

To apply for reexamination, submit your *Examination Result Notice* along with $25 for the reexamination fee to the DRE Examinations Office. As with exam rescheduling, credit card payments are accepted by fax, mail, or phone.

▶ Applying for the California Salesperson License

Once you have passed your salesperson exam you can apply for your license—and you only have one year to do so. Your license application will be mailed to you automatically with your exam results. As with your exam application, you must complete the license application completely and honestly. You will need to submit it with the following:

- proof of legal presence in the United States (such as a birth certificate or resident alien card)
- a properly completed *State Public Benefits Statement* (Form RE 205)

- fingerprints (see following section for details)
- appropriate fees

License Application Fees

If you are submitting the transcripts for the two additional course requirements now, or if you submitted them with your exam application and the Real Estate Principles requirement, your license application fee is $120. However, if you did not submit proof for the remaining two courses with your exam application and are unable to do so now, the fee is $145.

Note: You will only be eligible for an 18-month Conditional License at this time.

Money Saving Tip

If possible, submit proof for the two remaining courses with your exam or license application—you will save $25.

Fingerprinting

The DRE requires that all licensees submit fingerprints. The fee is $56. **California residents** are to submit fingerprints via the California Department of Justice's (DOJ) Live Scan Program. You will be mailed a *Live Scan Service Request Form* with your license application and must follow these procedures:

1. Find a Live Scan service provider on the DOJ's website at: http://caag.state.ca.us/fingerprints/publications/contact.pdf or call the DRE at 916-227-0931. A list of Live Scan providers will also be available at the exam site.
2. Pay the $56 fee directly to the Live Scan provider.
3. After having your fingerprints scanned by a Live Scan provider, complete Part 3 of your *Live Scan Service Request Form* and submit it along with your license application to the DRE.

Out-of-state applicants must submit two official sets of ink fingerprints on the *FBI Applicant Fingerprint Card,* which is mailed to you with your license application.

1. Take both *FBI Applicant Fingerprint Cards* to a local law enforcement agency to have your ink fingerprints taken.
2. Make check or money order payable to the DRE (*not* the local law enforcement agency administering your prints) in the amount of $56.
3. Submit both fingerprint cards along with your license application and check or money order to the DRE.

Note to all applicants: If you are past due on child support payments, you may have restrictions or extra fees assigned to your license. See the special section on the DRE website for Child Support Obligors.

▶ How to Prepare for the Exam

You have made it this far—you have completed at least one or more of the required real estate courses and have made the decision to read this book—so you have already shown that you have the commitment it will take to prepare for the exam. This book is designed to be a valuable tool in preparing you for the big day.

Test-Taking Techniques

Chapter 2, The LearningExpress Test Preparation System, does exactly as the title suggests—it teaches you how to prepare for test effectively. In this chapter, you will learn to:

- set up a realistic study-plan
- use your study time and exam time efficiently
- overcome test anxiety

The best approach for effective studying is to be disciplined, stay on your study schedule, and do not procrastinate.

Study Materials

Utilize all of your study materials. By reviewing information from a variety of sources, you are more likely to cover all of the material that might be included on the exam. This book is a great source of information and can be used as a foundation for your study plan. In addition, the DRE publishes a *Real Estate Law Book* and *Reference Book*, available on their website. Your study materials should also include your notes, exams, and texts from your real estate courses.

▶ Using this Book

In addition to this chapter and the Test Preparation System, this book contains three content and review chapters and four practice exams. We suggest that you take the first practice exam (Chapter 3) before moving on to the content and review material. This way, you will be able to better assess your personal strengths and weaknesses, allowing you to direct your time where you need it the most.

Chapter 4, the California Real Estate Refresher Course, is an overview of real estate concepts and criteria that will be covered on the exam.

Chapter 5 is dedicated to Real Estate Math Review. This chapter reviews the types of problems and computations you will face on the exam, allowing you to practice and polish your math skills.

Chapter 6 is a Real Estate Glossary, providing an excellent list of real estate terminology needed for the exam and your career.

Although you should focus most of your efforts on the areas where you need the most improvement, you should read all of the chapters in this book to ensure that you do not miss out on valuable information. You will find that some of the information and terminology in Chapters 4 through 6 is repeated, but this will only help to reinforce your knowledge.

Use the other three practice tests in the book (Chapters 7, 8, and 9) to gauge your progress as you go along, so you can continue to focus your concentration where needed. As we have already mentioned, the DRE does not disclose the number of questions that will be on future exams. Based on the usual exam content and time allotted for the actual exam, the practice tests in this book each have 150 questions. There is no guarantee that there will be 150 questions on the real exam.

Do not forget about the bonus CD-ROM included with this book. It includes practice questions, so you can practice on a computer if you wish. The CD-ROM is designed to be user-friendly; however, please consult the "How to Use the CD-ROM" section located in the back of the book, should you have any questions.

► Important Note

This book covers the most commonly used key terms and concepts that are likely to be covered on the exam. However, it would be impossible to include everything; thus, we suggest that you utilize a variety of study materials. Please note that real estate laws and regulations change from time to time, so it is important that you be aware of the most up-to-date information (consult the *Real Estate Law Book*, published and available by the DRE). Our book is intended to be just one of the many study tools you will use, and is designed to reinforce and round-out your knowledge of real estate sales. In addition, information about application processes, fees, and practices may change. For the most accurate and up-to-date information, go to www.dre.ca.gov.

► The Path to Success

Each person has his or her own personal goals and individual path to take to achieve those goals. Desire, dedication, and know-how are essential, no matter what path you take. You have already shown that you have the desire and dedication, just by reading this chapter. You are well on your way to a new career in real estate! You have shown that you are serious; now let this book help give you the know-how you need to pass your exam.

2 ▶ The LearningExpress Test Preparation System

CHAPTER SUMMARY

Taking the California Real Estate Sales Exam can be tough. It demands a lot of preparation if you want to achieve a top score. Your career depends on your passing the exam. The LearningExpress Test Preparation System, developed exclusively for LearningExpress by leading test experts, gives you the discipline and attitude you need to be a winner.

FACT: TAKING THE real estate licensing exam is not easy, and neither is getting ready for it. Your future career as a real estate salesperson depends on your getting a passing score, but there are all sorts of pitfalls that can keep you from doing your best on this exam. Here are some of the obstacles that can stand in the way of your success:

- being unfamiliar with the format of the exam
- being paralyzed by test anxiety
- leaving your preparation to the last minute
- not preparing at all!
- not knowing vital test-taking skills: how to pace yourself through the exam, how to use the process of elimination, and when to guess
- not being in tip-top mental and physical shape
- messing up on exam day by arriving late at the test site, having to work on an empty stomach, or shivering through the exam because the room is cold

What's the common denominator in all these test-taking pitfalls? One word: control. Who's in control, you or the exam?

Here's some good news: The LearningExpress Test Preparation System puts you in control. In nine easy-to-follow steps, you will learn everything you need to know to make sure that you are in charge of your preparation and your performance on the exam. Other test-takers may let the test get the better of them; other test-takers may be unprepared or out of shape, but not you. You will have taken all the steps you need to take to get a high score on the real estate licensing exam.

Here's how the LearningExpress Test Preparation System works: Nine easy steps lead you through everything you need to know and do to get ready to master your exam. Each of the steps listed below includes both reading about the step and one or more activities. It's important that you do the activities along with the reading, or you won't be getting the full benefit of the system. Each step tells you approximately how much time that step will take you to complete.

Step 1. Get Information	50 minutes
Step 2. Conquer Test Anxiety	20 minutes
Step 3. Make a Plan	30 minutes
Step 4. Learn to Manage Your Time	10 minutes
Step 5. Learn to Use the Process of Elimination	20 minutes
Step 6. Know When to Guess	20 minutes
Step 7. Reach Your Peak Performance Zone	10 minutes
Step 8. Get Your Act Together	10 minutes
Step 9. Do It!	10 minutes
Total	**3 hours**

We estimate that working through the entire system will take you approximately three hours, though it's perfectly OK if you work faster or slower. If you take an afternoon or evening, you can work through the whole LearningExpress Test Preparation System in one sitting. Otherwise, you can break it up, and do just one or two steps a day for the next several days. It's up to you—remember, you are in control.

▶ Step 1: Get Information

Time to complete: 50 minutes
Activity: Read Chapter 1, "The California Real Estate Sales Exam"

Knowledge is power. The first step in the LearningExpress Test Preparation System is finding out everything you can about the California Real Estate Sales Exam. Once you have your information, the other steps in the Learning-Express Test Preparation System will show you what to do about it.

Part A: Straight Talk About the California Real Estate Sales Exam

Why do you have to take this exam, anyway? You have already been through your pre-license course; why should you have to go through a rigorous exam? It's simply an attempt on the part of your state to be sure you have the knowledge and skills necessary for a licensed real estate agent. Every profession that requires practitioners to exercise financial and fiduciary responsibility to clients also requires practitioners to be licensed—and licensure requires an exam. Real estate is no exception.

It's important for you to remember that your score on the California Real Estate Sales Exam does not determine how smart you are, or even whether you will make a good real estate agent. There are all kinds of things an exam like this can't test: whether you have the drive and determination to be a top salesperson, whether you will faithfully exercise your responsibilities to your clients, or whether you can be trusted with confidential information about people's finances. Those kinds of things are hard to evaluate, while a computer-based test is easy to evaluate.

This is not to say that the exam is not important! The knowledge tested on the exam is knowledge you will need to do your job. And your ability to enter the profession you've trained for depends on your passing this exam. And that's why you are here—using the LearningExpress Test Preparation System to achieve control over the exam.

Part B: What's on the Test

If you haven't already done so, stop here and read Chapter 1 of this book, which gives you an overview of the California Real Estate Sales Exam. Then, go to www.dre.cahwnet.gov and read the most up-to-date information.

▶ Step 2: Conquer Test Anxiety

Time to complete: 20 minutes
Activity: Take the Test Stress Quiz

Having complete information about the exam is the first step in getting control of the exam. Next, you have to overcome one of the biggest obstacles to test success: test anxiety. Test anxiety not only impairs your performance on the exam itself, but also keeps you from preparing! In Step 2, you will learn stress management techniques that will help you succeed on your exam. Learn these strategies now, and practice them as you work through the exams in this book, so they will be second nature to you by exam day.

Combating Test Anxiety

The first thing you need to know is that a little test anxiety is a good thing. Everyone gets nervous before a big exam—and if that nervousness motivates you to prepare thoroughly, so much the better. It's said that Sir Laurence Olivier, one of the foremost British actors of this century, felt ill before every performance. His stage fright didn't impair his performance; in fact, it probably gave him a little extra edge—just the kind of edge you need to do well, whether on a stage or in an examination room.

Test Stress Quiz

You only need to worry about test anxiety if it is extreme enough to impair your performance. The following questionnaire will provide a diagnosis of your level of test anxiety. In the blank before each statement, write the number that most accurately describes your experience.

0 = Never   1 = Once or twice   2 = Sometimes   3 = Often

___ I have gotten so nervous before an exam that I simply put down the books and didn't study for it.

___ I have experienced disabling physical symptoms such as vomiting and severe headaches because I was nervous about an exam.

___ I did not show up for an exam because I was scared to take it.

___ I have experienced dizziness and disorientation while taking an exam.

___ I have had trouble filling in the little circles because my hands were shaking too hard

___ I have failed an exam because I was too nervous to complete it.

___ **Total: Add up the numbers in the blanks above.**

Your Test Stress Score

Here are the steps you should take, depending on your score. If you scored:

0–2: your level of test anxiety is nothing to worry about; it's probably just enough to give you that little extra edge.

3–6: your test anxiety may be enough to impair your performance, and you should practice the stress management techniques listed in this section to try to bring your test anxiety down to manageable levels.

7+: your level of test anxiety is a serious concern. In addition to practicing the stress management techniques listed in this section, you may want to seek additional help.

Above is the Test Stress Quiz. Stop and answer the questions to find out whether your level of test anxiety is something you should worry about.

Stress Management Before the Test

If you feel your level of anxiety getting the best of you in the weeks before the test, here is what you need to do to bring the level down again:

- **Get prepared.** There's nothing like knowing what to expect and being prepared for it to put you in control of test anxiety. That's why you are reading this book. Use it faithfully, and remind yourself that you are better prepared than most of the people taking the test.
- **Practice self-confidence.** A positive attitude is a great way to combat test anxiety. This is no time to be humble or shy. Stand in front of the mirror and say to your reflection, "I am prepared. I am full of self-confidence. I am going to ace this test. I know I can do it." Say it into a tape recorder and play it back once a day. If you hear it often enough, you will believe it.

- **Fight negative messages.** Every time someone starts telling you how hard the exam is or how it's almost impossible to get a high score, start saying your self-confidence messages above. Don't listen to the negative messages. Turn on your tape recorder and listen to your self-confidence messages.
- **Visualize.** Imagine yourself reporting for duty on your first day as a real estate salesperson. Think of yourself talking with clients, showing homes, and best of all, making your first sale. Visualizing success can help make it happen—and it reminds you of why you are going to all this work in preparing for the exam.
- **Exercise.** Physical activity helps calm your body down and focus your mind. Besides, being in good physical shape can actually help you do well on the exam. Go for a run, lift weights, go swimming—and do it regularly.

Stress Management on Test Day

There are several ways you can bring down your level of test anxiety on test day. They will work best if you practice them in the weeks before the test, so you know which ones work best for you.

- **Deep breathing.** Take a deep breath while you count to five. Hold it for a count of one, then let it out on a count of five. Repeat several times.
- **Move your body.** Try rolling your head in a circle. Rotate your shoulders. Shake your hands from the wrist. Many people find these movements very relaxing.
- **Visualize again.** Think of the place where you are most relaxed: lying on the beach in the sun, walking through the park, or whatever. Now close your eyes and imagine you are actually there. If you practice in advance, you will find that you only need a few seconds of this exercise to experience a significant increase in your sense of well-being.

When anxiety threatens to overwhelm you right there during the exam, there are still things you can do to manage the stress level:

- **Repeat your self-confidence messages.** You should have them memorized by now. Say them silently to yourself, and believe them!
- **Visualize one more time.** This time, visualize yourself moving smoothly and quickly through the test answering every question right and finishing just before time is up. Like most visualization techniques, this one works best if you have practiced it ahead of time.
- **Find an easy question.** Find an easy question, and answer it. Getting even one question finished gets you into the test-taking groove.
- **Take a mental break.** Everyone loses concentration once in a while during a long test. It's normal, so you shouldn't worry about it. Instead, accept what has happened. Say to yourself, "Hey, I lost it there for a minute. My brain is taking a break." Put down your pencil, close your eyes, and do some deep breathing for a few seconds. Then you will be ready to go back to work.

Try these techniques ahead of time, and see if they work for you!

▶ Step 3: Make a Plan

Time to complete: 30 minutes
Activity: Construct a study plan

Maybe the most important thing you can do to get control of yourself and your exam is to make a study plan. Too many people fail to prepare simply because they fail to plan. Spending hours on the day before the exam poring over sample test questions not only raises your level of test anxiety, it also is simply no substitute for careful preparation and practice over time.

Don't fall into the cram trap. Take control of your preparation time by mapping out a study schedule. On the following pages are two sample schedules, based on the amount of time you have before you take the California Real Estate Sales Exam. If you are the kind of person who needs deadlines and assignments to motivate you for a project, here they are. If you are the kind of person who doesn't like to follow other people's plans, you can use the suggested schedules here to construct your own.

Even more important than making a plan is making a commitment. You can't review everything you learned in your real estate courses in one night. You have to set aside some time every day for study and practice. Try for at least 20 minutes a day. Twenty minutes daily will do you much more good than two hours on Saturday.

Don't put off your study until the day before the exam. Start now. A few minutes a day, with half an hour or more on weekends, can make a big difference in your score.

Schedule A: The 30-Day Plan

If you have at least a month before you take the California Real Estate Sales Exam, you have plenty of time to prepare—as long as you don't waste it! If you have less than a month, turn to Schedule B.

Time	Preparation
Days 1–4	Skim over the written materials from your training program, particularly noting 1) areas you expect to be emphasized on the exam and 2) areas you don't remember well. On Day 4, concentrate on those areas.
Day 5	Take the first practice exam in Chapter 3.
Day 6	Score the first practice exam. Use "Exam 1 for Review" on page 68 to see which topics you need to review most. Identify two areas that you will concentrate on before you take the second practice exam.
Days 7–10	Study the two areas you identified as your weak points. Don't forget, there is the California Real Estate Refresher Course in Chapter 4, the Real Estate Math Review in Chapter 5, and the Real Estate Glossary in Chapter 6. Use these chapters to improve your score on the next practice test.
Day 11	Take the second practice exam in Chapter 7.
Day 12	Score the second practice exam. Identify one area to concentrate on before you take the third practice exam.
Days 13–18	Study the one area you identified for review. Again, use the Refresher Course, Math Review, and Glossary for help.
Day 19	Take the third practice exam in Chapter 8.
Day 20	Once again, identify one area to review, based on your score on the third practice exam.
Days 20–21	Study the one area you identified for review. Use the Refresher Course, Math Review, and Glossary for help.
Days 22–25	Take an overview of all your training materials, consolidating your strengths and improving on your weaknesses.
Days 26–27	Review all the areas that have given you the most trouble in the three practice exams you have taken so far.
Day 28	Take the fourth practice exam in Chapter 9. Note how much you have improved!
Day 29	Review one or two weak areas by studying the Refresher Course, Math Review, and Glossary.
Day before the exam	Relax. Do something unrelated to the exam and go to bed at a reasonable hour.

Schedule B: The 10-Day Plan

If you have two weeks or less before you take the exam, use this 10-day schedule to help you make the most of your time.

Time	Preparation
Day 1	Take the first practice exam in Chapter 3 and score it using the answer key at the end. Use "Exam 1 for Review" on page 68 to see which topics you need to review most.
Day 2	Review one area that gave you trouble on the first practice exam. Use the California Real Estate Refresher Course in Chapter 4, the Real Estate Math Review in Chapter 5, and the Real Estate Glossary in Chapter 6 for extra practice in these areas.
Day 3	Review another area that gave you trouble on the first practice exam. Again, use the Refresher Course, Math Review, and Glossary for extra practice.
Day 4	Take the second practice exam in Chapter 7 and score it.
Day 5	If your score on the second practice exam doesn't show improvement on the two areas you studied, review them. If you did improve in those areas, choose a new weak area to study today.
Day 6	Take the third practice exam in Chapter 8 and score it.
Day 7	Choose your weakest area from the third practice exam to review. use the Refresher Course, Math Review, and Glossary for extra practice.
Day 8	Review any areas that you have not yet reviewed in this schedule.
Day 9	Take the fourth practice exam in Chapter 9 and score it.
Day 10	Use your last study day to brush up on any areas that are still giving you trouble. Use the Refresher Course, Math Review, and Glossary.
Day before the exam	Relax. Do something unrelated to the exam and go to bed at a reasonable hour.

▶ Step 4: Learn to Manage Your Time

Time to complete: 10 minutes to read, many hours of practice!
Activity: Practice these strategies as you take the sample tests in this book

Steps 4, 5, and 6 of the LearningExpress Test Preparation System put you in charge of your exam by showing you test-taking strategies that work. Practice these strategies as you take the sample tests in this book, and then you will be ready to use them on test day.

First, you will take control of your time on the exam. It's a terrible to know there are only five minutes left when you are only three-quarters of the way through the test. Here are some tips to keep that from happening to *you*.

- **Follow directions.** Read all of the directions carefully and ask questions before the exam begins if there's anything you don't understand.
- **Pace yourself.** Wear a watch to the exam. This will help you pace yourself. For example, when one-quarter of the time has elapsed, you should be a quarter of the way through the test, and so on. If you are falling behind, pick up the pace a bit.
- **Keep moving.** Don't waste time on one question. If you don't know the answer, skip the question and move on. You can always go back to it later.
- **Don't rush.** Though you should keep moving, rushing won't help. Try to keep calm and work methodically and quickly.

▶ Step 5: Learn to Use the Process of Elimination

Time to complete: 20 minutes
Activity: Complete worksheet on Using the Process of Elimination

After time management, your next most important tool for taking control of your exam is using the process of elimination wisely. It's standard test-taking wisdom that you should always read all the answer choices before choosing your answer. This helps you find the right answer by eliminating wrong answer choices. And, sure enough, that standard wisdom applies to your exam, too.

Let's say you are facing a question that goes like this:

Alicia died, leaving her residence in town and a separate parcel of undeveloped rural land to her brother Brian and her sister Carrie, with Brian owning one-quarter interest and Carrie owning three-quarters interest. How do Brian and Carrie hold title?

a. as tenants in survivorship
b. as tenants in common
c. as joint tenants
d. as tenants by the entirety

You should always use the process of elimination on a question like this, even if the right answer jumps out at you. Sometimes the answer that jumps out isn't right after all. Let's assume, for the purpose of this exercise, that you are a little rusty on property ownership terminology, so you need to use a little intuition to make up for what you don't remember. Proceed through the answer choices in order.

So you start with answer **a**. This one is pretty easy to eliminate; this tenancy doesn't have to do with survivorship. Make a note that answer choice **a** is incorrect.

Choice **b** seems reasonable; it's a kind of ownership that two people can share. Even if you don't remember much about tenancy in common, you could tell it's about having something "in common." Make a mental note, "good answer, I might use this one."

Choice **c** is also a possibility. Joint tenants also share something in common. If you happen to remember that joint tenancy always involves equal ownership rights, you mentally eliminate this choice. If you don't, make a note, "good answer" or "well, maybe," depending on how attractive this answer looks to you.

Choice **d** strikes you as a little less likely. Tenancy by the entirety doesn't necessarily have to do with two people sharing ownership. This doesn't sound right, and you have already got a better answer picked out in choice **b**. If you are feeling sure of yourself, you can elimnate this choice.

If you're pressed for time, you should choose answer **b**. If you have the time to be extra careful, you could compare your answer choices again. Then, choose one and move on.

If you are taking a test on paper, like the practice exams in this book, it's good to have a system for marking good, bad, and maybe answers. We're recommending this one:

X = bad
✓ = good
? = maybe

If you don't like these marks, devise your own system. Just make sure you do it long before test day—while you're working through the practice exams in this book—so you won't have to worry about it just before the exam.

Even when you think you are absolutely clueless about a question, you can often use process of elimination to get rid of one answer choice. If so, you are better prepared to make an educated guess, as you will see in Step 6. More often, the process of elimination allows you to get down to only two possibly right answers. Then you are in a strong position to guess. And sometimes, even though you don't know the right answer, you find it simply by getting rid of the wrong ones, as you did in the example above.

Try using your process of elimination on the questions in the worksheet Using the Process of Elimination below. The questions aren't about real estate work; they're just designed to show you how the process of elimination works. The answer explanations for this worksheet show one possible way you might use the process to arrive at the right answer.

The process of elimination is your tool for the next step, which is knowing when to guess.

Using the Process of Elimination

Use the process of elimination to answer the following questions.

1. Ilsa is as old as Meghan will be in five years. The difference between Ed's age and Meghan's age is twice the difference between Ilsa's age and Meghan's age. Ed is 29. How old is Ilsa?
   a. 4
   b. 10
   c. 19
   d. 24

2. "All drivers of commercial vehicles must carry a valid commercial driver's license whenever operating a commercial vehicle." According to this sentence, which of the following people need NOT carry a commercial driver's license?
   a. a truck driver idling his engine while waiting to be directed to a loading dock
   b. a bus operator backing her bus out of the way of another bus in the bus lot
   c. a taxi driver driving his personal car to the grocery store
   d. a limousine driver taking the limousine to her home after dropping off her last passenger of the evening

3. Smoking tobacco has been linked to
   a. increased risk of stroke and heart attack.
   b. all forms of respiratory disease.
   c. increasing mortality rates over the past ten years.
   d. juvenile delinquency.

4. Which of the following words is spelled correctly?
   a. incorrigible
   b. outragous
   c. domestickated
   d. understandible

Answers

Here are the answers, as well as some suggestions as to how you might have used the process of elimination to find them.

1. d. You should have eliminated answer a right away. Ilsa can't be four years old if Meghan is going to be Ilsa's age in five years. The best way to eliminate other answer choices is to try plugging them in to

the information given in the problem. For instance, for answer **b**, if Ilsa is 10, then Meghan must be 5. The difference in their ages is 5. The difference between Ed's age, 29, and Meghan's age, 5, is 24. Does 24 = 2 times 5? No. Then answer **b** is wrong. You could eliminate answer **c** in the same way and be left with answer **d**.

2. c. Note the word *not* in the question, and go through the answers one by one. Is the truck driver in choice **a** "operating a commericial vehicle"? Yes, idling counts as "operating," so he needs to have a commercial driver's license. Likewise, the bus operator in answer **b** is operating a commercial vehicle; the question doesn't say the operator has to be on the street. The limo driver in **d** is operating a commercial vehicle, even if it doesn't have passenger in it. However, the cabbie in answer **c** is *not* operating a commercial vehicle, but his own private car.

3. a. You could eliminate answer **b** simply because of the presence of the word *all*. Such absolutes hardly ever appear in correct answer choices. Choice **c** looks attractive until you think a little about what you know—aren't *fewer* people smoking these days, rather than more? So how could smoking be responsible for a higher mortality rate? (If you didn't know that *mortality rate* means the rate at which people die, you might keep this choice as a possibility, but you would still be able to eliminate two answers and have only two to choose from.) And choice **d** is not logical, so you could eliminate that one, too. And you are left with the correct choice, **a**.

4. a. How you used the process of elimination here depends on which words you recognized as being spelled incorrectly. If you knew that the correct spellings were *outrageous*, *domesticated*, and *understandable*, then you were home free. You probably knew that at least one of those words was wrong!

▶ Step 6: Know When to Guess

Time to complete: 20 minutes
Activity: Complete worksheet on Your Guessing Ability

Armed with the process of elimination, you are ready to take control of one of the big questions in test-taking: Should I guess? The first and main answer is *yes*. Some exams have what's called a "guessing penalty," in which a fraction of your wrong answers is subtracted from your right answers—but the California Real Estate Sales Exam doesn't work like that. The number of questions you answer correctly yields your raw score. So you have nothing to lose and everything to gain by guessing.

The more complicated answer to the question "Should I guess?" depends on you—your personality and your "guessing intuition." There are two things you need to know about yourself before you go into the exam:

- Are you a risk-taker?
- Are you a good guesser?

You will have to decide about your risk-taking quotient on your own. To find out if you are a good guesser, complete the worksheet Your Guessing Ability. Frankly, even if you are a play-it-safe person with lousy intuition, you're still safe in guessing every time. The best thing would be if you could overcome your anxieties and go ahead and mark an answer. But you may want to have a sense of how good your intuition is before you go into the exam.

Your Guessing Ability

The following are ten really hard questions. You are not supposed to know the answers. Rather, this is an assessment of your ability to guess when you don't have a clue. Read each question carefully, just as if you did expect to answer it. If you have any knowledge at all of the subject of the question, use that knowledge to help you eliminate wrong answer choices.

1. September 7 is Independence Day in
   a. India.
   b. Costa Rica.
   c. Brazil.
   d. Australia.

2. Which of the following is the formula for determining the momentum of an object?
   a. $p = mv$
   b. $F = ma$
   c. $P = IV$
   d. $E = mc^2$

3. Because of the expansion of the universe, the stars and other celestial bodies are all moving away from each other. This phenomenon is known as
   a. Newton's first law.
   b. the big bang.
   c. gravitational collapse.
   d. Hubble flow.

4. American author Gertrude Stein was born in
   a. 1713.
   b. 1830.
   c. 1874.
   d. 1901.

5. Which of the following is NOT one of the Five Classics attributed to Confucius?
   a. the I Ching
   b. the Book of Holiness
   c. the Spring and Autumn Annals
   d. the Book of History

6. The religious and philosophical doctrine that holds that the universe is constantly in a struggle between good and evil is known as
   a. Pelagianism.
   b. Manichaeanism.
   c. neo-Hegelianism.
   d. Epicureanism.

7. The third Chief Justice of the U.S. Supreme Court was
 a. John Blair.
 b. William Cushing.
 c. James Wilson.
 d. John Jay.

8. Which of the following is the poisonous portion of a daffodil?
 a. the bulb
 b. the leaves
 c. the stem
 d. the flowers

9. The winner of the Masters golf tournament in 1953 was
 a. Sam Snead.
 b. Cary Middlecoff.
 c. Arnold Palmer.
 d. Ben Hogan.

10. The state with the highest per capita personal income in 1980 was
 a. Alaska.
 b. Connecticut.
 c. New York.
 d. Texas.

Answers

Check your answers against the correct answers below.

1. c.
2. a.
3. d.
4. c.
5. b.
6. b.
7. b.
8. a.
9. d.
10. a.

► How Did You Do?

You may have simply gotten lucky and actually known the answer to one or two questions. In addition, your guessing was more successful if you were able to use the process of elimination on any of the questions. Maybe you didn't know who the third Chief Justice was (question 7), but you knew that John Jay was the first. In that case, you would have eliminated answer **d** and therefore improved your odds of guessing right from one in four to one in three.

According to probability, you should get $2\frac{1}{2}$ answers correct, so getting either two or three right would be average. If you got four or more right, you may be a really terrific guesser. If you got one or none right, you may be a really bad guesser.

Keep in mind, though, that this is only a small sample. You should continue to keep track of your guessing ability as you work through the sample questions in this book. Circle the numbers of questions you guess on as you make your guesses; or, if you don't have time while you take the practice exams, go back afterward and try to remember which questions you guessed on. Remember, on an exam with four answer choices, your chances of getting a right answer is one in four. So keep a separate "guessing" score for each exam. How many questions did you guess on? How many did you get right? If the number you got right is at least one-fourth of the number of questions you guessed on, you are at least an average guesser, maybe better—and you should always go ahead and guess on the real exam. If the number you got right is significantly lower than one-fourth of the number you guessed on, you would, frankly, be safe in guessing anyway, but maybe you would feel more comfortable if you guessed only selectively, when you can eliminate a wrong answer or at least have a good feeling about one of the answer choices.

▶ Step 7: Reach Your Peak Performance Zone

Time to complete: 10 minutes to read; weeks to complete!
Activity: Complete the Physical Preparation Checklist

To get ready for a challenge like a big exam, you have to take control of your physical, as well as your mental, state. Exercise, proper diet, and rest will ensure that your body works with, rather than against, your mind on test day, as well as during your preparation.

Exercise

If you don't already have a regular exercise program going, the time during which you are preparing for an exam is actually an excellent time to start one. And if you are already keeping fit—or trying to get that way—don't let the pressure of preparing for an exam fool you into quitting now. Exercise helps reduce stress by pumping wonderful good-feeling hormones called endorphins into your system. It also increases the oxygen supply throughout your body, including your brain, so you will be at peak performance on test day.

A half hour of vigorous activity—enough to raise a sweat—every day should be your aim. If you are really pressed for time, every other day is OK. Choose an activity you like, and get out there and do it. Jogging with a friend always makes the time go faster, or take a radio.

But don't overdo it. You don't want to exhaust yourself. Moderation is the key.

Diet

First of all, cut out the junk. Go easy on caffeine and nicotine, and eliminate alcohol and any other drugs from your system at least two weeks before the exam. Promise yourself a binge the night after the exam, if need be.

What your body needs for peak performance is simply a balanced diet. Eat plenty of fruits and vegetables, along with protein and carbohydrates. Foods that are high in lecithin (an amino acid), such as fish and beans, are especially good "brain foods."

The night before the exam, you might "carbo-load" the way athletes do before a contest. Eat a big plate of spaghetti, rice and beans, or whatever your favorite carbohydrate is.

Rest

You probably know how much sleep you need every night to be at your best, even if you don't always get it. Make sure you do get that much sleep, though, for at least a week before the exam. Moderation is important here, too. Extra sleep will just make you groggy.

If you are not a morning person and your exam will be given in the morning, you should reset your internal clock so that your body doesn't think you are taking an exam at 3:00 A.M. You have to start this process well before the exam. The way it works is to get up half an hour earlier each morning, and then go to bed half an hour earlier that night. Don't try it the other way around; you will just toss and turn if you go to bed early without having gotten up early. The next morning, get up another half an hour earlier, and so on. How long you will have to do this depends on how late you are used to getting up. Use the Physical Preparation Checklist on the next page to make sure you are in tip-top form.

► Step 8: Get Your Act Together

Time to complete: 10 minutes to read; time to complete will vary
Activity: Complete the Final Preparations worksheet

You are in control of your mind and body; you are in charge of test anxiety, your preparation, and your test-taking strategies. Now it's time to take charge of external factors, like the testing site and the materials you need to take the exam.

Find Out Where the Exam Is and Make a Trial Run

Do you know how to get to the testing site? Do you know how long it will take to get there? If not, make a trial run, preferably on the same day of the week at the same time of day. Make note, on the worksheet Final Preparations on page 32, of the amount of time it will take you to get to the exam site. Plan on arriving 30–45 minutes early so you can get the lay of the land, use the bathroom, and calm down. Then figure out how early you will have to get up that morning, and make sure you get up that early every day for a week before the exam.

Gather Your Materials

The night before the exam, lay out the clothes you will wear and the materials you have to bring with you to the exam. Plan on dressing in layers; you won't have any control over the temperature of the examination room. Have a sweater or jacket you can take off if it's warm. Use the checklist on the Final Preparations worksheet to help you pull together what you will need.

Don't Skip Breakfast

Even if you don't usually eat breakfast, do so on exam morning. A cup of coffee doesn't count. Don't do doughnuts or other sweet foods, either. A sugar high will leave you with a sugar low in the middle of the exam. A mix of protein and carbohydrates is best: cereal with milk and just a little sugar, or eggs with toast, will do your body a world of good.

Physical Preparation Checklist

For the week before the exam, write down 1) what physical exercise you engaged in and for how long and 2) what you ate for each meal. Remember, you are trying for at least half-an-hour of exercise every other day (preferably every day) and a balanced diet that's light on junk food.

Exam minus 7 days

Exercise: _____ for ____ minutes

Breakfast: _____

Lunch: _____

Dinner: _____

Snacks: _____

Exam minus 6 days

Exercise: _____ for ____ minutes

Breakfast: _____

Lunch: _____

Dinner: _____

Snacks: _____

Exam minus 5 days

Exercise: _____ for ____ minutes

Breakfast: _____

Lunch: _____

Dinner: _____

Snacks: _____

Exam minus 4 days

Exercise: _____ for ____ minutes

Breakfast: _____

Lunch: _____

Dinner: _____

Snacks: _____

Exam minus 3 days

Exercise: _____ for ____ minutes

Breakfast: _____

Lunch: _____

Dinner: _____

Snacks: _____

Exam minus 2 days

Exercise: _____ for ____ minutes

Breakfast: _____

Lunch: _____

Dinner: _____

Snacks: _____

Exam minus 1 day

Exercise: _____ for ____ minutes

Breakfast: _____

Lunch: _____

Dinner: _____

Snacks: _____

▶ Step 9: Do It!

Time to complete: 10 minutes, plus test-taking time
Activity: Ace the California Real Estate Sales Exam!

Fast forward to exam day. You are ready. You made a study plan and followed through. You practiced your test-taking strategies while working through this book. You are in control of your physical, mental, and emotional state.

Final Preparations

Getting to the Exam Site

Location of exam: _____

Date: _____

Departure time: _____

Do I know how to get to the exam site? Yes _____ No _____
If no, make a trial run.

Time it will take to get to exam site: _____

Things to Lay Out the Night Before

Clothes I will wear   _____

Sweater/jacket   _____

Watch   _____

Photo ID   _____

No. 2 pencils   _____

Calculator   _____

_____   _____

_____   _____

You know when and where to show up and what to bring with you. In other words, you are better prepared than most of the other people taking the California Real Estate Sales Exam with you. You are psyched.

Just one more thing. When you are done with the exam, you will have earned a reward. Plan a celebration. Call up your friends and plan a party, or have a nice dinner for two—whatever your heart desires. Give yourself something to look forward to.

And then do it. Go into the exam, full of confidence, armed with test-taking strategies you have practiced until they're second nature. You are in control of yourself, your environment, and your performance on the exam. You are ready to succeed. So do it. Go in there and ace the exam. And look forward to your future career as a real estate salesperson!

3 ▶ California Real Estate Sales Exam 1

CHAPTER SUMMARY

This is the first of the four practice tests in this book based on the California Real Estate Sales Exam. Take this first test to see how you would do if you took the exam today, and to get a handle on your strengths and weaknesses.

LIKE THE OTHER practice tests in this book, this test is based on the actual California Real Estate Sales Exam. See Chapter 1 for a complete description of this exam.

Take this exam in as relaxed a manner as you can, without worrying about timing. You can time yourself on the other three exams. You should, however, make sure that you have enough time to take the entire exam in one sitting. Find a quiet place where you can work without interruptions.

The answer sheet you should use is on the following page, and is followed by the exam. After you have finished, use the answer key and explanations to learn your strengths and your weaknesses. Then use the scoring section at the end of this chapter to see how you did overall.

► California Real Estate Sales Exam 1 Answer Sheet

1.	ⓐ ⓑ ⓒ ⓓ		51.	ⓐ ⓑ ⓒ ⓓ		101.	ⓐ ⓑ ⓒ ⓓ
2.	ⓐ ⓑ ⓒ ⓓ		52.	ⓐ ⓑ ⓒ ⓓ		102.	ⓐ ⓑ ⓒ ⓓ
3.	ⓐ ⓑ ⓒ ⓓ		53.	ⓐ ⓑ ⓒ ⓓ		103.	ⓐ ⓑ ⓒ ⓓ
4.	ⓐ ⓑ ⓒ ⓓ		54.	ⓐ ⓑ ⓒ ⓓ		104.	ⓐ ⓑ ⓒ ⓓ
5.	ⓐ ⓑ ⓒ ⓓ		55.	ⓐ ⓑ ⓒ ⓓ		105.	ⓐ ⓑ ⓒ ⓓ
6.	ⓐ ⓑ ⓒ ⓓ		56.	ⓐ ⓑ ⓒ ⓓ		106.	ⓐ ⓑ ⓒ ⓓ
7.	ⓐ ⓑ ⓒ ⓓ		57.	ⓐ ⓑ ⓒ ⓓ		107.	ⓐ ⓑ ⓒ ⓓ
8.	ⓐ ⓑ ⓒ ⓓ		58.	ⓐ ⓑ ⓒ ⓓ		108.	ⓐ ⓑ ⓒ ⓓ
9.	ⓐ ⓑ ⓒ ⓓ		59.	ⓐ ⓑ ⓒ ⓓ		109.	ⓐ ⓑ ⓒ ⓓ
10.	ⓐ ⓑ ⓒ ⓓ		60.	ⓐ ⓑ ⓒ ⓓ		110.	ⓐ ⓑ ⓒ ⓓ
11.	ⓐ ⓑ ⓒ ⓓ		61.	ⓐ ⓑ ⓒ ⓓ		111.	ⓐ ⓑ ⓒ ⓓ
12.	ⓐ ⓑ ⓒ ⓓ		62.	ⓐ ⓑ ⓒ ⓓ		112.	ⓐ ⓑ ⓒ ⓓ
13.	ⓐ ⓑ ⓒ ⓓ		63.	ⓐ ⓑ ⓒ ⓓ		113.	ⓐ ⓑ ⓒ ⓓ
14.	ⓐ ⓑ ⓒ ⓓ		64.	ⓐ ⓑ ⓒ ⓓ		114.	ⓐ ⓑ ⓒ ⓓ
15.	ⓐ ⓑ ⓒ ⓓ		65.	ⓐ ⓑ ⓒ ⓓ		115.	ⓐ ⓑ ⓒ ⓓ
16.	ⓐ ⓑ ⓒ ⓓ		66.	ⓐ ⓑ ⓒ ⓓ		116.	ⓐ ⓑ ⓒ ⓓ
17.	ⓐ ⓑ ⓒ ⓓ		67.	ⓐ ⓑ ⓒ ⓓ		117.	ⓐ ⓑ ⓒ ⓓ
18.	ⓐ ⓑ ⓒ ⓓ		68.	ⓐ ⓑ ⓒ ⓓ		118.	ⓐ ⓑ ⓒ ⓓ
19.	ⓐ ⓑ ⓒ ⓓ		69.	ⓐ ⓑ ⓒ ⓓ		119.	ⓐ ⓑ ⓒ ⓓ
20.	ⓐ ⓑ ⓒ ⓓ		70.	ⓐ ⓑ ⓒ ⓓ		120.	ⓐ ⓑ ⓒ ⓓ
21.	ⓐ ⓑ ⓒ ⓓ		71.	ⓐ ⓑ ⓒ ⓓ		121.	ⓐ ⓑ ⓒ ⓓ
22.	ⓐ ⓑ ⓒ ⓓ		72.	ⓐ ⓑ ⓒ ⓓ		122.	ⓐ ⓑ ⓒ ⓓ
23.	ⓐ ⓑ ⓒ ⓓ		73.	ⓐ ⓑ ⓒ ⓓ		123.	ⓐ ⓑ ⓒ ⓓ
24.	ⓐ ⓑ ⓒ ⓓ		74.	ⓐ ⓑ ⓒ ⓓ		124.	ⓐ ⓑ ⓒ ⓓ
25.	ⓐ ⓑ ⓒ ⓓ		75.	ⓐ ⓑ ⓒ ⓓ		125.	ⓐ ⓑ ⓒ ⓓ
26.	ⓐ ⓑ ⓒ ⓓ		76.	ⓐ ⓑ ⓒ ⓓ		126.	ⓐ ⓑ ⓒ ⓓ
27.	ⓐ ⓑ ⓒ ⓓ		77.	ⓐ ⓑ ⓒ ⓓ		127.	ⓐ ⓑ ⓒ ⓓ
28.	ⓐ ⓑ ⓒ ⓓ		78.	ⓐ ⓑ ⓒ ⓓ		128.	ⓐ ⓑ ⓒ ⓓ
29.	ⓐ ⓑ ⓒ ⓓ		79.	ⓐ ⓑ ⓒ ⓓ		129.	ⓐ ⓑ ⓒ ⓓ
30.	ⓐ ⓑ ⓒ ⓓ		80.	ⓐ ⓑ ⓒ ⓓ		130.	ⓐ ⓑ ⓒ ⓓ
31.	ⓐ ⓑ ⓒ ⓓ		81.	ⓐ ⓑ ⓒ ⓓ		131.	ⓐ ⓑ ⓒ ⓓ
32.	ⓐ ⓑ ⓒ ⓓ		82.	ⓐ ⓑ ⓒ ⓓ		132.	ⓐ ⓑ ⓒ ⓓ
33.	ⓐ ⓑ ⓒ ⓓ		83.	ⓐ ⓑ ⓒ ⓓ		133.	ⓐ ⓑ ⓒ ⓓ
34.	ⓐ ⓑ ⓒ ⓓ		84.	ⓐ ⓑ ⓒ ⓓ		134.	ⓐ ⓑ ⓒ ⓓ
35.	ⓐ ⓑ ⓒ ⓓ		85.	ⓐ ⓑ ⓒ ⓓ		135.	ⓐ ⓑ ⓒ ⓓ
36.	ⓐ ⓑ ⓒ ⓓ		86.	ⓐ ⓑ ⓒ ⓓ		136.	ⓐ ⓑ ⓒ ⓓ
37.	ⓐ ⓑ ⓒ ⓓ		87.	ⓐ ⓑ ⓒ ⓓ		137.	ⓐ ⓑ ⓒ ⓓ
38.	ⓐ ⓑ ⓒ ⓓ		88.	ⓐ ⓑ ⓒ ⓓ		138.	ⓐ ⓑ ⓒ ⓓ
39.	ⓐ ⓑ ⓒ ⓓ		89.	ⓐ ⓑ ⓒ ⓓ		139.	ⓐ ⓑ ⓒ ⓓ
40.	ⓐ ⓑ ⓒ ⓓ		90.	ⓐ ⓑ ⓒ ⓓ		140.	ⓐ ⓑ ⓒ ⓓ
41.	ⓐ ⓑ ⓒ ⓓ		91.	ⓐ ⓑ ⓒ ⓓ		141.	ⓐ ⓑ ⓒ ⓓ
42.	ⓐ ⓑ ⓒ ⓓ		92.	ⓐ ⓑ ⓒ ⓓ		142.	ⓐ ⓑ ⓒ ⓓ
43.	ⓐ ⓑ ⓒ ⓓ		93.	ⓐ ⓑ ⓒ ⓓ		143.	ⓐ ⓑ ⓒ ⓓ
44.	ⓐ ⓑ ⓒ ⓓ		94.	ⓐ ⓑ ⓒ ⓓ		144.	ⓐ ⓑ ⓒ ⓓ
45.	ⓐ ⓑ ⓒ ⓓ		95.	ⓐ ⓑ ⓒ ⓓ		145.	ⓐ ⓑ ⓒ ⓓ
46.	ⓐ ⓑ ⓒ ⓓ		96.	ⓐ ⓑ ⓒ ⓓ		146.	ⓐ ⓑ ⓒ ⓓ
47.	ⓐ ⓑ ⓒ ⓓ		97.	ⓐ ⓑ ⓒ ⓓ		147.	ⓐ ⓑ ⓒ ⓓ
48.	ⓐ ⓑ ⓒ ⓓ		98.	ⓐ ⓑ ⓒ ⓓ		148.	ⓐ ⓑ ⓒ ⓓ
49.	ⓐ ⓑ ⓒ ⓓ		99.	ⓐ ⓑ ⓒ ⓓ		149.	ⓐ ⓑ ⓒ ⓓ
50.	ⓐ ⓑ ⓒ ⓓ		100.	ⓐ ⓑ ⓒ ⓓ		150.	ⓐ ⓑ ⓒ ⓓ

► California Real Estate Sales Exam 1

1. Property is said to be divided into two classes. These are
   a. real property and personal property.
   b. real property and appurtenances.
   c. rural property and urban.
   d. public property and private property.

2. Police power is one of the rights the government maintains in land. Police power refers to
   a. the fact that every community has to have a police department or force of some kind.
   b. restrictions placed on the land, some examples are zoning ordinances, height restrictions, density ratings, and building set backs.
   c. the fact that the government can take real property back for the benefit of the whole, but with just compensation.
   d. the concept that states real property is returned to the state if an owner dies without a will, and without any heirs.

3. Capitalization rates are determined using the
   a. comparable approach.
   b. reproduction cost approach.
   c. income approach to value.
   d. market sales approach.

4. Bill Whisper buys a new home for $300,000. Bill puts 20% down and gets a new loan to cover the balance of the purchase price. Bill is required to pay two points on his new loan. Bill's points will be
   a. $4,800.
   b. $9,600.
   c. $2,400.
   d. $0, the buyer pays the points.

5. Which of the following are considered to be real property?
   a. items that are immovable by law
   b. items declared real property by a former owner
   c. under surface crops such as potatoes, peanuts, turnips, and carrots
   d. apple trees

6. Which of the following are the two types of encumbrances?
   a. money and non-money encumbrances
   b. leases and tax encumbrances
   c. money and easement encumbrances
   d. encroachments and easements

7. A preliminary title report
   a. is the initial report prepared by the title insurance company. It is not the final report, the final report is updated as the issuance of the title insurance is finalized.
   b. is all that is necessary to be sure of clear title.
   c. shows only obvious, immediate problems.
   d. is only issued when requested.

8. A new loan in the amount of $400,000 at 6% interest, amortized for 30 years, and payable in equal monthly installments of $2,398.20, is made on the purchase of a home. The interest for the first payment on that loan is
   a. $3,000.
   b. $24,000.
   c. $2,400.
   d. $2,000.

9. A single person owning a parcel of real property is called
   a. severalty.
   b. partnership.
   c. limited singularity.
   d. fee simplicity.

10. When two real estate licensees work for the same broker, and one lists a property for sale and the other sells the property to a buyer they will likely choose which agency position?
    a. buyer's agent or sellers agent at the licensee's discretion
    b. dual agents
    c. seller or buyer, at the licensee's discretion, as long as the agency is disclosed
    d. seller or buyer at the discretion of the principles

11. Jim and Linda Myers are looking for their first home. The lender tells them that a good rule of thumb is that their maximum monthly payment can be approximately 30% of their gross monthly earnings. Jim earns $60,000 a year and Linda earns $70,000 a year. Based on the lenders guidelines the maximum monthly payment for Jim and Linda is
    a. $3,000.
    b. $2,850.
    c. $3,250.
    d. $4,000.

12. The right of survivorship is found in
    a. community property with right of survivorship.
    b. joint tenancy.
    c. partnership in severalty.
    d. both a and b.

13. When groups of buyers combine their purchasing power to acquire ownership of property, they normally hold title as
    a. joint tenants.
    b. community property.
    c. community property with right of survivorship.
    d. tenants in common.

14. The grantor is the one who
    a. grants ownership to the new owner known as the grantee.
    b. receives the ownership from the trustee.
    c. receives the ownership from the grantee.
    d. grants ownership to the trustor.

15. There are three basic types of property descriptions. They are
    a. lot, block and tract, government description, and postal survey.
    b. government survey, lot, block and tract, and metes and bounds.
    c. address, assessors parcel number, and government survey.
    d. government survey, address, and metes and bounds.

16. If a husband and wife own real property and the method of holding title has not been selected it is assumed in law to be held as
    a. community property.
    b. tenants in common.
    c. joint tenancy.
    d. severalty.

17. Legal descriptions can be combined to create a usable description for a property. What is true concerning the three acceptable methods of describing property?
   a. It is common in rural areas to combine two or more of the three accepted methods of legal descriptions.
   b. Legal descriptions can never be combined.
   c. Metes and bounds are often combined with government survey.
   d. Lot, block, and tract are usually combined with government survey.

18. The government maintains four rights in land. These are
   a. police power, eminent domain, escheat, and taxation.
   b. eminent domain, taxation, escheat, and reversion.
   c. police power, taxation, reservation, and revision.
   d. taxation, police power, taxation, and reversion.

19. Private deed restrictions are encumbrances. Examples of private deed restrictions include a
   a. covenant never to use the land to sell alcoholic beverages.
   b. covenant not to remove a tree.
   c. covenant not to grow grapes for the production of wine.
   d. all of the above

20. Water rights can be thought of in three areas. These are
   a. underground water rights, riparian water rights, and rights of appropriation.
   b. riparian water rights, underground water rights, and water edge water rights.
   c. rights of appropriation, rights of reparation, and rights of eminent domain.
   d. underground water rights, surface water rights, and drainage water rights.

21. Any real estate relationship in which one party acts for or represents another is known as a(n)
   a. special relationship.
   b. personal relationship.
   c. extemporaneous relationship.
   d. agency relationship.

22. The greatest ownership that any person can have in real property is
   a. leasehold estate.
   b. fee simple absolute.
   c. fee simple defeasible.
   d. life estate.

23. The real estate agent is required to disclose their agency position
   a. when the principle believes the agent is "their agent."
   b. before any agreement is entered into.
   c. prior to the close of escrow.
   d. immediately upon the acceptance of an offer to purchase.

24. Encumbrances can be thought of in two categories:
    a. those that are assumable and those that are not assumable.
    b. those that affect the title, and those that affect the physical condition.
    c. those owned by others and those belonging to the legal owner of the property.
    d. those belonging to the government and those belonging to private parties.

25. Percolating water, often referred to as underground water, on an owners land, belongs to
    a. the owner only.
    b. all owners proportionately if they can get access.
    c. the land owner in common with adjacent owners under the concept of reasonable use.
    d. all land owners in the state for beneficial use only.

26. From the perspective of a third party, agency can be created by
    a. ostensibly acting as the agent.
    b. ratification.
    c. celebration.
    d. both **a** and **b**.

27. Herb and Anna Lyons call you to take a listing on their personal residence. You determine that the Market Value of their home is $450,000. Expenses of sale, including your 6% commission is $8\frac{1}{2}$% of the selling price. Herb and Anna tell you that they have an existing First Trust Deed of $157,275. They need to know how much money they should net at the close of escrow. You work out a preliminary net sheet. Your preliminary net sheet indicates that the Lyons will net how much?
    a. $195,525
    b. $292,725
    c. $411,750
    d. $254,475

28. When a licensee is guilty of misrepresentation but the broker knew nothing of this event, the broker will likely be
    a. not responsible at all.
    b. responsible for lack of supervision.
    c. responsible for lack of training.
    d. not responsible because the licensee should have been aware of the misrepresentation.

29. Under the concept of escheat, the property returns to the state if
    a. the owner dies without a will, and has no heirs.
    b. the owner dies without any heirs.
    c. the owner has a will but no heirs to leave their assets to.
    d. the owner has all of their assets in a family trust.

30. The agency relationship can be created in three ways. These are
   a. agreement, ratification, and estoppel.
   b. payment, ratification, and assignment.
   c. written agreement, oral agreement, and believing there is an agreement.
   d. ratified estoppel, implied ratification, and constructive implication.

31. The grant deed has certain warranties which are that
   a. the grantor will transfer any later, or after acquired title, to the grantee.
   b. the grantor has not previously conveyed the property to another.
   c. the grantor has not encumbered the property except as disclosed.
   d. all of the above

32. The most logical way for a husband and wife to hold title in a family trust is
   a. community property with right of survivorship.
   b. joint tenancy.
   c. tenants in common.
   d. community property.

33. The United States was surveyed using the government survey system, sometimes referred to as the rectangular survey system. This system is comprised of
   a. base lines and meridians, and develops into townships.
   b. townships that are six miles square.
   c. townships that contain 36 square miles.
   d. all of the above.

34. The creation of agency may be
   a. express or implied.
   b. ostensible or actual.
   c. sensible or senseless.
   d. possible or probable.

35. Right of Appropriation is a concept where
   a. water is allocated evenly to adjacent owners.
   b. water belongs to the state and is distributed by an appropriate water company.
   c. water is sold to the state, who distributes the water equitably.
   d. the state retains a right to allocate water to non-riparian owners.

36. Jerry and Hannah Stewart buy a new home for $500,000. The Stewarts put $75,000 cash as a down payment, the seller carries a $75,000 Second Trust Deed, and the Stewart's get a new First Trust Deed and note for the remainder of the purchase price. What is the loan to value (LTV) ratio of the new First Trust Deed?
   a. 70%
   b. 95%
   c. 80%
   d. 75%

37. The listing agent of a real property is bound by law to disclose their agency position on which of the following?
   a. a high-rise office building
   b. a four-unit apartment building
   c. a hundred-unit apartment building
   d. a small shopping center

38. An agency relationship is created when
   a. the principle believes the licensee is representing them as an agent.
   b. the contract is signed.
   c. the agency disclosure and confirmation are ratified.
   d. the licensee and the principle have agreed to create an agency relationship.

39. Floyd and Dorothy Comfort are buying a new home. They find a home they want for $460,000. They offer to purchase the home for $450,000 with $250,000 cash down payment. They get a commitment for a new First Trust Deed and note in the amount of $200,000 at 6% interest, amortized for 30 years, and payable in equal monthly installments of $1,199.10. Escrow is opened and everything goes well. The lender orders the appraisal and the Comforts pay for the appraisal through escrow. Escrow is set to close in one week and the appraisal comes in for $435,000. Which one of the following statements is true?
   a. The escrow must tell the Comforts about the low appraisal immediately.
   b. The lender ordered the appraisal, the lender will be the only one with authority to disclose the amount of the appraisal, the escrow will close as scheduled.
   c. The appraiser must inform the Comforts immediately.
   d. The real estate agent must inform the Comforts immediately.

40. A real estate agent writes an offer to purchase, and receipt for deposit to purchase a home he has shown a buyer with whom he has been working. The real estate agent should disclose his or her agency position
   a. before the buyer signs the offer.
   b. when the agent thinks the buyer is looking at him as their agent.
   c. before the buyer signs an Exclusive Authorization and Right to Acquire agreement.
   d. all of the above

41. When a real estate licensee sells a property that has been listed by his office, the only agency position that they can take is
   a. dual agency.
   b. singular agency.
   c. seller agent.
   d. buyer agent.

42. Riparian water rights are restricted to
   a. absolute use.
   b. reasonable use.
   c. occasional use.
   d. fair and responsible use.

43. A licensee is taking a listing on a home that he or she will attempt to sell. The seller asks if the licensee can charge a lower commission fee. The licensee can legally tell the owner
   a. the local Board of Realtors forbids listings for less than 6%.
   b. the California Association or Realtors will not allow members to list properties for less than a 6% commission.
   c. the National Association of Realtors will not allow members to list properties for less than a 6% commission.
   d. that his or her broker will not allow licensees to take a listing for less than 6% of the selling price of the listing.

44. Sid Zimmerman is a licensed real estate salesperson. Sid works for Whole Area Brokerage, Incorporated. Sid has an agreement with Whole Area Brokerage Company, Incorporated that includes a 60/40 commission split. Sid is to get 60% of any commissions that he generates, and Whole Area, Inc. gets 40% of any commissions that Sid generates. Sid lists a home for sale for $425,000. The listing agreement includes a 6% commission. Sid sells his listing to a buyer he has been working with. How much of a commission will Sid get at the close of escrow?
   a. $25,500
   b. $15,300
   c. $7,650
   d. $10,200

45. If a real estate broker or agent gives advice to a principle, with whom they have no formal business relationship, who relies on their advice, and the principle subsequently acts on the advice, suffering a loss, the agent is
   a. responsible but not liable.
   b. liable for the advice as a gratuitous agent.
   c. declared the listing agent.
   d. not responsible as no agreement existed.

46. The cost approach to value is most reliable when evaluating
   a. older neighborhoods.
   b. commercial properties.
   c. special use properties.
   d. new properties.

47. Escrow companies that are licensed by the California Department of Corporations operate as
   a. sole ownership companies.
   b. partnerships.
   c. limited partnerships.
   d. corporations.

48. Regulation Z requires the disclosure of the interest rate as
   a. the nominal rate.
   b. the annual percentage rate.
   c. the effective rate.
   d. both **b** and **c**.

49. California property taxes increase
   a. annually.
   b. daily.
   c. monthly.
   d. upon sale.

50. Salesperson Marion, who works for Blue Rug Realty, takes an Exclusive Agency Listing on a home owned by Mr. and Mrs. Iverson. She lists the home for $400,000. This listing includes a 6% commission if she sells the listing. Marion holds open houses every weekend for six weeks. She runs ads in the local newspaper. She puts a for sale sign on the front lawn with her personal telephone number on it. Mrs. Iverson mentions to a co-worker that they are trying to sell their home. The co-worker tells Mrs. Iverson that her daughter and son-in-law are looking for a home to purchase. Mrs. Iverson invites her co-worker's daughter and her husband to look at her home. They decide to buy the home for $400,000. They enter into a contract, go into escrow, and thirty days later the escrow closes. The Iverson's owe Blue Rug Realty

a. $24,000.

b. $14,400.

c. $9,600.

d. nothing, they sold the home themselves.

51. Mary transfers the ownership of a property to Millie. Mary tells Millie not to record the grant deed. Maurice is there when the transfer occurs. Mary issues another grant deed to Maurice. Mary tells Maurice not to record the grant deed. Maurice records the grant deed anyway. As a result,

a. Mary owns the property.

b. Maurice owns the property.

c. Millie owns the property.

d. Maurice and Millie own the property.

52. Herb Gunderson is a broker. Herb lists the home of Jack and Mary Wagoner. Mr. Wagoner tells Herb that he has personally installed R-13 insulation in all of the outside walls, R-30 in the attic, and R-30 under the floor on the ground floor. Jim Bessler, a member of the Board of Realtors that Herb belongs to, sells the home to buyers that he is working with. Jim and Herb are very excited about the listing and relay the existence of the insulation the seller has installed. The seller and buyer close escrow in 37 days. The buyer looks in the attic and notices no insulation, he then looks underneath the home and there is no insulation, further inspections show that the home is completely void of insulation.

a. Herb is liable.

b. Herb and Jim are liable.

c. Herb, Jim, and the Seller are liable.

d. Only the Seller is liable.

53. John and Ruby Oster make an offer on a $475,000 home. They propose to put $50,000 down and obtain a new First Trust Deed and note in the amount of $425,000 at 6% interest, amortized for thirty years, and payable in equal monthly installments of $2,548.08. The lender informs you during escrow that the Oster's cannot qualify for a fixed rate loan. The lender further informs you that the Oster's can qualify for an adjustable rate mortgage of $425,000 and a start rate of $3\frac{1}{2}$ % interest, with a first year monthly payment of $1,908.44. The margin is 2%, with a lifetime cap of 7%. The note allows for a maximum annual increase or decrease in the payment of $7\frac{1}{2}$%. What should you tell the Osters if they ask you when the payment can increase and how much it can increase?
  a. You should refer them to their attorney.
  b. You should tell them that they should talk to their loan agent, as you are not qualified as a real estate licensee to advise consumers about loans.
  c. You should explain that the amount of the monthly loan payment can increase every year, and the maximum that it can increase this first year is $143.14.
  d. You should advise them to pass this loan offer up and try and save more money for the down payment.

54. When a real estate licensee working under the license of a real estate broker lists a home for sale, the listing belongs to
  a. the licensee who listed the property.
  b. the broker.
  c. both the licensee and the broker.
  d. this is up to the owner and the licensee.

55. Ella and Yolanda are trying to get the listing on Mr. and Mrs. Greg's home. Ella feels she has the greatest chance to get the listing because she went to high school with Mrs. Greg. Yolanda talks the Gregs into listing with her and her company because they sell more homes than Ella and Ella's company. Ella complains to the Board of Realtors and insists that this matter be arbitrated. The arbitration committee will likely decide that
  a. Yolanda wins, as she is the procuring cause.
  b. Ella wins, because she has known the owners longer.
  c. Ella wins, because Yolanda should never have told the Gregs that her company is more active than Ella's company.
  d. Yolanda will have to split her commission with Ella.

56. Agency is created when
  a. the principle delegates the right to act, in the principles behalf, to a second person known as the agent, and that agent acts.
  b. the principle pays a third party to perform a certain act on their behalf.
  c. the agent acts as if they are representing the rights of another.
  d. the principle tells someone to contact "my agent."

57. The broker/salesperson uses a comparative market analysis (CMA) to
  a. determine the market value of a certain property.
  b. determine the trends in a regional analysis.
  c. get an idea of the probable increase in taxes for a clients home.
  d. get an idea of the use of the Consumer Price Index.

58. Comparable sales are used to determine the current market value of a property called the "subject property." Which of the following statements regarding adjustments is true?
  a. Adjustments are made to the subject property to make it as similar to the comparable as possible.
  b. Adjustments are never made to the subject property.
  c. Adjustments are made to the subject property and the comparable properties, as needed.
  d. Adjustments are never made to properties being compared.

59. Market analysis is a useful tool that can be used to determine
  a. rents, marketing time, market value, purchasing trends, and average age.
  b. rents, marketing time, market value, and business trends.
  c. market value and market rents.
  d. market value, rents, permitted land uses, and zoning.

60. A market analysis differs from a regional analysis in that
  a. a market analysis is for the immediate area.
  b. a regional analysis is for an area greater than that covered by a market analysis.
  c. a market analysis and a regional analysis are the same thing.
  d. a market analysis is for a smaller area, while the regional analysis is for a larger geographical area that may include the market analysis mentioned.

61. The elements of valuation are
  a. PETE.
  b. demand, utility, soundness, and tradability.
  c. demand, undesirability, scarcity, and transferability.
  d. utility, transferability, scarcity, and demand.

62. The principle of substitution states that
  a. a property will not sell for more than a similar property in the same area.
  b. most three-bedroom home buyers, will buy a four-bedroom home if they can't find a three bedroom.
  c. floor plans can be substituted in most cases.
  d. area and style can be easily substituted.

63. A real estate agent can be
  a. general only.
  b. general or specific.
  c. detailed or vague.
  d. specific only.

64. The principles of progression and regression state that
  a. more expensive areas will decline more rapidly in recessions.
  b. expensive homes will always maintain their value regardless of location.
  c. less expensive homes adjacent to more expensive homes will cause the more expensive home to lose value (regression). Less expensive homes located next to more expensive homes will cause the less expensive home to gain value (progression).
  d. when economic booms are evident less expensive areas will increase in value more rapidly than more expensive areas.

65. The principle of conformity states that
   a. property conforms because of its location.
   b. properties achieve their greatest contribution when they conform.
   c. a property will not sell for more than a similar property in a similar area.
   d. properties contribute according to their conformation.

66. Daniel and Sarrah Rambolt want to buy a new home. They find a $300,000 home they like. They can put $60,000 down, and get a new loan of $240,000 at 6% interest, payable in equal monthly installments of $1,438.92. Their annual taxes are estimated to be $3,750. Their hazard (fire) insurance is estimated to be $1,050 a year.

   1. What will their total monthly housing cost be?

   2. Based on a 30% front end ratio, how much money will they have to earn monthly?

   a. Monthly housing cost is $1,438.92. Monthly earnings have to be $4,796.40.
   b. Monthly housing cost is $1,526.42. Monthly earnings have to be $6,129.74.
   c. Monthly housing cost is $1,838.92. Monthly earnings have to be $6,129.74.
   d. Monthly housing cost is $1,751.42. Monthly earnings have to be $5,838.07.

67. Agency relationships may be created by
   a. implication.
   b. ratification.
   c. implementation.
   d. compensation.

68. The value most sought by real estate practitioners is
   a. market value.
   b. market price.
   c. immediate value.
   d. value to their buyer.

69. The market approach to value, also called the comparable approach to value, is most accurate when determining the value of
   a. new property.
   b. existing housing.
   c. income property.
   d. special use properties, like theaters.

70. Real estate agents are generally
   a. general agents.
   b. specific agents.
   c. detailed agents.
   d. general and specific agents.

71. The grant deed is used to
   a. transfer the ownership of real property.
   b. transfer the ownership of real property between family members.
   c. give property to non-profit organizations only.
   d. transfer the ownership of residential real property only.

72. The cost approach to value considers which two types of cost?
   a. reproduction cost and replacement cost
   b. land costs and city fees
   c. the cost of the separate elements of the building, and the cost of the land
   d. the cost of the land, and changes in zoning laws

73. The cost approach to value entertains the cost of
   a. the land and the depreciated improvement.
   b. the replacement cost of the land and the improvement on a square foot basis.
   c. the highest and best use of the land.
   d. the entire property as if new.

74. An agent is someone who
   a. works for another agent.
   b. is authorized to represent and act on behalf of another person.
   c. is an employee of a principle who helps make decisions.
   d. works for another to accomplish general or specific tasks at the agent's discretion.

75. Lenders speak in ratios of loan to property value (LTV). If a lender will make an 80% loan to value and the subject property appraises for $300,000, what is the amount of the loan this lender will make?
   a. $275,000
   b. $260,000
   c. $240,000
   d. $290,000

76. For a quitclaim deed to be valid, the grantor of a quitclaim deed has to
   a. own at least half of the subject property.
   b. have no interest in the subject property.
   c. be the legal spouse of the grantee.
   d. have lived on the property for at least three of the previous five years.

77. Market value and market price differ in which respect?
   a. Market value is the probable price the property will sell for, market price is the price the property actually sold for.
   b. Market value and market price are the same thing.
   c. Market value is the price the property sold for, market price is the price the property should have sold for.
   d. Market price is what the seller is asking for the property, market value is the price the property will likely sell for.

78. Interest rates on loans are quoted with an actual interest rate and an Annual Percentage Rate (APR). The difference between these two rates is
   a. actual monthly interest, and the interest rate for all interest costs for the life of the loan.
   b. the monthly calculation and the annual calculation.
   c. the actual monthly rate and the daily rate.
   d. the total interest costs and the nominal interest rate.

79. Most residential real estate loans in California are made through
   a. mutual savings banks.
   b. mortgage loan brokers.
   c. mortgage companies.
   d. commercial banks.

80. Interest rates on loans have names that denote the type of return. Which of the following statements is true?

   a. The stated rate on a loan is called the nominal rate.

   b. The stated rate on a loan is called the amortization rate.

   c. The rate on a loan is always based on compounded interest.

   d. The nominal rate and the effective rate are the same thing.

81. California Title Insurance Companies are regulated by the

   a. California Department of Real Estate.

   b. California Office of Real Estate Appraisers.

   c. California Department of Insurance.

   d. California Department of Corporations.

82. A broker putting several investors he knows into the ownership of a small income property would likely hold title to the property as

   a. community property.

   b. severalty.

   c. tenants in common.

   d. tenants in severalty.

83. Broker Aaron runs an ad in the local newspaper. The ad reads "Duplex in prestigious area. Under priced because of partnership problems, their loss is your gain." What is the legal status of this advertisement?

   a. This is legal if the property is under priced.

   b. This is legal if the property is under priced and there is a partnership problem.

   c. This ad could get the right buyer to purchase a property that will be the best investment of their life.

   d. You cannot advertise any property as under priced or below market.

84. Jerry and Myrna McCoy purchase a home for $375,000. They put $75,000 down and get a commitment for a new First Trust Deed and note in the amount of $300,000 at 5.5% interest, amortized for 30 years, and payable in equal monthly installments of $1,703.37. The escrow is for 60 days, the mortgage broker suggests that the McCoys buy a locked-in rate guarantee for $275. They decline the purchase of the locked in rate guarantee. Forty days into the escrow the rates jump to 6%. Which of the following is most true?

   a. The McCoys will still get the 5.5% loan.

   b. The McCoys will have to find another lender.

   c. The McCoys should have purchased the locked in rate.

   d. The McCoys will lose the home because of this rate change.

85. The information about a parcel of real property is stored in computers at the title company, this data or information is referred to as

   a. chain of title.

   b. property data bank.

   c. multiple listing service.

   d. title plant.

86. The recorded public history of a particular parcel of real property is called the

   a. chronological history of the situs.

   b. chain of title.

   c. complete public record.

   d. preliminary title report.

87. There are two listings that must have a termination date. The two listings are

    a. exclusive authorization and right to sell listing and the exclusive agency listing.

    b. agency listing and exclusive licensee listing.

    c. open listing and net listing.

    d. exclusive agency listing and open listing.

88. Title Insurance has four basic functions. These are to

    a. review risks that may not be part of the public record, interpret legality, help correct any defects in the title, and insure a marketable title.

    b. guarantee clear title, furnish a list of known imperfections, cover losses not covered in other policies, and protect against prescriptive easements.

    c. discover encroachments, discover undesirable easements, find fraud in the chain of tile, and insure a marketable title.

    d. issue a preliminary title report, inspect the property for problems, review the public record, and review risks that may not be part of the public record

89. The comparable method of valuation is embedded in all three approaches to value. This is obvious in the cost approach when

    a. realizing the square foot cost of property was determined by prior sales.

    b. determining the capitalization rate for a building by comparing similar capitalization rates on similar properties.

    c. seeking the gross rent multiplier by comparing the recent sales of income producing properties.

    d. All of the above involve comparison.

90. When a new owner purchases real property with the use of a loan there is/are normally

    a. one title insurance policy.

    b. two title insurance policies.

    c. three title insurance policies.

    d. four title insurance policies.

91. Riparian rights are those rights reserved for

    a. owners whose land borders on a river or other water course.

    b. all owners under the concept of reasonable use.

    c. owners within a reasonable distance from the watercourse.

    d. the state that maintains these water rights.

92. The most inclusive title insurance policy available in California is

    a. the CLTA policy.

    b. the short-term rate.

    c. ALTA-R.

    d. the expanded CLTA.

93. There are two policies of title issued when there is a purchase money loan. These policies are for the

    a. buyer and seller.

    b. buyer, seller, and tenants, if any.

    c. buyer and lender.

    d. buyer and possible creditors.

94. The escrow officer is licensed by

    a. the Department of Real Estate.

    b. the Department of Escrow Services.

    c. escrow officers are not licensed.

    d. the Department of Corporations.

95. The listing agreement where the listing broker gets paid if the property sells no matter who sells the property is the
   a. exclusive authorization and right to sell.
   b. exclusive agency listing.
   c. net listing.
   d. open listing.

96. Brokers can conduct escrows
   a. on transactions in which they have an interest.
   b. on any real estate transaction.
   c. only if they have a company licensed by the California Department of Corporations.
   d. real estate brokers cannot have an interest in an escrow company.

97. The most recurring number in a series of numbers, or values, is important in appraisal and the comparative market analysis used by REALTORs. This number indicates the most common value in a neighborhood, and helps to find the value of property in that neighborhood. What is the most recurring number called?
   a. average
   b. mode
   c. mean
   d. median

98. There are four types of listings used in California. These are
   a. open listing, exclusive authorization and right to sell, exclusive agency, and net listing.
   b. open listing, exclusive listing, exclusive agency, and net listing.
   c. net listing, exclusive brokerage listing, exclusive authorization and right to sell listing, and net listing.
   d. open agency, exclusive authorization and right to sell, net agency listing, and open agency listing.

99. Delivery is extremely important in the transfer of real property. Delivery refers to the method the grantee is made aware of the intention of the grantor to pass title to the grantee. Which of the following best describes delivery?
   a. the intention of the parties rather than the act of physically delivering the documents
   b. simply handing the documents to the grantee
   c. the grantor intends to pass title to the grantee, but the grantee is unaware of the transfer
   d. placing the document in a safe deposit box for delivery to the grantee upon the grantors' death is a valid delivery.

100. Bob transfers the ownership of a residential property to Mary using a grant deed. Mary moves into the home as her permanent residence but does not record the grant deed. Bob grants the same property to Betty. Betty records the grant deed. As a result,
a. Betty owns the property.
b. Mary is the owner of the property.
c. Bob retains ownership of the property.
d. the first to record is first in title.

101. The preliminary title report should list
a. the name of the owner and the description of the property, outstanding taxes, bonds, and other assessments, identity of any covenants, conditions and restrictions, and any recorded liens or encumbrances that must be eliminated before loans can be made.
b. liens, encumbrances, owners of record, and pending lawsuits.
c. easements, encroachments, liens, and taxes.
d. the name of the owner, the description of the property, outstanding taxes and bonds, other assessments, covenants, conditions and restrictions, pending legislation that could affect the property, and existing encroachments.

102. Upon the sale of their principle residence, a married couple is entitled to an exemption of $500,000 if
a. they have lived in the property for two of the past five years.
b. they are over 55 years of age.
c. this is the only real property they own.
d. they have never used this exemption before.

103. The acronym that most real estate practitioners use to remember the four rights the government retains is
a. DUST.
b. PETE.
c. REIT.
d. FNMA.

104. The taxes due on the gain from the sale of income producing property can be deferred by
a. selling the property to a family member.
b. using the 1031 Internal Revenue Code Tax Deferred Exchange (IRC).
c. transferring the property to a family trust before it is sold.
d. gradually selling small percentages of the property to third parties.

105. One element of desirability for a husband and wife holding title to property as community property is
a. the tax basis is adjusted to the fair market value at the time of death of either spouse.
b. one half of the tax basis of the property is adjusted to fair market value at time of death of either spouse.
c. there is an absolute right of survivorship.
d. this is not a desirable method of holding title.

106. In California, real property taxes are based on
a. county assessors appraisal of the property.
b. the current value of property in the neighborhood the property is located in.
c. one percent (1%) of the last similar sale in the neighborhood.
d. one percent (1%) of the purchase price of the property, plus annual adjustments.

107. A California statute that allows supplemental taxes to be placed on a property to support needed improvements in a specific area are known as
   a. *ad valorem* taxes.
   b. Mello/Roos.
   c. special improvement bonds.
   d. supplemental taxes.

108. Title Insurance insures for
   a. the future.
   b. the past.
   c. the value of any loss from zoning errors.
   d. fire damage only.

109. For a real estate agency relationship to exist it is NOT necessary to have
   a. a license.
   b. a written contract.
   c. a commission.
   d. all of the above

110. A tax payer is allowed to deduct which of the following as tax deductions because of the ownership of their principle residence?
   a. property taxes
   b. insurance
   c. interest on loans
   d. both **a** and **c**

111. Which of the following statements is true regarding a salesperson's handling of trust accounts?
   a. The salesperson has nothing to do with trust accounts.
   b. The salesperson has to have a trust account and keep a chronological log of funds received and placed in the trust account, returned to the giver of the trust funds, or given to third parties.
   c. It is illegal for a salesperson to have a trust account.
   d. Trust accounts are only necessary if the salesperson receives checks or money orders made out to them, or if they are given cash.

112. There are three possible agency positions for a real estate licensee to take. These are
   a. dual agency, buyer agency, or seller agency.
   b. broker agency, consumer agency, or general agency.
   c. specific agency, general agency, or all-inclusive agency.
   d. singular agency, multiple agency, or secular agency.

113. In California, it is unlawful to discriminate
   a. on the basis of race, color, religion, sex, marital status, national origin, ancestry, familial status, or mental or physical handicaps.
   b. on the basis of race, color, and creed.
   c. in most residential buildings.
   d. in most areas.

114. The proceeds from the refinance of an income producing property
a. is taxable upon receipt of the proceeds.
b. is taxable if the proceeds exceed the adjusted tax basis of the property.
c. is not taxable.
d. raises the tax basis of the income property.

115. Harold is renting one of his apartment units in a predominantly white neighborhood. Harry and Wanda Iverson inquire about the apartment. They look at the rental, and are interested in renting the apartment. Harry and Wanda are African-American. Harold explains to them that this is a predominantly white neighborhood, and they simply wouldn't be happy there. Fortunately, he has another apartment for rent in a more diverse neighborhood which is nicer, less expensive, and should better fit their needs. This is known as
a. good business.
b. helping the Iversons achieve a better life style.
c. racial discrimination and steering.
d. trying to help.

116. The Unruh Civil Rights Act deals with discrimination in
a. the sale, rental, lease, and financing of all types of housing.
b. the placement of loans.
c. service of customers at businesses.
d. the hiring practices of employers.

117. Sarah and Saul Weinstein want to rent an apartment from Herb Stanton, the owner of a sixteen-unit apartment building. Herb has two apartment units available to be rented. Herb believes that Sarah and Saul are Jewish. Because Herb believes that the majority of his tenants are not Jewish, he shows the Weinsteins the smaller apartment by the swimming pool and explains that the apartment is a bit noisy because of the pool filter. Which of the following is true?
a. Herb can show the Weinstein's any apartment he likes.
b. Herb is steering and discriminating.
c. Herb is not discriminating, he offered them an apartment.
d. Herb is not discriminating, he is discouraging.

118. Brian, a salesperson for Hallmark Realtors, takes a listing on a home. The owners of the home tell Brian he can have the listing "only if you promise not to sell to minorities." Brian takes the listing and agrees to these terms.
a. Brian is breaking several laws against discrimination, the California Real Estate Commissioners Rules and Regulations, and violating the Realtors Code of Ethics. If discovered, Brian and Hallmark Realtors could lose their real estate licenses.
b. Brian should explain that this is a discriminatory practice that he cannot be part of such practices, but he understands and will do his best to accomplish the sellers' goals.
c. The issue never came up, no minorities wanted to see the property.
d. As long as Brian doesn't prohibit minorities from looking at the property he is not in violation of any laws.

119. Jim Hawkins, a real estate broker who runs a property management company makes an appointment to show property to Albert Henderson. When Jim arrives at the property he notices a Latino man waiting impatiently in front of the building and he assumes this is Al. Jim has an agreement with the owners of this building stating that he will not rent to minorities. He drives back to his office. Al calls later to ask why he didn't meet him. Jim explains that he rented the property to some people he had been negotiating with.

    a. Jim is in violation of several laws because he avoided the meeting when he assumed Al was the Latino man waiting.

    b. Jim is acting responsibly if he was actually in negotiations with others and he rented the property to them.

    c. Jim is in violation because of his agreement with the owners, and because he avoided Al because of his ethnicity.

    d. Jim should have stopped and explained to Al that the owners will not rent to minorities.

120. Bill Williams interviews Sarah and Nathanial Johnson to rent an apartment. The Johnsons are African-Americans. Bill likes Sarah but takes an immediate dislike to Nathanial. Bill explains that he doesn't think that they will be able to establish a workable relationship. Additionally, in his management business, Bill rents to several African-American couples and families.

    a. Bill is within his rights, he doesn't have to rent to the Johnsons if he doesn't think they can get along.

    b. Bill has to rent to the Johnsons because they are African-American.

    c. Bill is in violation of several laws and should lose his brokers license.

    d. Personal dislike is just an excuse for discrimination.

121. The annual increase in real property taxes in California is based on

    a. current taxes plus 2% of the current taxes.

    b. current taxes plus the 2% of the difference in the current value and purchase price.

    c. one percent (1%) of the current value.

    d. one percent (1%) of the purchase price plus 5% annual increases of the current property taxes.

122. An ad that reads "Apartment for rent, quiet, homelike atmosphere, one block from Beth Shalom Temple, like owning your own little home"

    a. This ad would be considered discriminatory and considered steering.

    b. This ad is legal, it is simply giving people a general idea of the location.

    c. This ad could be desirable if the area near Beth Shalom Temple is a very desirable area.

    d. The ad is poor because it doesn't have anyone to contact.

123. The exclusive authorization and right to acquire is an agreement entered into by
    a. the agent and the seller.
    b. the agent and the buyer.
    c. the agent, the buyer, and the seller.
    d. this agreement cannot be used in California.

124. An ad that reads "we buy homes—call for quick action" is legal if
    a. the broker tries to talk people into a listing and can't buy the home.
    b. the broker explains to the seller that if he buys the home he will buy it under market and resell the home, or he can offer it for sale at a higher price if the owner gives him the listing.
    c. the broker looks at the home but decides not to buy that home.
    d. Both **b** and **c** are true.

125. The capitalization approach to value is used to find the value of
    a. income producing properties.
    b. new residential property.
    c. raw land.
    d. special use properties.

126. "Salespersons wanted. Our average salesperson has a six-digit income." This is a good ad if
    a. the company has no salespersons.
    b. the company has an adequate number of salespersons earning incomes to justify the six figure claim.
    c. the company has several salespersons who will soon be earning very high incomes.
    d. the company used to have the top producers in the area.

127. Real estate records have to be kept by the broker for
    a. two years.
    b. three years.
    c. four years.
    d. five years.

128. The two powers that allow government to control the use of land are
    a. escheat and police power.
    b. taxation and zoning.
    c. police power and the power of eminent domain.
    d. land use regulations and master plans.

129. The transfer disclosure statement is required by law in California. The transfer disclosure statement is a
    a. statement of conditions known to exist, made by the seller, verified by the listing agent, verified by the selling agent, and reviewed by the buyer.
    b. statement of existing problems that the seller is aware of, that the seller gives to the listing agent who decides whether these need to be shared with other parties in the transaction.
    c. guarantee of the condition of the title of the property as far as the seller can ascertain.
    d. warranty of the condition of the property for the benefit of the buyer.

130. Puffing is
    a. a sales exaggeration that does not lead to misrepresentation.
    b. the same as misrepresentation.
    c. exaggerating the size of the improvements.
    d. a term used to describe extremely steep terrain.

131. Multiple Listing Services (MLS) are
   a. computer services where subscribing REALTORs place their listings in the computer data banks and share the opportunity to sell and benefit monetarily from each others listings.
   b. services for listing groups of undesirable buyers and sellers.
   c. services where vendors and repairmen can register their services, the costs of their services, as well as provide recommendations from former clients.
   d. groups of real estate licensees who meet monthly for breakfast to exchange ideas on marketing and sales techniques.

132. The Quitclaim Deed is often recommended by attorneys. The Quitclaim Deed
   a. transfers whatever right, title, or interest the grantor had in the property at the time of the execution of the Quitclaim Deed.
   b. transfers all future rights subsequently obtained by the grantor.
   c. transfers any responsibility for loans on property.
   d. transfers only community property rights.

133. The Holden Act prohibits
   a. discriminatory loan practices.
   b. discrimination in rental practices of residential properties.
   c. discrimination against same sex partners.
   d. discrimination against customers in businesses for race, color, religion, sex, marital status, national origin, ancestry, family status, or physical and mental handicaps.

134. The grantee is the one who
   a. receives the title in the granting.
   b. grants the title of real property to the grantor.
   c. receives the trust deed as evidence of title.
   d. gives the grant deed to the beneficiary.

135. James Border held a straight note in the amount of $100,000. Over the past five years James has received $45,000 in interest payments. What is the interest rate on this note?
   a. 10%
   b. 9%
   c. 4.5%
   d. 8.7%

136. The form of ownership that would give an investor the greatest flexibility when selling his or her interest would be
   a. a general partnership.
   b. ownership in severalty.
   c. joint tenancy.
   d. a limited partnership.

137. The listing agreement that gives a specific real estate broker the right to sell a listing but where the owner reserves the right to sell the property himself without paying the listing broker a commission is called a(n)
   a. open listing.
   b. exclusive agency listing.
   c. exclusive authorization and right to sell.
   d. net listing.

138. Loan records have to be kept by a real estate broker for
- **a.** two years.
- **b.** three years.
- **c.** four years.
- **d.** five years.

139. A listing agreement that gives several real estate brokers the right to sell a property, and promises to pay the broker who is first to produce a buyer, but where the owner retains the right to sell the property themselves without any obligation to pay brokers with whom the owner has listing agreements, is called a(n)
- **a.** open listing.
- **b.** exclusive agency listing.
- **c.** exclusive authorization and right to sell.
- **d.** net listing.

140. All listing agreements should be in writing EXCEPT
- **a.** an open listing.
- **b.** an exclusive authorization and right to sell.
- **c.** net listings.
- **d.** all listings should be in writing.

141. When a real estate licensee presents an offer to a seller and the seller counteroffers part of the offer
- **a.** no offer exits.
- **b.** most of the offer exists.
- **c.** the original offer is void.
- **d.** the counteroffer is void.

142. Encumbrances are held by
- **a.** the owner of the property.
- **b.** the government only.
- **c.** someone who is not the legal owner of the property.
- **d.** utility companies only.

143. When a real estate licensee writes a deposit receipt and right to purchase, the licensee is required by law to
- **a.** read the agreement in its entirety to the buyer and to the seller.
- **b.** present the offer to the seller.
- **c.** present the offer if it is a reasonably good offer.
- **d.** make sure the listing agent has a copy of the offer.

144. Encumbrances associated with a property include
- **a.** topography that limits the type of building that is possible.
- **b.** loans, easements, zoning restrictions, and building codes.
- **c.** limits to restrictions based on zoning and building codes.
- **d.** locational limitations and restrictions.

145. Broker Andy manages a 100-unit apartment building. His monthly fee is based on 6% of $1,000 per month in rent. Normally Broker Andy earns $6,000 a month. In December, Broker Andy was in Hawaii for a vacation. He did not make any arrangements with his staff to pay him the $6,000 management fee for December. At the end of January, the management account owed Broker Andy $12,000—$6,000 for December and $6,000 for January. Which of the following is TRUE?
   a. Broker Andy charges too much for the management of this building.
   b. Broker Andy is guilty of commingling.
   c. Broker Andy is guilty of conversion.
   d. Broker Andy is handling the management account in a businesslike manner.

146. Julie Bryant sells a home to Bob and Myra Johnson. They ask Julie how they should hold title to the property. Julie should reply,
   a. "Most of my clients hold property as Community Property with the right of survivorship. Is that how you would like to hold title?"
   b. "I'm not allowed to advise you on methods of holding title to real property. You should consult an attorney."
   c. "I have an information sheet from the title company that explains how to hold title. Most of my clients hold title as Joint Tenants. Is that how you want to hold title?"
   d. "Don't worry about how you are going to hold title. The escrow people will make that decision for us."

147. A limited partner may limit his or her liability to creditors in the event of a business failure.
   a. The limited partner is liable for the amount of his investment. He or she has no further obligations incurred from this investment other than his initial investment.
   b. The limited partner will have to come up with an amount equal to his initial investment.
   c. The limited partner will be liable for whatever liabilities the partnership has incurred.
   d. The limited partner is not liable for anything. He or she should get his initial investment back.

148. An owner of an apartment building wants Mary Watson, who has rented apartment #17 for the last three years, to move. The notice that will be required for Mary is
   a. a three-day notice to pay or quit.
   b. a three-day notice to perform covenants or quit.
   c. a thirty-day notice to vacate.
   d. a sixty-day notice to vacate.

149. Jim Anston owns a twenty-unit apartment building. Jim has a strict "no pets" policy. Mindy Ralston applies for a tenancy on a vacant unit that Jim has advertised. Mindy has a small dog. Mindy explains to Jim that she wants the unit but can't part with her dog. Jim has been trying to find a tenant like Mindy for some time. He explains that she will be the only person in the complex that is allowed to have a dog. Jim sends a letter stating that the building is still a "no pets" building, except for Mindy. What is TRUE concerning the other tenants?

    a. All of the tenants can get a dog. Jim can restrict the size and weight to approximately the size of Mindy's dog.

    b. Jim is within his rights. He can sanction one tenant to have a small dog.

    c. Jim should have sent the letters to the other tenants as "Registered Mail." Until he does that, they can get any dog they want.

    d. The tenants can get any dog they desire. Jim has opened the flood gate.

150. All evictions in California begin with a(n)

    a. three day notice to pay or quit.

    b. unlawful detainer action.

    c. summons and complaint.

    d. writ of execution followed by a summons and complaint.

▶ Answers

1. a. The definition of property is broken down into two basic categories: real and personal.

2. b. This choice best describes police power, which is one of the four rights maintained by the government.

3. a. Capitalization rates are estimated from the sale of other income-producing properties, this would be a comparable approach to finding the capitalization rate. So, while the capitalization rate is used in the Income Approach, or Capitalization Approach to value, they are determined using the Comparable Approach.

4. a. Bill would pay two points of $240,000. A point is 1%, two points are 2%. Bill's loan is $240,000, 2% times $240,000 would be $4,800, which is the answer. There are several ways to find Bill's loan. An easy way is to figure Bill's down payment:

    $300,000   Purchase Price
    <u>Times 20%</u>   Down
    $60,000   Bill's Down Payment

Since Bill's down payment is $60,000, you would subtract the down payment from the purchase price and come up with a loan of $240,000 or;

Purchase Price	$300,000
Less Down Payment	$ 60,000
New Loan	$240,000

Points are figured on the amount of the loan. Two points equal 2% so you multiply the loan by the points, or;

Loan Amount	$240,000
Times % of Points	2%
Dollar Amount of Points	$ 4,800

5. a. The definition of real property expands to include items that are immovable by law.

6. a. Encumbrances are broken down into two categories: money and non-money.

7. a. The preliminary title report is a quick scan of the property to see if there is any obvious problem. As the escrow proceeds and the closing date approaches, the title insurance search increases in depth and scope. Often, unwanted uninsurable situations will occur at the closing of the escrow. This normally stops the immediate closing until the title is deemed "clear."

8. d. The first month's interest is $2,000. *(Remember when you are taking California real estate tests that they never ask a mathematical question that you cannot figure out with a piece of paper and a pencil. In other words they do not require you to have a calculator.)*

The answer is calculated by multiplying the face amount of the loan, $400,000, by the interest rate, 6%, and dividing by the months in a year, 12.

1. Find the first year's interest;
   Loan Amount times the interest rate = first year's interest;
   $400,000 \times 6\% = \$24,000$
2. Find the first month's interest
   First Year's interest equals the first year's interest divided by the months in a year
   $\$24,000 \div 12 = \$2,000$

That answer is **d.**

9. a. When a single individual owns a piece of real property it is called *ownership in severalty*.

10. b. Since both the listing agent and the selling agent are working for the same broker, and anything they do is an extension of the brokers' acts, the broker is the listing agent and the selling agent, and therefore dual agency is the logical agency choice.

11. c. Jim and Linda's incomes are given to you as an annual income. The lender gave the criteria on a monthly basis.

1. Add Jim and Linda's Income.

Jim's Annual Income	$ 60,000
Linda's Annual Income	$ 70,000
Jim and Linda's Combined Annual Income	$130,000

2. This annual income has to be reduced to a monthly income. You will divide Jim and Linda's annual income by 12 months.
   Annual Income ÷ 12 Months = Monthly Income
   $\$130,000 \div 12 \text{ Months} = \$10,833.33$
3. 30% of the Gross Monthly Income can be used for the loan payment. You will multiply the gross monthly income, $10,833.33 by 30%, and come up with the estimated monthly loan payment.
   Monthly Income × 30% = Estimated Monthly Loan Payment
   $\$10,833.33 \times 30\% = \$3,250$
4. $3,250 is answer **c.**

12. d. In California, the right of survivorship in real property ownership is found in community property with the right of survivorship and joint tenancy.

13. d. When unrelated groups of people buy real property, they normally hold it as *tenants in common*.

14. a. The grantor signs the grant deed naming the grantee in the document and conveys the grant deed to the grantee.

15. b. The three basic types of legal description are government survey or rectangular survey, lot, block and tract, and metes and bounds.

16. a. In California, when a husband and wife fail to indicate the method of holding title it is assumed to be held as community property.

17. c. If two methods of legally describing real property are used it is part of a township description combined with a metes and bounds description.

18. a. The four rights retained by the government are police power, eminent domain, taxation, and escheat. This is known by the acronym PETE.

19. d. All of the choices in this question are covenants, or promises, placed in deeds as restrictions on use by future owners of land.

20. a. Water rights are thought of in these three areas: underground, riparian, and appropriation.

21. d. The question is practically the definition of agency relationship.

22. b. The greatest ownership in any real property is fee simple absolute.

23. b. Before entering into any real estate agreement, the agent should disclose his or her agency relationship with the principle. This agency position is ratified, or disclosed again with each subsequent real estate agreement entered into with the principle.

24. d. Encumbrances can be thought of in two categories of ownership, those belonging to the government, and those belonging to private parties.

25. c. Percolating water belongs to adjacent land owners in common with the owner of the land where the water is.

26. d. An ostensible agency is created when a third party reasonably assumes that an agency exists because of the acts of the principle. For instance, a seller (principle) of a property may lead the buyer to believe that someone is their agent. If the buyer (third party) believes this to be true, then the seller could be bound by the acts of the agent. *Ratification* best describes the approval of a transaction that has already taken place. For instance, an agent finds a buyer for land that a seller owns. An offer is presented and the seller accepts. The seller has ratified the existence of the agency, even though there was no listing agreement.

27. d. The estimated net will be $254,475.

1. Estimate the expenses of sale:

   Sales Price × Percentage of Estimated Costs = Estimated Expenses of Sale

   $$\$450,000 \times 8\tfrac{1}{2}\% = \$38,250$$

2. Estimate the estimated net:

Estimated Selling Price:	$450,000
Less Expenses of Sale:	$ 38,250
Less Loans of Record:	$157,275
Estimated Net From Sale:	$254,475

   Herb and Anna should net $254,475 at close of escrow.

28. b. Brokers are liable for the acts of the licensees that work under their broker's license.

29. a. Two facts have to be present for escheat to take place. First, the owner has to die intestate (without a will). Second, the owner cannot have any heirs. If there is no will and if the state cannot find any heirs, the property then escheats to the state.

30. a. Agreement, ratification, and estoppel are the three ways that agency can be created.

31. d. Choices **a**, **b**, and **c**, are a description of what the grant deed warranties.

32. d. The most logical way for a husband and wife to hold title in a family trust is community property.

33. d. All of the answers are part of the government survey or rectangular survey method of survey.

34. a. The creation of agency can be either express (written), or implied (acted like).

35. d. The right of appropriation is the right of the state to allocate water as it is needed by the citizens.

36. a. The loan to value (LTV) ratio of any loan is that loan divided by the purchase price of the property in question.
Figure out the amount of the First Trust Deed:

Purchase Price	$500,000
Less Down Payment	$ 75,000
Less Other Loans	$ 75,000
First Trust Deed	$350,000

First Trust Deed ÷ Purchase Price =
Loan to Value of First Trust Deed
$350,000 ÷ $500,000 = 70%
The loan to value is 70%, choice **a.**

37. b. Disclosure of agency in California is required for residential properties of one to four units only.

38. a. Technically, the agency relationship is created when the principle thinks the agent is acting on their behalf. Disclosure should occur at this point, but since it is vague, the normal point of disclosure is just before entering into any agreement.

39. b. The lender ordered the appraisal and is the only person entitled to the information contained in the appraisal. The escrow will close as scheduled. The appraiser is only allowed, by law, to tell the party that ordered the appraisal, the escrow is not allowed to disclose this information and the agent probably doesn't know and can't get the information.

40. d. All three choices are points that would require the disclosure of agency to the principle. Normally the disclosure is made just before writing the first contract, in this case the offer to purchase and receipt for deposit.

41. a. When a real estate licensee sells a property that has been listed by another agent in the office in which they place their license, *dual agency* is the likely agency that will exist. Generally, the broker is the agent for both the buyer and the seller, and this would normally constitute dual agency.

42. b. Riparian water rights, or adjacent water rights, are subject to reasonable use.

43. d. The only time a licensee can tell an owner that a commission has to be a certain percentage of the sale is if his or her broker will not allow a listing without a minimum commission.

44. b. $425,000 × 6% = $25,500;
$25,500 × 60% = $15,300

45. b. When a principle relies on a licensee as "their agent" it is not necessary that the agent is paid for their services. Therefore, they are a gratuitous agent.

46. d. The cost approach is the most valuable method when determining the value of new buildings.

47. d. Escrow companies that are licensed by the Department of Corporations operate as Corporations.

48. d. Regulation Z requires that the interest rates on loans be stated as the effective rate (stated rate), and the annual percentage rate.

49. a. California property taxes increase annually.

50. d. The Iversons owe nothing. This is an exclusive agency listing, the seller retains the right to sell the property without paying a commission.

51. c. Millie owns the property because Maurice was aware of the delivery. Recordation was not necessary as far as Maurice and Mary are concerned.

52. d. When a seller, or principle, tells their agent something that appears factual, the agent can repeat with confidence what the principle has told them. If the principle was lying, the agent is not liable. The principle is liable. On the other hand, if the agent knowingly lies about a fact, both the agent and the principle are liable.

53. c. The loan payment could increase as much as $7\frac{1}{2}$% annually and that this first year that would amount to $143.13.

 1. Find the new maximum monthly payment:

 Old Monthly Payment × Annual Payment Increase = New Monthly Payment

 $\$1,908.44 \times 7\frac{1}{2}\% = \$2,051.57$

 2. Find the maximum increase for the first year:

 New Monthly Payment – Old Monthly Payment = Monthly Difference

 $\$2,051.57 - \$1,908.44 = \$143.13$

54. b. All real estate actions of salespersons are the actions of their broker.

55. a. The person who gets the signature is the procuring cause, the person who caused the thing to happen. That person is responsible for the outcome. In this case the procuring cause, Yolanda, wins because she gets the listing. The theory of procuring cause is that Ella couldn't get the Greg's to agree, Yolanda did get the Greg's to agree.

56. a. Agency is created when the principle delegates the right to act, in the principles behalf, to a second person known as the agent, and that agent acts. This agent would be known as the "procuring cause."

57. a. The comparative market analysis (CMA) is the most common method of determining current market value.

58. b. Adjustments in the comparable market analysis, or market approach to value, are always made to the comparables, never to the subject property.

59. c. Market value, probable selling price, and market rents are best determined using a market analysis.

60. d. The market analysis is for the immediate market, a neighborhood of similar homes, quality, and demand. A regional analysis is more useful in determining the success of a shopping mall, car mart, or property that will serve the inhabitants of a large area.

61. d. The elements of valuation are found with the acronym DUST: demand, utility, scarcity, and transferability.

62. a. A property will not sell for more than a similar property in the same area. That is the principle of substitution.

63. b. Normally, real estate agents are specific. However, the real estate agent can be a general agent under certain circumstances.

64. c. The principles of progression and regression state that a property located adjacent to more expensive properties will tend to increase in value (progression), while more expensive property adjacent to less expensive property will suffer a loss in value (regression).

65. b. The principle of conformity states that property will achieve its greatest value when located adjacent to properties of the same value.

66. c. The monthly housing cost is $1,838.92. The monthly earnings have to be $6,129.74.

 1. What will their total month housing cost be?

 The monthly housing cost will be the loan payment, $\frac{1}{12}$ of the taxes, and $\frac{1}{12}$ of the insurance. Or;

$1,438.92 + (\frac{\$3,750}{12}) + (\frac{\$1,050}{12}) =$

$1,438.92 + $312.50 + $87.50 = $1,838.92

More simply:

Monthly House Payment:	$1,438.92
Plus Monthly Taxes:	$ 312.50
Plus Monthly Insurance:	$ 87.50
Total Monthly Housing Cost:	$1,838.92

2. Based on a 30% front-end ratio, how much money will they have to earn monthly? Lenders speak in front-end ratios and back-end ratios. This means that the front end is the total housing cost. If 30% of the front-end cost is $1,838.92, then the Rambolts will have to earn $1,838.92 divided by 30% or in this case;

Total Monthly Housing Costs (Front End Ratio = Minimum Monthly Earning

$1,838.92 × 30% = $6,129.74

The answer is **c**. Monthly housing cost is $1,838.92. Monthly earnings have to be $6,129.74.

67. b. Agency relationships can be created by agreement, ratification, or estoppel.

68. a. The value most sought by real estate practitioners is market value.

69. b. The market approach, or comparable approach to value, is most accurate when used to determine the value of existing housing.

70. b. Real estate agents are normally specific agents, engaged to perform a specific task, not all business tasks.

71. a. The grant deed is used to transfer ownership of real property.

72. a. The cost approach considers two costs. The replacement cost is the cost to rebuild the property with contemporary materials. Reproduction cost is the cost to try and reproduce a property as it was originally built.

73. a. The cost approach estimates the cost (new) of building the replacement, then subtracts the estimated depreciation, and finally adds the value of the land in coming up with the value.

74. b. The definition of an agent is someone who is authorized to represent and act on behalf of another person.

75. c. The Loan to Value Ratio, (LTV) is stated as a percentage of the whole price. An 80% LTV on a $300,000 property would be $300,000 × 80% = $240,000.

76. b. It is not required that the grantor of a quitclaim deed have an interest in a property they are giving a quitclaim deed on. If they do, the quitclaim deed will divest them of that interest.

77. a. Market price is the price a property sells for. Market value is the maximum price a property should sell for if it is exposed to all the probable buyers in a market, for a reasonable time and the seller and buyer are acting, without duress, in their own best interest.

78. a. The annual percentage rate is a measurement of all the interest that is paid on a loan for the life of the loan. It is meant to be a shopping rate. The consumer can pick the lowest APR and that should be the best loan from an interest rate standpoint.

79. a. Mutual savings banks make most real estate loans in California.

80. a. The stated rate is the rate at which the borrower is told they are getting the loan, it is the basic rate on the face amount of the loan. The basic rate and the nominal rate are synonymous.

81. c. California title insurance companies are regulated by the California Department of Insurance.

82. **c.** When several people invest in a piece of property they normally take title as tenants in common.

83. **b.** Legal if the property is under priced, a partnership breakup is forcing the sell, and finally that the seller(s) have been made aware of the ad and approved.

84. **c.** The McCoys should have purchased the guaranteed lock. It isn't likely the lender will hold the 5.5% rate, and they don't have to as there was no guarantee with the loan. If the McCoys try to find another lender they will likely pass the close date of the escrow before the new loan is approved. The McCoys won't lose the home, but they will have a higher interest rate on their loan.

85. **d.** Information kept by title insurance companies is commonly called a *title plant*.

86. **b.** The history of any parcel of real property is known as the *chain of title*.

87. **a.** There are two listing agreements that have to have a termination date. The two are the exclusive listings, the exclusive authorization and right to sell, and the exclusive agency listing.

88. **a.** The four basic functions of title insurance are to 1) review risks that are not part of the public record, 2) interpret legal issues, 3) help cure any defects in the title, and 4) insure the title.

89. **d.** The comparable method is part of all three methods. Most information concerning value is obtained from similar values of similar data or objects. We normally know square foot cost from the cost of buildings that have already been built, or by adding up the cost of materials, land, labor, and profit. All of which are comparables. Capitalization rates are gotten from the sale of similar buildings. Gross rent multipliers are realized from the same data.

90. **b.** When a parcel of property is purchased with a loan there are normally two policies of title insurance issued. One is for the buyer, and one is for the lender.

91. **a.** Water rights are reserved for owners whose land borders on a river or other water course.

92. **c.** The most inclusive title insurance policy available in California is the ALTA-R.

93. **c.** When there is a loan procured in a purchase of real property there are normally two title of policy insurance policies issued. One is for the buyer, and the second is for the lender.

94. **c.** Escrow officers are not currently licensed. The escrow company is licensed by the Department of Corporations, the escrow officer holds no required license.

95. **a.** The exclusive authorization and right to sell is the listing agreement where the listing broker gets paid regardless of who sells the property.

96. **a.** Brokers can conduct the escrow in transactions where they have an interest. Interest means they are the listing or selling broker. In this case, the escrow is licensed by the Department of Real Estate.

97. **b.** The mode is the most often recurring number. This helps establish a common value for a neighborhood.

98. **a.** Listed are the four types of listings available in California.

99. **a.** Delivery refers to the intention of the parties: Did the grantor want to grant and did the grantee want to receive.

100. b. One of the oldest proofs of delivery is the taking of possession. Since Mary took possession of the property she would be deemed the owner even if she didn't record the deed. Betty should have inspected the property and inquired what rights the tenant had.

101. a. This is a summary of what the preliminary title report should list. Name of the owner, legal description of the property, outstanding taxes, any bonds, or other assessments, covenants, conditions and restrictions, any recorded liens or encumbrances which would include recorded easements.

102. a. The requirement of the exemption is that the seller has lived at the property for two for the past five years. Since there is a husband and wife they are entitled to a $500,000 exemption.

103. b. PETE is the acronym that is most commonly used to remember the four rights the government retains in real property: police power, eminent domain, taxation, and escheat.

104. b. The taxes on monetary gain from the sale of income-producing property can be deferred by using the 1031 Internal Revenue Tax Code Deferred Exchange.

105. a. There are several benefits to a married couple who hold real property as community property. One of these benefits is that the tax basis of the property is moved to the market value at the time of death of either partner.

106. d. Proposition 13, which limited property taxes to 1% of the purchase price of real property, is also allowed for annual 2% increases in the property tax.

107. b. The Mello/Roos law allows supplemental taxes on new property or on existing property by a vote of the people.

108. b. Title insurance covers things that have occurred in the past, past judgments, title passed by incompetent people, etc. Title insurance covers up to the close of escrow, anything that occurs after the close of escrow or passing of title is not insured.

109. d. All of the information is correct, as the creation of an agency relationship is not dependent on any of the answers.

110. d. Both property taxes and interest on loans paid on a taxpayer's principle residence can be used as a tax deduction.

111. c. Salespersons are not allowed to have a trust fund account. They can be a signature on a trust fund account if they have two years experience and a letter from their broker designating them as a signature on a specific trust account.

112. a. This is a list of the three possible agency positions for an agent to take.

113. a. The Unruh Civil Rights Act makes it illegal to discriminate in a business facility, based upon race, color, religion, ancestry, or national origin. The Rumford Act makes it illegal to discriminate in the area of housing based upon race, color, religion, national origin, ancestry, sex, family status, and age. The federal laws tend to mirror the California state laws and do, from time to time, add to the list of discriminatory offenses, including discrimination against families with children under 18 years of age (exemption is a retirement community), and handicapped home buyers or tenants.

114. c. The proceeds from a refinance of investment real property are not taxable as income.

115. c. Harold is discriminating and steering. He is discriminating because he is trying to get Harry and Wanda to move somewhere else, and steering because he is suggesting the place they should move. Harold should treat Harry and Wanda as he would any tenant he was interviewing and processing.

116. c. The Unruh Act covers discrimination in service to customers at businesses.

117. b. Herb is discriminating by showing only one of the two available units to the Weinsteins.

118. a. Brian is breaking several laws and rules. Brian will lose his real estate license if this is discovered by regulatory agencies.

119. c. Jim can't agree with the owner's demands. He would have to explain that he is "color blind" by law, he cannot avoid Al because of his color, he is required by law to process Al as he would any other tenant, and he cannot use any guideline for Al that he would not use for any other applicant.

120. a. Bill Williams is obligated by law to treat everyone the same. He cannot deny a qualified tenant the right to rent and occupy the facility, if the refusal is based upon discrimination as defined in both state and federal law. However, Mr. Williams was within his rights to refrain from renting to the Johnsons because his reasons were not based on discrimination.

121. a. The annual increase in property taxes allowed on real property in California is 2% of the current taxes.

122. a. This ad would be considered discriminatory and would be viewed as trying to steer Jewish people to the apartment while discouraging non-Jewish apartment lookers.

123. b. The exclusive authorization and right to acquire is an agreement used between a real estate agent and a buyer.

124. d. Both **b** and **c** are true. The ad would be legal if in fact the broker could purchase the home, and if he decides to buy the home he would be required to explain to the seller that he intends to sell the home at a profit in the immediate or near future.

125. a. The capitalization approach to value is used to determine the value of income producing properties.

126. b. The ad is legal if the company has a number of salespersons earning incomes to justify the six-figure income claim.

127. b. Records for real estate transactions must be kept for three years from the close of escrow or three years from the last action on that file.

128. c. The two powers that allow the government to control land use are police power and eminent domain.

129. a. In the case Easton *v.* Strassburger, the California Court of Appeals ruled that brokers are supposed to be aware of all material facts that negatively affect the value of the real property. The agent has a duty to inspect the facility and disclose all material facts. The obligation to inspect rests with both the listing and selling agents, who are obligated to conduct a reasonable, competent, and diligent inspection.

130. a. This choice is a good definition of *puffing*.

131. a. This is the best definition offered for *multiple listing services.*

132. a. This is the definition of the *Quitclaim Deed.*

133. a. The Holden Act covers discrimination in "red lining," or loan discrimination in California.

134. a. The grantee is the one who receives the title in the granting.

135. b. Nine percent would have to be the answer for this question.

Steps to solution: Notice that the note is listed as a straight note; this means that it is interest only. The total interest earned for the last five years is $45,000. Your first step will be to reduce the interest payments to annual payments. This is because interest rates on straight notes are figured on an annual basis.

1. Find the interest per year:

Total Interest ÷ Years = Annual Interest

$45,000 ÷ 5 = $9,000

2. Find the annual interest rate:

Annual Interest ÷ Face Amount of Note = Annual Interest Rate

$9,000 ÷ $100,000 = 9%

136. b. Ownership in severalty, that is, severed from anyone else's interest, would give the individual owner complete freedom to dispose of the property.

137. b. This is the definition of an *exclusive agency listing.*

138. c. Records for loan transactions have to be kept for four years from the close of escrow or the last activity on that file.

139. a. The open listing can be given to several brokers while the seller retains the right to personally sell the property without being liable to any persons holding an open listing.

140. d. All listings should be in writing.

141. c. When an offer is counteroffered, the original offer has been rejected, and is void.

142. c. Encumbrances are normally held by someone who does not own the property.

143. b. The licensee is required by law to present all written offers. This is binding on the listing.

144. b. This choice is a good example of *encumbrances.*

145. b. Broker Andy is guilty of commingling. He is not allowed to have more than $200 in this Trust Fund Account at any given time. Broker Andy is also not allowed to have his commission for management in the account for more than 30 days.

146. b. "I'm not allowed to advise you on methods of holding title to real property, you should consult an attorney," should be her answer. Real estate agents, unless they are attorneys, are not allowed to advise buyers on methods of holding title to real property.

147. a. The limited partner is liable for the amount of his investment. He has no further obligations incurred from this investment other than his initial investment.

148. d. Tenants who have lived in an apartment for more than one year are entitled to a sixty-day notice to vacate. If they have lived in an apartment for less than one year, then a thirty-day notice will suffice.

149. a. All of the tenants can get a dog. Jim can restrict the size and weight to approximately the size of Mindy's dog. This is "the one size fits all" rule. If you allow one tenant to do something you have allowed all of the tenants to do the same thing.

150. b. All evictions begin with an unlawful detainer action.

Scoring

Evaluate how you did on this practice exam by first finding the number of questions you answered correctly. Only the number of correct answers is important—questions you skipped or got wrong don't count against your score. At the time this book was printed, a passing score for the exam was 70%, although the test you take may have more or fewer than 150 questions. On this practice exam, a passing score would be 105 correct.

Use your scores in conjunction with the Learning-Express Test Preparation System in Chapter 2 of this book to help you devise a study plan using the California Real Estate Refresher Course in Chapter 4, the Real Estate Math Review in Chapter 5, and the Real Estate Glossary in Chapter 6. You should plan to spend more time on the sections that correspond to the questions you found hardest and less time on the lessons that correspond to areas in which you did well.

For now, what is much more important than your overall score is how you performed on each of the areas tested by the exam. You need to diagnose your strengths and weaknesses so that you can concentrate your efforts as you prepare. The different question types are mixed in the practice exam, so in order to diagnose where your strengths and weaknesses lie, you will need to compare your answer sheet with the following table, which shows which of the categories each question falls into.

Once you have spent some time reviewing, take the second practice exam in Chapter 7 to see how much you have improved.

EXAM 1 FOR REVIEW

Subject Area	Question Numbers
Property Ownership and Land Use Controls and Regulation	1, 2, 5, 6, 9, 15, 18, 19, 20, 22, 24, 25, 29, 31, 33, 35, 42, 91, 105, 106, 107, 110, 128, 134, 136, 142, 144
Laws of Agency	21, 23, 26, 30, 34, 37, 38, 40, 41, 45, 52, 54, 56, 63, 67, 74, 109, 112
Valuation and Market Analysis	3, 46, 57, 58, 59, 60, 61, 62, 64, 65, 68, 69, 72, 73, 77, 89, 97, 125
Financing	4, 8, 11, 27, 36, 39, 48 , 53, 66, 75, 78, 79, 80, 84, 102, 104, 135, 138, 147
Transfer of Property	7, 12, 13, 14, 16, 17, 51, 71, 76, 85, 86, 90, 100, 132
Practice of Real Estate and Mandatory Disclosures	10, 47, 49, 70, 81, 82, 83, 88, 92, 93, 94, 96, 101, 103, 108, 111, 113, 114, 115, 116, 117, 118, 119, 120, 121, 122, 124, 126, 127, 129, 130, 131, 133, 143, 145, 146
Contracts	28, 32, 43, 44, 50, 55, 87, 95, 98, 99, 123, 137, 139, 140, 141, 148, 149, 150

California Real Estate Refresher Course

CHAPTER SUMMARY

If you want to review real estate concepts, terminology, and California real estate law for your exam, this is the chapter you need. It covers the most commonly tested concepts on the California exam. Using this chapter, you can review just what you need to know for the test.

OW YOU USE this chapter is up to you. You may want to proceed through the entire outline in order, or perhaps, after taking the first practice exam, you know that you need to brush up on just one or two areas. In that case, you can concentrate only on those areas.

Following are the major sections of the California Real Estate Sales Exam and the page on which you can begin your review of each one.

Property Ownership and Land Use Controls and Regulations

Practice of Real Estate and Mandated Disclosures

Contracts

▶ Property Ownership and Land Use Controls and Regulations

Classes of Property

Property can be divided into two classes: **real property** and **personal property.** In California, the terms **real property** and **real estate** frequently mean the same thing. In this course, and in the California real estate salesperson's examination, the terms may be used interchangeably to refer to both the **land** and the **rights of ownership,** but typically, real property refers to rights of ownership and real estate refers to the **profession**, such as **the Real estate Law** (those laws regarding the regulation of real estate **licencees**).

The **bundle of rights of ownership** interests in real property includes the **right to possess, use, exclude others, encumber** (**easements** and **liens**), and **transfer title** to someone else by **sale, gift, will,** or **exchange.**

Property Characteristics

Personal property is everything that is **not real property.** Items of personal property (also called **chattels**) include:

- **tangibles**, such as a car, clothing, or jewelry
- **intangibles**, such as a patent, which is considered intellectual property

Real property is the earth itself, including:

- what is beneath the surface (including minerals and other substances)
- the air space above the surface

Items Appurtenant

Appurtenances are rights or property that ordinarily are transferred with land and used for its benefit, such as **easements.** Appurtenant means "belongs to" or "goes with" or "runs with" the land.

Items Afixed to the Property

Fixtures are man-made additions to land, such as buildings, fences, and other improvements. Items that become fixtures are **personal property** before they are attached to the land; if severed, they become personal property again.

That Which Are Immoveable by Law

The five tests that courts use to determine whether or not an item is a fixture and thus part of the real property can be remembered by the word **MARIA.**

Method of attachment
Agreement of the parties, which can override all other considerations
Relationship of the parties—in a residential sale or lease, legislatures and courts tend to favor the buyer/tenant
Intention of the party who attached the item to land or building
Adaptability of the item for another use or location

Trade fixtures are equipment or furnishings used in a business. Trade fixtures are attached to the real estate while in use but are removable by the tenant at the end of the lease term. Trade fixtures are always considered personal property.

Growing things can be **real** property or personal property, depending on how they are grown.

Fructus naturales are plants and trees that occur naturally or as part of the landscaping and are part of the real estate.

Fructus industriales (**emblements**) are annually cultivated crops and are personal property. Corn would be considered personal property, but orange trees would be considered real property as trees are perennial; the oranges may be considered personal property if commerically grown.

Encumbrances

An **encumbrance** is a right or interest in a property that does not belong to an owner or a tenant. Encumbrances consist of **liens** and items which affect the use and physical condition of the property.

An encumbrance (**cloud on the title**) is anything that affects title to real estate. It is **voluntary** if it is imposed with the consent of the titleholder. It is **involuntary** if it can be imposed without the consent of the titleholder.

A **lien** is a claim to property to ensure payment of a debt.

A **mechanic's lien** is an example of an involuntary use of real estate to secure payment of a debt. State law specifies the requirements for creating and enforcing a mechanic's lien. In general, a mechanic's lien is available to anyone who provides material or labor for an improvement to real estate, including design services. An architect, surveyor, contractor, carpenter, plumber, electrician, landscaper, and many other participants in the construction process are all entitled to a mechanic's lien if they have not been paid for their services or materials.

There are statutory time periods for:

- providing **preliminary notice** to the property owner (as well as the general contractor and construction lender, if any) of the right to file a mechanic's lien—20 days from the time work begins or materials are supplied
- A **Notice of Completion** must be filed by the contractor within ten days of completing the work. All subcontractors have 30 days after the Notice of Completion to file a mechanic's lien for non-payment.
- All **general contracts** have 60 days after the Notice of Completion to file a mechanic's lien for non-payment.
- If there is no Notice of Completion, all parties have 90 days after completion of the work to file a mechanic's lien.

When a mechanic's lien is properly created, it takes priority over all other subsequent liens, except for **tax liens**.

Foreclosure (**sale**) of the real estate may be postponed by the property owner during a court hearing on the merits of the case, provided the property owner posts a **bond** to ensure payment to the claimant.

The property owner can be protected against the lien claim of someone who performs work that was not authorized by filing and posting on the property a **notice of nonresponsibility** within ten days of discovery of the work.

A **judgment** is a determination of a court that may impose an obligation for payment on a property owner. An **Abstract of Judgment** must be recorded for a judgment to become a **lien**.

A **writ of attachment** is a pre-judgement lien and is difficult to obtain. Under a writ of attachment the courts take custody of the defendants' real and personal property to assure payment at the close of a legal proceeding.

A *lis pendens* is a document that can be recorded to warn anyone examining the title to the specified real property that the property is the subject of a legal action.

If a judgment is made in favor of a claimant, an abstract of judgment can be recorded in any county in which the debtor may own property creating a **general lien**. If the judgment is not **satisfied** (**paid off**) in timely fashion, a **writ of execution** can be requested of the court. The writ of execution directs the sheriff to sell the specified property to satisfy the judgment. **Certain** property (such as the debtor's **homestead**) may be exempt from forced sale. A **Declaration of Homestead** does not prevent a forced sale of the property. It does however protect, within limits, the equity in a home. So, a **foreclosure** can take place. However, some of the equity from the foreclosure will go to the homeowner. There is more information on this topic under **Deeds**.

An **easement** is a **non-possessory interest** in real property, a right to use land for a limited purpose, such as the right to travel over a shared driveway. An easement may be acquired by **express grant** or **express reservation** in a **deed** or as described below. (Don't confuse an easement with a **license**, which is a temporary permission to come onto someone's land. The holder of a concert ticket has a license to enter the concert hall for the performance.)

The **dominant tenement** is a parcel of land that benefits from an easement over an adjoining parcel. An **easement appurtenant** is one that runs with the land because it is transferred when title to the dominant tenement is transferred.

The **servient tenement** is the parcel of land that is burdened with the easement; that is, the parcel over which the owner of the dominant tenement is allowed to travel.

An **easement in gross** is a personal right and exists apart from ownership of any adjoining or attached parcels of land. An example of this is an **utility easement**.

An **easement by implication of law** is created when an owner of land sells a parcel that would otherwise be landlocked except for a route over other adjoining land still owned by the seller of the landlocked parcel.

An **easement by necessity** is created when a parcel is landlocked and there is no method of ingress or egress other than over someone else's land. In that case, the most efficient route must be taken.

An **easement by prescription** is obtained in a manner similar to that of **adverse possession** (Adverse possession will be discussed later in this chapter.). The right to be obtained is a right of use rather than ownership, but the use must be without the permission of the property owner and must continue for the statutory period; five years in California. Property taxes (unlike adverse possession) are not paid by the user of the easement, however.

An **easement by condemnation** can be created for a public purpose (such as installation of utility lines) by means of the government's **right of eminent domain**, the right of the government to take, after fair compensation, private property that will be used for the public good. (Refer to **Deeds** for more information.)

An **easement** can be terminated by:

- **deed** from the owner of the **dominant** tenement to the owner of the servient tenement
- **express agreement** of the owners of the dominant and servient tenements
- **abandonment**, in the case of an **easement by prescription**

- **nonuse** (only if obtained by **prescription**)
- **merger**, when one owner aquires both the dominant and servient tenements.
- **excessive use**
- **destruction** of the servient tenement
- adverse possession of the easement property
- **lawsuit**, as by an **action to quiet title**

An **encroachment** occurs when a property improvement extends onto an adjoining parcel of land.

An encroachment may be so slight as to be unnoticeable or unobjectionable, as with a fence line that deviates by only one or a few inches from the defined property boundary.

Though usually occurring at ground level, there may be an encroachment into an adjoining property owner's air space by the roofline or other part of a building.

The remedy may be removal of the encroachment or money damages. But if no legal action is taken (or permission granted) by the owner of the burdened land within three years, such action is barred by the **statute of limitations**. For encroaching vegetation (trees, bushes, etc.), there is no statute of limitations.

Types of Ownership

Estates in Real Property

Estates in real property are **freehold** or **nonfreehold** (sometimes called **less-than-freehold**).

Freehold estates of ownership include the fee simple estate and the life estate.

Fee simple (**fee simple absolute**) is the highest (most complete) form of ownership. But it may be subject to a condition or limitation, in which case it is a **defeasible fee** (**determinable fee**). A **fee simple estate** is inheritable.

A **life estate** lasts only for the lifetime of the holder of the estate (or another identified living person, when a life estate *pur autre vie* is created). The holder of a **life estate** has all the responsibilities of ownership while the estate is in effect and may not destroy the premises. A life estate is not inheritable unless it is a life estate *pur autre vie* and the person against whose life the estate is measured survives the original holder of the life estate. A life estate usually is followed by a **remainder** interest in a party or parties named in the document that created the life estate. If no remainder interest was created, the property returns by reversion to the creator of the life estate (or that person's heirs).

Merger of a **fee interest and life estate** occurs when the same party acquires ownership of both interests. If that happens, the life estate is extinguished.

Nonfreehold estates are leasehold interests and are considered **personal property** (**chattels real**).

The **lessor** (owner of the **leased fee**) permits the **lessee** (holder of the **leasehold interest**) to use the property for the period and under the **terms** specified in the lease. The **terms of the lease** may allow it to be transferred during the **lease term**.

Forms of Ownership

Ownership in severalty (**tenancy in severalty**) is ownership by one party, which can be an individual or business. (The owner's interest is severed from that of anyone else.) The **owner in severalty** receives all of the benefits of ownership, such as income from space rental or sale or **lease of mineral rights**. In return, the owner in severalty is solely responsible for payment of property and other taxes and must bear the burden of property maintenance and other costs.

Concurrent ownership is ownership by more than one party. The rest of this section discusses forms of concurrent ownership.

A **tenancy in common** has the following attributes:

- Individual interests can be acquired at different times.
- Ownership interests can be equal or unequal. **Benefits** (income) and **burdens** (expenses) of ownership are divided in the same proportion.
- Each owner has an undivided right to use of the entire property, unless the parties agree otherwise.
- Each owner can transfer, encumber, or will his/her interest without affecting the rights of the other owners. The new owner will be a **tenant in common** with the other owners.
- A **partition action** can be brought to terminate the tenancy and divide the property (or the proceeds of a sale of the property) according to each co-owner's proportionate share.
- A creditor may force a sale of a co-owner's interest to satisfy a debt. The new owner of that share will be a tenant in common with the other owners.

A **joint tenancy** has the following attributes:

- Individual interests must be acquired at the same time (**unity of time**).
- Individual interests must be acquired by the same document (**unity of title**).
- Ownership interests are always equal (**unity of interest**), as are each co-owner's share of the benefits (**income**) and burdens (**expenses**) of ownership.
- Each owner has an undivided interest; that is, the right to use of the entire property (**unity of possession**).

The **four unities** of **time**, **title**, **interest**, and **possession** must exist to establish **joint tenancy**.

A properly created joint tenancy will carry with it the **right of survivorship**. This means that a joint tenant cannot will his/her ownership interest; when a co-owner dies, the surviving co-owners share equally in the deceased owner's interest. A joint tenant can sell his/her interest at any time.

A **partition action** can be brought to sever a joint tenancy and divide the property (or the proceeds of a sale of the property). In California, a recorded document, such as a deed , can be used to sever a joint tenancy as to that co-owner's share.

Creditors may force a sale of a share of jointly owned property to reach an individual owner's interest. If there were more than two co-owners in the joint tenancy, the share that is sold (either by the creditor or the co-owner) is held in a tenancy in common and the remaining shares are still held in joint tenancy as to those interests only.

A **tenancy by the entirety** has the following attributes:

- It is allowed in some states (but not California) as a form of joint tenancy that is available only to married couples.
- It is terminated by agreement of the spouses, dissolution (divorce), or death.
- A transfer of property held in tenancy by the entirety requires the agreement of both spouses.
- Creditors of only one spouse may be unable to reach property owned in tenancy by the entirety.

California, which is a **community property** state, does not recognize either **dower** or **curtesy interests**.

Community property is recognized in California, as well as in Arizona, Idaho, Louisiana, Nevada, New Mexico, Texas, and Washington. Other states (such as Michigan and Wisconsin) have adopted similar forms of marital property ownership. Each of these states has a unique variation of community property. The following rules apply in California:

- Community property is an ownership option only for a married couple. It is the option that will be assumed if no other choice is specified when spouses take title to property.
- In California, the legal presumption is that California real property and all personal property (wherever located) that is acquired during marriage is community property. There is an exception for property acquired by gift or inheritance by one spouse only, or by the sale of one spouse's separate property (**non-community property**).
- Out-of-state real property acquired during marriage by spouses who subsequently move to California is considered **quasi-community property**. The same rule applies when real estate or personal property (wherever located) is exchanged for California real estate.
- Separate property that is **commingled** with community property (combined with, as occurs with funds held in a joint checking or savings account) is treated as community property.
- Both spouses have the right to manage community property. A **transfer** or **encumbrance** of real estate held as community property requires the signature of both spouses.
- Only a creditor of both spouses can reach community property.

By taking title as Community Property, each spouse can will their one-half share of the community property to whomever they wish. If a spouse dies **intestate** (without a will), then the surviving spouse inherits their share.

By taking title as **Community Property with Right of Survivorship**, neither spouse can will their share, the surviving spouse interits the decedent's share.

A **tenancy in partnership** is the way in which property is owned by a partnership created to conduct business for profit.

In a **general partnership**, all of the following occur:

- All partners are entitled to actively participate in partnership business.
- All partners are equally liable for partnership debts.
- All partners have equal right of control of partnership property.
- All partners must agree to the transfer of partnership property. (Sale of real estate also requires signatures of spouses of partners.)
- Partnership income is taxed to individual partners and not the partnership.
- Personal creditors of the partners cannot reach partnership property.

In a **limited partnership**, all of the following occur.

- One or more **general partners** actively manage the business and have the full responsibility of partners, as listed above.
- One or more **limited partners**, as defined by state law, are inactive (not involved in day-to-day business management), in exchange for which they are not liable for partnership obligations beyond the amount invested.
- Partnership income is taxed to individual partners and not the partnership.

A **joint venture** is similar in form to a general partnership, but created to carry out a single project. Individuals or firms may contribute their work product, rather than money.

A **corporation** is an artificial entity created by state law.

- **Shareholders** are owners of stock in the corporation.
- **Bylaws** grant authority to specified officers to transact business.
- Shareholders are not personally liable for corporate debts.
- A shareholder's interest is inheritable.
- The corporation is taxed, as are individual shareholders when they receive stock **dividends**, so double taxation results.

An **S corporation** is created under **Subchapter S** of **the Internal Revenue Service Code**.

- It can have no more than 35 shareholders.
- It allows corporate income to be taxed only to individual owners (shareholders), thus avoiding double taxation.

A **limited liability company** (**LLC**) is defined by state law, and each state's law has unique differences.

- It offers the limited liability of a corporation.
- Its income is taxed directly to its owners, thus avoiding double taxation.

A **syndicate** is a group formed by a syndicator to combine funds for real estate investment. The form of ownership may be a partnership, **corporation**, **limited liability company**, **tenancy in common**, or other arrangement.

A **trust** may be created to hold and manage **real estate**.

- A **real estate investment trust** (**REIT**) is defined by both federal and state law.
- A REIT must have more than 100 investors.
- A REIT allows ownership shares to be publicly traded.
- A REIT must distribute 95% of its profits each year.

A **living trust** is used to hold title to the property of the **trustor** (owner), who is also the trust's **beneficiary**. On the death of the trustor, title passes to a **contingent beneficiary** identified in the trust instrument, thus avoiding probate.

Descriptions of Property

In order for some or all of the rights of ownership of real property to be transferred, the property must be described in sufficient detail to exclude all other parcels.

The **metes and bounds** system is one of the oldest methods of land measurement and description used in this country. The **bounds** (boundary lines) of property are measured from a specified point of beginning along measurements called **metes**, with each change of direction marked by a compass angle. **Markers** denote each turning point; in modern descriptions, **natural monuments** (the old oak tree) have been replaced by **benchmarks** (metal pins). The description ends with the return to the point of beginning.

The **U.S. government survey system** (**rectangular survey system**) was developed to have a more uniform method of delineating property boundaries.

Property is identified by reference to the intersection of a **meridian** (**principal meridian**) running north-south and a baseline running east-west. In California, there are three such intersections:

- Humboldt Base and Meridian Lines
- Mt. Diablo Base and Meridian Lines
- San Bernardino Base and Meridian Lines

Land is separated into rectangles called **townships** of six miles square (six miles to a side, or 36 square miles). Townships are counted in **tiers** north or south of a baseline and ranges east or west of a meridian. A township is divided into 36 sections. A **section** is one mile square (one square mile) and contains 640 acres. An **acre** contains 43,560 square feet.

Sections are numbered as shown in the following figure.

The **subdivision system** (**lot and block system**) uses **parcel numbers** noted on a **subdivision map** (**plat map**). The deed to each **parcel** references the book and page number in the recorder's office where the subdivision map can be found.

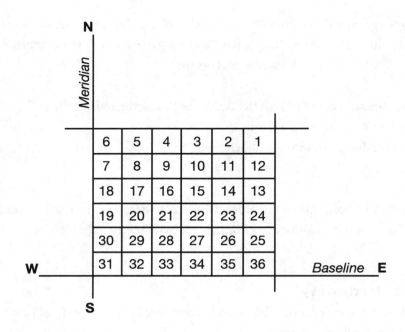

Government Rights in Land

The **police power** of government is its right to regulate for the benefit of the public health, safety, morals, and welfare. Exercise of their police power by the states in the context of land use generally is passed on to local governing bodies (counties, cities) by enabling acts. Federal regulations also exist.

Planning is used to establish permissible land uses in defined areas.

Every county and municipality is required by California law to formulate a **general plan** (also called the **master plan**) that sets the pattern for future land development. Establishment of a general plan is a time-consuming process that involves recommendations of consultants as well as public review and comment.

The general plan covers such topics as:

- land use
- availability of utilities and means of transportation
- housing
- conservation
- open space
- noise
- safety concerns (protection from fire as well as seismic and other geological hazards)

The general plan can be revised, but each change requires further public review and comment. There must be a solid waste management plan. Coastal development is also a concern in affected areas.

A **planning commission** may carry out a continuous process of review and enforcement.

Zoning is the primary method of carrying out the goals of the general plan. When an area is **zoned**, designated parcels are limited to specific property uses. Deviation from those uses requires petition to a board of **zon-**

ing adjustment (**board of zoning appeals**, **zoning appeals board**, or **zoning hearing board**). Further appeal is to the local governing body, such as the city council. Appeal beyond the local level will be to the state court system. The ultimate arbiter of an appeal on constitutional grounds (such as an unlawful taking of property without payment of just compensation) is the **U.S. Supreme Court.**

A **nonconforming** use is one that was in existence before the zoning regulation went into effect. Such property improvements typically will be allowed to remain, though subject to strict rules regarding future modifications.

A **variance** will be granted for a minor deviation from a zoning requirement, if to do otherwise would deny a property owner a use expected by owners of comparable properties. An example would be a steeply sloping residential building lot that requires the house to be placed closer to the front property line than would ordinarily be permitted.

A **conditional use** (**special use**) permit allows a property use that is not specified for the zoned area but is nevertheless considered of sufficient benefit to property owners to be allowed. An example would be a child care center located in an area zoned for residential use.

Rezoning is a change in permitted uses that may be the result of a revision of the general plan or consent of the governing body. **Downzoning** is a change to a more limited range of property uses, such as a change from multi-family residential to single-family residential. **Upzoning** is a change to a broader range of uses, such as a change from residential to commercial.

Spot zoning is a change of zoning that affects only one or a few properties and is generally not permitted.

Subdivision development is subject to both California and federal regulations on the formation, marketing, and sale of parcels.

Property used in the commission of a drug-related crime is subject to forfeiture and sale.

The Interstate Land Sales Full Disclosure Act is a federal law that applies to **interstate offerings** (marketing of parcels to buyers in other states) of 25 or more parcels of less than five acres each. This federal law requires disclosure to prospective purchasers of the nature and extent of the ownership interest they will acquire. The disclosure must include:

- the type of title that will be transferred
- findings of soil and other reports
- the number of parcels in the finished development
- the **amenities** that will be provided (from utilities to clubhouse and other facilities)
- the proximity of the development to necessary services, such as police and fire departments

California's Subdivided Lands Law is administered by the **Real Estate Commissioner**. The law regulates the financing and marketing to consumers of **parcels** in any residential **subdivision** of five or more parcels of up to 160 acres of land each.

The **Commissioner** issues a public report describing the property being offered, as well as the status of improvements and financing. Applicable **subdivisions** include:

- a **standard subdivision** with separate **parcels** and no **common areas**
- a **common interest subdivision** with separately owned parcels as well as one or more common areas (open land or facilities such as a club house or swimming pool), including **condominiums, community apartment projects, time-share projects, stock cooperative projects** and **limited equity housing cooperatives**
- an **undivided interest subdivision** in which each owner is a tenant in common
- a **land project**, which has 50 or more parcels in an area of fewer than 1,500 registered voters within the subdivision or within two miles of its boundaries

California's Subdivision Map Act provides authority to local jurisdictions to set requirements for **subdivision** approval, including public hearings. The law applies to any subdivision of land into two or more parcels.

A **tentative subdivision** map prepared by the developer will describe the property and provide specifications on streets, public areas, provision of utilities, source of water supply, storm water drainage, and proposed property use.

The final map will include all local requirements.

The California Environmental Quality Act of 1970 (CEQA) may require preparation of an **environmental impact report (EIR)** before a subdivision can be approved either by the **Real Estate Commissioner** or the local jurisdiction.

Any California development with an earthquake fault area must comply with the **Alquist-Priolo Earthquake Fault Zoning Act**. This **zoning** act helps control the development of residential and other properties designed for human occupancy, within a quarter mile of earthquake faults.

The Seismic Hazards Mapping Act applies to California property located in a defined **seismic hazards zone**.

The Coastal Zone Conservation Act applies to California property within a defined **coastal zone**.

Building codes are minimum construction standards for building, framing, plumbing, electrical wiring, and other components. In California, both state and local **building codes** must comply with the **Uniform Building Code** established by the **Building Officials and Code Administrators International, Inc. (BOCA)**.

A **building permit** is issued when plans are approved for either new construction or a remodeling.

A **plan** must conform with **setback** (minimum distance from property boundaries or other buildings), **dimension** (length, width, height), **size** (square or cubic footage), **design**, and **applicable state** as well as local requirements, such as installation of sprinkler systems in high fire-risk areas. A **building permit** is required no matter who performs the work. Building contractors are licensed by the state.

When work is underway, the local **building inspector** or **codes director** will examine the construction project at various stages of progress for compliance with the minimum standards.

A **certificate of occupancy (CO)** is issued on completion only after all requirements have been satisfied.

Public Controls

Manufactured homes (formerly called **mobile homes**) are subject to construction requirements of the federal **Department of Housing and Urban Development (HUD)**.

The structural integrity and components of HUD-code homes, as they are called, are not subject to local requirements. But such homes are subject to local rules regarding building placement as well as the grading of the site, foundation work and manner of installation of the home, plumbing and electrical connections, and other site-related features.

California's Mobilehome Accommodation Structures Law sets requirements for structures used with manufactured homes. **The Mobilehome Parks Act** regulates parks used for manufactured homes. In the **California Real Estate Law** (found in the **Business and Professions Code**), a mobile home is defined as a "structure transportable in one or more sections, designed and equipped to contain not more than two dwelling units to be used with or without a foundation system."

Licensees must be aware that membership in an organization must not lead to illegal activities. **The Sherman Antitrust Act**, a federal law, prohibits certain business practices that could place unfair restrictions on free competition in the marketplace. Prohibitions against restraint of trade that directly effect the real estate industry include the following:

- There can be no **price fixing**. Agency fees or commissions are always subject to negotiation between principal and agent before an agency relationship is established. Agents for different companies are not allowed to agree to predetermined fees, or to agree on a range of fees for specific services. Even discussion of such matters could subject agents to civil and criminal penalties that could result in fines and/or imprisonment.
- Agencies cannot agree to provide service only in a designated geographic area.
- Agencies cannot agree to boycott certain companies or other agencies.
- Agents are not to form exclusive organizations (such as property listing services) that arbitrarily prevent nonmembers from gaining access to sales and marketing information. Membership criteria must be designed so as not to unfairly exclude otherwise qualified agents from participation.

Environmental Hazards and Regulations

Environmental influences include any factor in the climate or terrain of an area that affects value. Effects can be local (proximity to an earthquake fault) or global (increased levels of pollution caused by smoke from widespread fires following a drought). Some influences are the result of human intervention, such as industrial, agricultural, or urban pollutants.

Environmental regulations intended to protect air, water, and land from contamination exist at both federal and state levels.

Federal laws include the **Clean Water Act, Clean Air Act, National Environmental Policy Act**, and others.

The Comprehensive Environmental Response, Compensation, and Liability Act (CERCLA), enacted in 1980, is the **Superfund Law** and is enforced by the **Environmental Protection Agency** (EPA).

The EPA has identified more than 30,000 inactive hazardous waste sites, and placed the most dangerous of these (those requiring immediate attention) on a **National Priority List** (NPL).

Expenses of cleanup work are paid in part by the **Hazardous Substances Response Fund** (**Superfund**), which is financed by taxes on industries (such as oil and chemical companies) with the greatest likelihood of causing contamination. Other federal as well as private funds are also used in this effort.

Other inactive industrial sites that may or may not be contaminated are described as **brownfields**. The EPA estimates that there are 450,000 such sites throughout the country. Documentation of such sites has begun in 40 state and regional jurisdictions.

Some states, such as California, have their own hazardous waste remediation laws. In the event of a property transfer, state law requires disclosure by the property owner of known or suspected contamination.

The federal **Toxic Substances Control Act** has resulted in recommendations from the EPA on detection and remediation or containment of

- **asbestos** insulation fibers
- naturally occurring **radon** gas that seeps into a building foundation
- **urea-formaldehyde** (**UF**) gas that may be released by some glues, resins, preservatives, and bonding agents found in plywood and other building products and furnishings

The Safe Drinking Water Act was amended in 1986 to prohibit use of materials containing lead in public water supplies as well as in residences connected to public water supplies. In 1988, the use of lead-based solder in plumbing applications within buildings was prohibited. Homes built before 1988 may still have pipe connections made with lead-based solder.

The Residential Lead-Based Paint Hazard Reduction Act of 1992 requires disclosure of the possible presence of lead-based paint in all houses built before 1978.

- Houses and other buildings built before 1978 are likely to have ceilings, walls, and other surfaces painted with lead-based paint.
- The EPA enforces the law.

Private Controls

Use of land may also be limited by a restriction that appears in the deed from **grantor** to **grantee**. By accepting the deed, the grantee agrees to be bound by the limitation.

Subdivision restrictions typically are listed in a Declaration of Restrictions that is recorded with the subdivision map and referred to in the deed to every individual lot buyer in the subdivision. Each landowner thus becomes bound by the listed obligations.

Restrictions are also termed **covenants, conditions, and restrictions** (**CC&Rs**). In practice, the term restriction can refer to any of the following.

A **covenant** is a promise of a property owner. The violation of a convenant can lead to a dollar damage award, enforced in court. A **condition** stipulates an action that a property owner must perform, or refrain from performing. The violation of a condition is the most serious and can lead to the reversion of the property to the creator of the condition. But a **restraint on alienation** (a condition that prevents a transfer of title) is unlawful. A

restriction stipulates a forbidden activity or property use. Many subdivisions make use of a homeowners' association to enforce deed restrictions and maintain common areas.

Water Rights

Water rights are defined by state law and depend on the water source and use. The most obvious source is surface water.

On a navigable body of flowing water, such as a river, the property owner's boundary extends to the **mean** (average) **high water line.** The state owns the land under the water. Owners of property bordering a flowing stream may have **riparian rights.** An owner of riparian rights also has the right to reasonable use of the water the property borders. **Littoral rights** belong to owners of property bordering a lake or other body of still or non-navigable water. The property owner's boundary typically extends to the center of the body of water.

Each property owner has the right to use a reasonable quantity of water, as long as the use is limited to that property of the owner. The government's right of appropriation may be used to take water for a public use. Water permits issued by local jurisdictions are used to ration scarce water resources in areas of growing population.

Use of **underground (subterranean) water** is vital in states that have insufficient water from surface sources for residential, agricultural, and commercial uses. **Percolating water** drains from the surface to underground strata. The **doctrine of correlative rights** limits the amount of water that can be taken to a proportionate share based on each owner's share of the surface area.

Special Categories of Land

Mineral rights belong to the owner of real property, unless they are retained by means of a reservation in the deed to the landowner, or assigned to someone else by means of a grant from the landowner. The right to remove specified minerals can also be assigned by the landowner by means of a **mineral lease.**

Oil and gas are subject to the **rule of capture.** The surface owner has the right to remove as much oil or gas as possible from wells on the owner's land. However, ownership cannot be claimed until these substances are reduced to possession.

▶ Laws of Agency

Law, Definition and Nature of Agency Relationships, Types of Agencies, and Agents

Agent—the traditional definition, found in the **California Civil Code**, is that the agent represents the interests of another person, called the **principal**, in dealings with third persons. In a real estate sales transaction, the traditional view is that:

- The **real estate agent** of the seller (**listing agent**) acts as a fiduciary to the seller.
- In the absence of an agreement to the contrary, any cooperating agent who brings a buyer to the transaction acts as a **subagent** of the listing agent and thus also owes the duties of a fiduciary to the seller.

Dual agent—an agent who represents both parties to a transaction. In California, a dual agent is always required to have the consent of both parties before acting in that capacity. In some states this type of representation is prohibited.

Subagency—the traditional view is that a cooperating agent is the subagent of the listing agent and thus represents the seller. The cooperating agent can reject the offer of subagency, however, and act as the buyer's agent instead.

Creation of Agency and Agency Agreements

Note: Some information relating to the creation of agency and agency agreements will also be discussed in Contracts.

The listing agreement is the contract that establishes the **agency** relationship of property owner and real estate agent. The object of the listing agreement usually is the sale of the described property. A written listing agreement will establish an **express agency**, rather than an **implied agency** that can be inferred by the conduct of the principal and agent. **Listing agreements** establish a **special agency** related only to the property described, rather than a **general agency**.

An **open listing** (**nonexclusive listing**) results in payment of a commission to the listing agent only if that person is the procuring cause of the sale. If the property is sold by any other agent, the listing agent is not entitled to a commission.

An exclusive agency listing prevents the property owner from listing the property with any other agent. This means that, in the event of sale, the listing agent will receive a commission even if another agent was the procuring cause of the sale. The owner is still entitled to sell the property to someone without the agent's assistance and avoid paying any commission.

An **exclusive authorization and right-to-sell listing** provides the greatest protection to the listing agent, who will be paid the commission no matter who sells the property.

An **option listing** gives the listing agent the right to purchase the property. This kind of agreement requires disclosure by the listing agent of the details of any planned subsequent transaction, including the agent's profit, and agreement of the property owner.

A **net listing** offers the property owner a guaranteed sales price, with the listing agent taking any part of the purchase price over that amount. This arrangement is frowned upon as it opens the agent to charges of misrepresentation of the true value of the property at the time the agreement is initiated. Within one month of closing the transaction the broker must inform in writing both the buyer and the seller the actual selling price involved in the sale. This is often simply disclosed by the escrow company's closing statement.

A **buyer agency** (**buyer broker**) agreement will establish the terms under which the agent will find property that meets the buyer's specifications and work to complete the transaction. The buyer agent's compensation must be specified. It can be a flat fee, an hourly rate, or (most often) a percentage of the purchase price to be paid at the time of closing.

Responsibilities of Agent to Seller/Buyer as Principal

The real estate listing agent owes the property owner (**principal**) the duties of a **fiduciary**. The agent must act in the owner's best interests. The buyer's agent owes the same responsibilities to the buyer.

The agent's duties to their principal include the following:

- loyalty
- good faith (fair dealing with all parties to the transaction)
- honesty
- full disclosure of material facts concerning the transaction
- due diligence in carrying out the terms of the agreement
- avoidance of any conflict of interest
- utmost care
- integrity
- obey lawful instructions
- no secret profits (The agent may not make any secret profit as a result of the transaction.)

The property owner owes the real estate agent and buyer honesty and disclosure of material facts concerning the property. The buyer also must pay the agreed-upon compensation on completion of a transaction.

Disclosure of Agency

Agency relationships must be disclosed by the agent to the principal prior to any agreement being signed by the principal. In the case of a seller, agency relationships must be disclosed prior to the listing. In the case of a buyer, agency relationships must be disclosed prior to a buyer broker agreement or the offer to purchase.

Dual agency is legal, but only if disclosed to all parties in a transaction.

Disclosure of Acting as Principal or Other Interest

Agents must disclose any interest they have in a property to their principal. They must also disclose if a family member has an interest in a property or is a buyer in a transaction in which the agent is participating.

Termination of Agency

A **listing agreement** can be terminated by:

- **expiration** of the time period specified in the agreement
- **performance**—a successful transaction or other fulfillment by the agent of the terms of the agreement
- **mutual consent of the parties** (**rescission**)
- **revocation** by property owner, who may be liable for damages (advertising expenses, and so on) to the agent
- **renunciation** by the agent
- death or **adjudicated incompetency** of either owner or agent
- **destruction** of the property

Commission and Fees

Commissions and fees charged by a real estate agent are always negotiable. Residential listing agreements must contain a notice that commissions are negotiable and not set by law in ten-point bold print.

▶ Valuation and Market Analysis

Definitions

The Appraisal Standards Board of the Appraisal Foundation has produced the **Uniform Standards of Professional Appraisal Practice (USPAP)**. These standards set the minimum requirements for appraisals. Some useful definitions are:

> **Appraisal**—the act or process of estimating value; an estimate of value
>
> **Cash flow analysis**—a study of the anticipated movement of cash into or out of an investment
>
> **Departure provision**—section of USPAP that allows the appraiser to perform an assignment that will vary from the specific guidelines set by USPAP. The guidelines are not intended to be binding, but any variations should be undertaken only after:

- appropriate determination by the appraiser that the **deviation** is warranted
- notification to the client that the appraisal will vary from recommended guidelines
- agreement of the client to the stated limitations on the work to be performed

> **Feasibility analysis**—a study of the cost-benefit relationship of an economic endeavor
>
> **Mass appraisal**—the process of valuing a universe of properties as of a given date utilizing standard methodology, employing common data, and allowing for statistical testing
>
> **Report**—any communication, written or oral, of an appraisal, review, or consulting service that is transmitted to the client upon completion of an assignment. The types of report include the:

- **self-contained appraisal report**—the most complete report, with a detailed presentation of the data collected and the valuation process
- **summary appraisal report**—a more concise presentation of the data and analysis
- **restricted appraisal report**—a report providing minimal data and analysis and limited to the use(s) specified
- **review**—the act or process of critically studying a report prepared by another

Appraisal Regulations

The Financial Institutions Reform, Recovery, and Enforcement Act of 1989 (FIRREA) requires most appraisals in federally related transactions to be performed by state licensed or certified appraisers. California instituted appraiser licensing and certification in 1992. Examples of federally related transactions are those involving any one of the following:

- lender chartered or insured by an agency of the federal government
- loan funded, insured, or guaranteed by any **federal agency**
- loan sold to a federal or quasi-federal organization

The Appraisal Foundation is a nonprofit corporation established in 1987 to assist the states by setting minimum standards for:

- appraisals
- appraiser education and training

Licensing is required in valuations of one- to four-unit residential property unless the property is of unusual size or complexity. Licensed appraisers also can handle appraisals of nonresidential property and complex residential property valued at less than $250,000.

As of January 1, 1998, **California's Office of Real Estate Appraisers** (**OREA**) has set the minimum requirements for the residential license at:

- 90 hours of education with at least 15 hours of USPAP
- 2,000 hours of experience
- passing the required examination

A **licensed residential appraiser** can conduct appraisals of one- to four-unit residential property up to a value of $1 million and nonresidential property valued at no more than $250,000.

Experience can be obtained by performing allowed activities under the supervision of an appraiser. A **trainee license** is available to applicants who have successfully completed 90 classroom hours of instruction so that they can gain experience working for a licensed or certified appraiser.

A **certified residential appraiser** is allowed to appraise one- to four-unit properties of any size or complexity and nonresidential property valued at no more than $250,000. Minimum requirements are the following:

- 120 hours of education with at least 15 hours of USPAP
- 2,500 hours/two-and-a-half years of experience
- passing of the required examination

A **certified general appraiser** is allowed to appraise any type of real property within the appraiser's qualifications. Minimum requirements are the following:

- 180 hours of education with at least 15 hours of USPAP
- 3,000 hours/two-and-a-half years of experience
- passing of the required examination

There are continuing education requirements in order to renew either a license or certification after four years.

Value

An appraisal will specify the type of value sought. The elements that establish value can be remembered by the acronym **DUST**:

Demand for the type of property
Utility (desirable use) the property offers
Scarcity of properties available
Transferability of the property to a new owner (lack of impediments to a sale)

Appraisals most often are used to estimate a property's market value. Market value can be defined as the most probable price that a buyer is willing to pay, and a seller is willing to accept, when all of the following apply:

- both parties are aware of the condition of the property
- neither party is acting under duress
- financing for the transaction is typical of what is available locally

Market value is an estimate of value only. The estimate is not necessarily what a property will actually sell for. Market value may be more or less than the amount the owner has spent on the property.

A property's **cost** is the expense to its owner of buying or improving it. A property's **sales price** is what someone else pays for it. The sales price frequently is less than the cost of the land and improvements. This happens when a property owner over-customizes or over-improves a property, failing to take into account the likely needs of a prospective purchaser.

Other values that may be sought include the following:

Assessed value—determination for property tax purposes
Book value—depreciated cost basis used for accounting and tax purposes
Insurance value—the maximum amount that an insurer will be willing to pay for an insured loss
Investment value—what an investor is willing to pay for the right to receive the cash flow produced by the property
Loan value—the maximum loan that can be secured by the property
Salvage value—what the component parts of a building or other improvement will be worth following demolition or removal
Utility value—what a particluar property is worth to a particular buyer

The principles of value that underlay the appraisal process include the following:

Anticipation—the expectation that property value will rise over time

Assemblage (**plottage**)—bringing a group of adjoining parcels under the same ownership, which may make them more valuable for a particular purpose, such as construction of a residential or commercial development.

Change—forces to which all property is subject, including

- **physical**—the action of the elements, which can occur gradually or in a brief period of time
- **political**—regulations that affect property use
- **economic**—employment level, business start-ups, expansions and failures, and other factors that influence the level of prosperity of a region
- **social**—demographic and other trends that affect the demand for property

Conformity—individual properties in a residential neighborhood tend to have a higher value when they are of similar architecture, design, age, and size. The same principle applies generally to commercial properties.

Competition—a result of increasing demand as well as a creator of increasing demand. For example, even though a regional mall may offer many stores selling similar products, it will benefit all store owners by bringing more shoppers to the area.

Contribution—the cost of an additional component should have a corresponding increase in the value of the property

Externalities—effect on value of factors outside a property. An example is any government action taken to increase housing affordability and thus purchases, such as the mortgage interest deduction for homeowners.

Highest and best use—the legally allowed property use that makes maximum physical use of a site and generates the highest income

Law of decreasing returns—in effect when property improvements no longer bring a corresponding increase in property value

Law of increasing returns—in effect as long as property improvements bring a corresponding increase in property value

Life cycle—applies to an individual property as well as a neighborhood. The **initial period of development** (**growth** or **integration**) becomes a **period of equilibrium** (when properties are at their highest and best use) followed by **decline** (**disintegration**), when property values go down as maintenance requirements increase and are not met. In areas that warrant the substantial expense of building **renovation**, there may then be a period of **revitalization**.

Progression—the benefit to a property of being located in an area of more desirable properties. The small, plain house on a street of mansions will benefit from proximity to them.

Regression—the detriment to a property of being located in a neighborhood of less desirable properties. The large, over-improved house on a street of small, plain houses will have a lower value than it would in a neighborhood of comparable houses.

Substitution—the principle underlying appraisal practice, that the typical buyer will want to pay no more for a property than would be required to buy another, equivalent property. This principle, when applied to income-producing property, is called **opportunity cost.** An investor will want to pay no more for real estate than another investment offering the same likely risk and potential reward.

Supply and demand—as the number of properties available for sale goes up relative to the number of potential buyers, prices will fall. As the number of properties declines while the number of potential buyers remains the same or increases, prices will rise.

Theory of distribution—consideration of the contribution to value of each of **the four factors of production—land (rent), labor (salaries), capital (interest),** and **management (profit).** When these factors are in balance, property value will be at its highest.

Methods of Estimating Value

Following are the steps in the appraisal process:

- State the problem. The nature of the appraisal assignment must be clearly understood. The assignment may be to find the market value of the subject property. If so, that should be stated.
- Determine the kinds and sources of data necessary. The appraiser must ask:

What are the characteristics of the subject property?

What economic or other factors will play a role in determining property value?

What approach(es) will be most appropriate in this appraisal and what kind of data will be necessary?

- Determine the highest and best use of the site.
- Estimate the value of the site.
- Estimate the property's value by each of the appropriate approaches (market data, cost, and/or income).
- Reconcile the different values reached by the different approaches to estimate the property's most probable market value. This process is called **reconciliation** or **correlation.**
- Report the estimate of value to the client. There are several types of documents that may be prepared.

The **narrative appraisal report** provides a lengthy discussion of the factors considered in the appraisal and the reasons for the conclusion of value.

The **form report** is used most often for single-family residential appraisals. The **Uniform Residential Appraisal Report (URAR)** is required by various agencies and organizations. Computerized appraisal generation and delivery by modem is possible and is increasingly expected by banks and other lenders.

The **self-contained report** defined by USPAP will be as complete as the narrative appraisal report.

Use of either the summary report or **restricted report** defined by USPAP will require the consent of the client.

An appraiser uses one or more of three approaches to reach an estimate of value.

The **market data** (**sales comparison**) **approach** makes use of data on sales of nearby, comparable properties to estimate the likely value of the property being appraised (**subject property**). This process of **paired data** (**paired sales**) **analysis** is the best method for valuing most residential property.

The sales price of a **comparable property** (**comp**) is adjusted down to compensate for the market value of a desirable feature that is present in the comp but not the subject property.

The sales price of a comp is adjusted up to allow for desirable features that are present in the subject property and not the comp.

Example: The house at 1230 River Road is being appraised. A comparable house at 1142 River Road sold last month for $230,000. The comp has a detached garage and the subject property does not. The estimated value of the garage is $9,600, which is subtracted from the sales price of $230,000 to derive an adjusted sales price for the comp of $220,400. After analyzing the sales prices of five comps in this way, and comparing the resulting adjusted figures, the appraiser estimates the value of the subject property as $220,000.

Land, whether or not it has any improvements (buildings) is often valued separately by using the market data approach.

The cost approach uses the following formula: reproduction cost of improvements minus depreciation on improvements plus land value equals property value. If a property (such as an older building) has features that could not be economically duplicated today, the replacement cost of a functionally equivalent structure will be found.

Building reproduction cost typically is found by one of the following methods.

- **Square-foot method**—the current cost per square foot of comparable construction is multiplied by the number of square feet in the subject building.
- **Index method**—a factor representing the change over time in construction prices is applied to the original cost of the building.
- **Unit-in-place method**—current price of each component part (foundation, framing, roofing, and so on) is added.
- **Quantity survey method**—detailed cost breakdown of each element of construction, including **direct** (**labor, materials**) and **indirect** (**permit, profit**) **costs.**

Depreciation for appraisal purposes is not the same as that used for tax purposes. The appraiser estimates the actual effect on value of depreciation from all causes, termed **accrued depreciation**. Depreciation can be **curable** or **incurable**; it is curable if the defect is one that could be corrected at a cost that does not exceed what the property will be worth (see **principle of contribution**). Causes of deterioration include:

- **Physical deterioration**—the effect of the elements and ordinary wear-and-tear. Generally curable.
- **External obsolescence**—economic, locational, or environmental influences that may have a negative effect on value. Generally incurable.
- **Functional obsolescence**—features that are no longer considered desirable, in design, manner of construction, or layout. A house with four bedrooms and only one bathroom suffers from functional obsolescence. Can be curable or incurable.

Depreciation can be estimated by using the:

- **Age-life method** (**straight line method**)—the rate of annual depreciation is determined by dividing the number one by the number of years that the building should be useful for its intended purpose, then multiplying the resulting percentage by the building's effective age. For example, a building with a total estimated useful life of 50 years depreciates at the rate of $\frac{1}{50}$, or 2% per year. If the building is 20 years old, but has been well maintained, the appraiser may decide that it shows an effective age of only 15 years. Its accrued depreciation would then be calculated as 30% (2% $\times$ 15 years).
- **Observed condition method**—each category of building component is separately considered and the effective appreciation of each is noted. For example, a roof that will need replacement within the next few years may be considered to have depreciated 90%. This approach requires that each component be separately valued and then separately depreciated.

The **income approach** is also called the income **capitalization approach**.

The simplest way to use property income to estimate market value is to use a **gross income multiplier** (**GIM**). Income produced by comparable properties is compared to their sales prices. A factor is created for each property by dividing the property's sales price by its annual gross income. Then, a factor is derived that can be applied to the market rent of the subject property—the rent the property would be capable of producing at today's going rates.

Example: Building A produces annual gross income of $20,000 and sold recently for $200,000. Building B produces annual gross of $32,000 and sold recently for $300,000. The GIM for Building A is $200,000 divided by $20,000, or 10. The GIM for Building B is $300,000 divided by $32,000, or 9.375. After analyzing several more properties, the appraiser concludes that a GIM of 10 is appropriate for the subject property. Applying that multiple to the subject property's annual market rent of $28,000, the appraiser reaches an estimate of value by this method of $280,000.

A **gross rent multiplier** (**GRM**) based on monthly market rent typically is used in the appraisal of a house. A much more detailed income valuation can be made using **direct capitalization**.

Market rent—the property's potential income if available for a new occupant at current rates—is estimated by analysis of comparable properties.

Effective gross income is found by totaling income from all sources and subtracting an allowance for vacancy and collection losses.

Net operating income is found by subtracting operating expenses from effective gross income. For appraisal purposes, operating expenses include **variable expenses** (such as salaries and utilities), **fixed expenses** (such as real estate taxes and insurance), and **reserves for replacement** (such as set-asides for a new roof and furnace) but not costs of financing, income tax payments, depreciation deductions and capital improvements.

Net operating income is divided by the **capitalization rate** (the desired return on the investment) to arrive at an **indication of value** (what an investor would be willing to pay for the income stream generated by the property).

The capitalization rate (**cap rate**) is found by building its component parts. An investor expects to receive a **profit** (**interest rate**) on the capital invested, as well as to have the capital itself returned by the time the investment is unusable.

Example: Mary wants to purchase an apartment building that has a remaining economic life of 40 years. She wants interest of 10% annually on her investment, as well as the return of the amount invested. The building's net operating income is $120,000 annually. Thus, each year the investment will have to have a cap rate of 10% plus $2\frac{1}{2}$% (100% divided by 40 years), or $12\frac{1}{2}$%. If we divide the net income of $120,000 by the $12\frac{1}{2}$% cap rate, the value of the property to this investor can be estimated at $960,000.

The **break-even point** (the point at which a property begins to generate profit) is found by adding operating expenses and the **debt service** (mortgage payment) on the property, and then dividing that total by the property's potential gross income.

Example: A property has operating expenses of $50,000 per year and requires debt service of $120,000 for the same period. The property can be expected to produce gross income of $190,000 per year. The property's break-even ratio is the total of all expenses of property ownership divided by the total income the property is expected to produce. In this example, the break-even ratio is created by adding $50,000 and $120,000 to arrive at $170,000, and then dividing $170,000 by $190,000. The resulting percentage is the break-even point—in this case, 89.5%.

This means that, when the property has an occupancy level of 89.5%, the expenses of owning it equal the income it generates. Below that point, the property has a **negative cash flow** (it costs more to own than it earns). Above that point, the property generates profit.

Discounted cash flow is another way to determine value by analyzing income projections. The income expected in each year of ownership is discounted to its present worth. The annual income figures are then added together to find the property's total present value.

► Financing

General Concepts

The most important factor in the increasing number of homeowners in this country is the availability of long-term financing at reasonable cost.

Financing Instruments are separate documents establish the fact that:

- a debt is owed (**the note**)
- the debt is **secured** by real estate (the **mortgage** or deed of **trust**)

The **promissory note** from borrower to lender records the amount borrowed and the terms of payment. You will find more information about promissory notes and securities under Contracts. **Principal** is the amount borrowed. **Interest** is the cost of a loan. With a **straight note**, only the interest is paid over the term of the loan, with the entire principal due at the end of the loan term. With an **installment note**, periodic payments of principal are made in addition to payments of interest.

When an installment note is **amortized**, payments (usually monthly) are equal and include both interest for the payment period and some of the principal owed. In the beginning of the loan term, the payments mostly go towards interest. As more of the principal is repaid, the amount paid towards interest decreases. By the last required payment, the entire amount owed has been repaid.

With a **fixed-rate note**, the interest rate is the same over the life of the loan. With an **adjustable-rate note**, the interest rate will vary over the life of the loan depending on changes and in an agreed-upon index. The **margin** is a rate added to the index rate. There will be a **cap** (maximum amount of increase) in the allowable rate increase for a stated period. There may also be a cap on the amount of the payment.

The required payment may increase or decrease as the interest rate rises or falls. If the interest rate goes up but payments do not, there may be **negative amortization**—that is, if the payment isn't sufficient to cover both interest and some of the principal owed, the amount of the debt will be increased.

A **balloon payment**, typically the final payment, is one that is at least twice the amount of any other payment. A **short-term loan** (say, three to five years) may have payments calculated on a 30-year loan term, but with the entire remaining balance due in the final balloon payment. This device can be useful when either one of the following is true:

- the borrower knows that the period of occupancy will be temporary and the property will be sold before the balloon payment is due
- interest rates are high and the borrower expects to refinance at a lower rate in a few years

Purchase money mortgage is a term used to describe either one of the following:

- any loan that is used to finance the purchase of real estate, that is, the loan used to make the purchase. (This does not include refinanced loans.)
- a credit from the seller for all or part of the purchase price (**seller financing**)

A **blanket mortgage** is one in which more than one parcel of real estate is used as **collateral**. An **open end mortgage** allows the borrower to increase the amount of the loan up to a predetermined limit.

A **reverse annuity mortgage** is one in which the borrower receives monthly payments from the lender in exchange for a lien on the specified property. The borrower must own the home outright or have substantial equity in it. Interest on the amount borrowed is added to the amount owed. The loan will be paid off when the property is sold, the borrower dies, or the loan period ends. This type of loan is used to allow elderly homeowners to benefit from the equity in their property without having to sell it.

Terms and Conditions

Some of the contract provisions that may be included in a promissory note are listed below:

- The **due-on-sale clause** (**alienation clause**) allows the lender to demand full payment of the remaining indebtedness if the property is sold.
- An **impound account** (**escrow account**) may require the borrower to make regular payments to be used to pay property taxes and insurance.
- **Late charges** will be incurred if the borrower is late in making a payment.
- A **prepayment penalty** provides an additional charge if the borrower makes any early loan payment. Most current loans allow prepayment of all or part of the loan balance without penalty.
- A **release clause** will benefit the borrower if the loan is secured by more than one lot or parcel. As the loan is paid off, the lender will release its security interest as to individual lots or parcels.

Types of Loans

Conventional loans are those made without any form of government-backed insurance or guarantee. The lender looks to the borrower and the **security** (the property) for assurance that the loan will be repaid by the borrower (or by forced sale of the property). Conventional loans are made by a variety of lenders. Conventional loans are those available from lending institutions, such as **S&Ls** and **commercial banks**. Conventional loans typically are **conforming loans**. This means that they meet the borrower and property qualification requirements of **FNMA** and are eligible for resale on the secondary market.

Borrowers who make a down payment of less than 20% of the sales price may be required to purchase **private mortgage insurance** (**PMI**). The insurance **premium** usually is a monthly charge added to the loan payment. It can be eliminated (with the lender's approval) when the borrower's equity in the home is at least 20% of the home's value.

Savings and loan associations (**S&Ls**) at one time made the majority of residential loans. Today, the number of S&Ls has been so greatly reduced that their share of the home mortgage market has dropped dramatically.

- Most transactions that would formerly have been handled by an S&L are now handled by savings banks.
- S&L deposits are now insured by the **Federal Deposit Insurance Corporation** (**FDIC**), the agency that has always insured bank deposits.

Sources of Financing

Commercial banks are currently the dominant residential lenders.

- They may be chartered by either the state or federal government, although the trend is toward federally chartered institutions.
- Their deposits are insured by the FDIC.

Mutual savings banks are owned by their depositors.

Mortgage companies (**mortgage bankers**) make loans that are then resold.

- The mortgage company typically will retain the loan servicing function.
- Mortgage bankers must be distinguished from mortgage brokers, who serve as middlemen between borrowers and lenders. In California, a real estate broker's license is necessary to act as a mortgage loan broker.

Life insurance companies have become important sources of investment funds for commercial and development properties. They are subject to regulation of the state in which they are authorized to do business.

Credit unions may make home loans, particularly home equity loans, to their members.

The primary mortgage market consists of lenders who deal directly with borrowers to make loans. The lender may or may not retain ownership of the loan after it is made.

A loan will be kept in the lender's portfolio if it is not sold to someone else.

Even when a lender sells a loan, it may retain the **loan servicing function**. The borrower's payments will continue to be made to the originating lender, who will charge a fee to the new owner in exchange for carrying out the collection function.

The right to payment on most residential loans is resold by the lender who originated the loan as part of what is termed the secondary mortgage market. When funds are returned to lenders, more loans can be made, interest rates are kept down, and property ownership is encouraged.

Loans that are sold often are treated as **mortgage-backed securities** (**MBS**). This means that they are sold individually or bundled into **pools** (**blocks**) for sale to an organization.

How to Deal with Lenders

Borrower qualification is the first concern of the lender. Compliance with FNMA's qualification requirements is necessary for a conforming loan that will be sold on the secondary mortgage market.

The **Uniform Residential Loan Application form** was created by FNMA and FHLMC to provide consistent data for evaluating the credit-worthiness of prospective borrowers.

Factors to be considered in the loan application process include income, employment history, and other financial obligations.

The **loan-to-value ratio** (percent of the property's value that will be borrowed) will determine whether or not private mortgage insurance (PMI) will be required.

Many expenses reported at closing are paid by either buyer or seller, some are shared equally, and others are divided on a proportionate basis. All expenses are subject to negotiation of the parties.

Who is responsible for expenses incurred on the day of closing?

Local custom or the agreement of the parties can dictate the party responsible for expenses incurred on the day of closing. Because the transfer of funds and title occurs on the day of closing, the buyer usually is responsible for that day's expenses. By the same reasoning, the buyer is also entitled to receive whatever benefit may accrue from ownership that day, such as the day's income if the property is a rental unit.

The **Uniform Settlement Statement** will indicate how each expense is to be apportioned.

- Unless the parties have agreed otherwise, the **escrow agent** will follow local custom as to the number of days in a year or month.
- For ease of calculation, a year of 360 days and standard month of 30 days may be assumed.
- Unless you are instructed otherwise, you should use a 360-day year and 30-day month for proration problems in the licensing examination.

Example: Property taxes on Graycastle are due on July 1 for the year beginning on that day and ending on the following June 30. Harold has paid $1,800 in property taxes for the current tax year on the home he is selling. The sale is to close on September 15. What amount will be credited to Harold and what amount will be debited to Jane, the buyer, for property taxes?

Jane is responsible for paying property taxes on $9\frac{1}{2}$ months of ownership (half of the month of September and the months from October through the following June. At the rate of $150 per month ($1,800 divided by 12 months), Jane must pay $1,425 ($150 multiplied by 9.5).

See Chapter 5, the Real Estate Math Review, for more help with proration problems.

Government Programs

Government-backed loans are those that receive some form of assurance of payment from an agency of the government.

FHA-insured loans are those that the **Federal Housing Administration** (**FHA**) insures.

- A one-time insurance payment is made by the purchaser at the time of the closing of the sale.
- FHA sets maximum loan amounts that it will lend depending on the state or county in which the property is located.
- The borrower of an FHA-insured loan must meet the financial qualifications set by FHA.
- The property being purchased must be appraised by a licensed appraiser.

- The interest rate to be paid is subject to negotiation between borrower and lender.
- Discount points can be charged and can be paid by either buyer or seller, as they agree.
- Because of the FHA insurance, a lower-than-usual down payment may be possible.
- FHA no longer allows any part of the borrower's down payment to be made with borrowed funds.
- FHA-insured loans made before December 15, 1989 are assumable without buyer qualification. FHA-insured loans made on or after December 15, 1989, require the new owner to qualify before the loan can be assumed.

VA-guaranteed loans carry the assurance of the **Department of Veteran Affairs** (**VA**) that the lender will be protected in the event of default by the borrower.

- VA-guaranteed loans are available to veterans of the U.S. Armed Forces or a U.S. ally who meet certain minimum service requirements.
- The **certificate of eligibility** is the VA's statement that the veteran is eligible for the loan guarantee program.
- The VA sets the loan amount that it will guarantee. The property purchased may be a greater amount, but the guarantee will not increase.
- The interest rate is subject to negotiation between the veteran and lender.
- The property must be appraised and the VA will then issue a **certificate of reasonable value** (**CRV**) based on that estimate.
- The **funding fee** depends on the category of veteran and the amount of the down payment, which can range from zero to 10% or more.
- The property may be sold and the VA loan assumed, but the veteran must receive a written release of liability from the VA to be relieved of obligation in the event of a future foreclosure.
- The veteran's entitlement can be reused on a subsequent home purchase, although the amount of the entitlement will be reduced if there has been an assumption of a prior loan guarantee.

The **Farmer's Home Administration** (**FmHA**) actually makes loans to purchase rural property. It also guarantees loans made by private lenders.

The **California Veterans Farm and Home Purchase Program** provides Cal-Vet loans through the **California Department of Veterans Affairs** (**CDVA**). The CDVA obtains loan funds from voter-approved bond issues, buys the property, and then sells it to the veteran on a land contract, holding title until the debt is repaid. A Cal-Vet loan can be used for a property purchase, to finance land and construction, to renovate a house, or to make improvements. The veteran must qualify for credit, loan terms are typically 30 years, and there is a loan application fee of $50, but no origination fee. The down payment must be at least 5% of the purchase price. On all Cal-Vet loans, the interest rate is subject to change annually based on the cost of bond funds, but is typically competitive with conventional loan rates.

Mortgages/Deeds of Trust/Notes

The term **mortgage** is used to refer to any instrument used to secure real estate in payment for a debt. In practice, the security instrument may take the form of either a mortgage or deed of trust. There are separate requirements for the creation and enforcement of the two forms of security instrument.

The mortgage creates a security interest in the identified real estate. The **mortgagor** is the property owner and the **mortgagee** is the lender. A mortgage must be recorded in the county clerk's or recorder's office in the county where the property is located in order to establish its priority.

A **first mortgage** (**senior mortgage**) takes priority over every other encumbrance filed after it. A **second mortgage** (**junior mortgage**) will be satisfied on default of the borrower only after the first mortgage debt has been repaid. There may even be a third mortgage or more. Each successive lien takes a weaker position.

On repayment of the loan by the borrower, the mortgagee executes a **release of mortgage** (**satisfaction of mortgage** or **discharge of mortgage**) that can be recorded to indicate that the lien is no longer effective.

On a default by the borrower, the traditional remedy for the holder of a mortgage was strict foreclosure in which the property could be sold immediately. The modern requirement is a foreclosure action that must be brought in court following statutory notice and other requirements.

If the security instrument is a **mortgage with power of sale**, the property may be sold without a court hearing, but state law still applies and there will be specific notice and other requirements. Even after the property has been sold at public auction, there is a **right of redemption** for the borrower within the statutory time period.

If the sales price at the foreclosure sale does not cover the amount owed on the loan, some states allow the lender to obtain a **deficiency judgment** against the borrower. This means that other assets can be claimed by the lender to satisfy the remaining indebtedness.

California provides homeowners and others with anti-deficiency protection in the event that the proceeds of sale on loan default do not cover the amount owed. This means that the lender has no recourse except the real estate. **Anti-deficiency protection** is available when the foreclosed loan (**purchase money mortgage** or **trust deed**) was used to pay all or part of the purchase price of an owner-occupied dwelling of no more than four units and the **mortgagee** (lender) was the seller of the property.

The **contract for deed** (**land contract**) is a form of seller financing in which title to the real estate is not given to the purchaser for a year or longer following the date of sale. This type of financing is often used in rural areas for purchases of vacant or improved land when the buyer doesn't want to deal with a conventional lender or when the buyer has difficulty finding or qualifying for any other form of financing. A Cal-Vet loan uses a contract for deed.

Because of former abuses of the contract for deed in which defaulting buyers lost all equity in the property, even when payments had been made for a substantial period of time, there are strict rules (including the disclosure requirements mentioned earlier) regarding the formation and enforcement of this type of instrument. Even when legal title is still held by the seller, a defaulting buyer may be found to have equitable title to the property and thus be entitled to an **ownership** (**equity**) **interest** in the proceeds of any foreclosure sale.

In California, the **deed of trust** is the preferred security instrument because in the event of default in payment of the underlying debt it does not require a judicial (court-ordered) foreclosure. The deed of trust executed at the time the loan is originated actually transfers title from the **trustor** (owner) to a **trustee** (third party), who holds title in trust for the benefit of the **beneficiary** (lender). The trustor remains in possession of the real estate while the deed of trust is in effect.

If the underlying debt is repaid, the trustee is notified by the beneficiary and title is returned to the trustor by means of a reconveyance deed from the trustee. In the event of a **default** in payment of the underlying note by the trustor, the trustee is authorized to sell the property to pay off the remaining debt. When the property is sold a trustee's deed is given to the new owner. As with a mortgage foreclosure, California law will dictate whether or not the lender is entitled to a **deficiency judgment** in the event that the proceeds of a forced sale do not cover the amount owed. A deficiency judgement cannot be obtained through a non-judicial foreclosure.

Financing/Credit Laws

The **Equal Credit Opportunity Act**, a federal law that has been in effect since 1975, prohibits discrimination in the granting of credit on the basis of age, sex, race, color, marital status, religion, or national origin.

Factors that can legitimately be considered are the applicant's income, stability of the source of the **income**, **total assets** and **liabilities**, and **credit rating** (past history of use of credit). The fact that all or part of the applicant's income comes from any public assistance program cannot be considered, however.

The lender also is prohibited from discriminating against any applicant who has exercised any right under any federal consumer credit protection law.

The borrower must be informed of the right to receive a copy of any appraisal report prepared as part of the loan process, and how and when it may be obtained.

The **Fair Credit Reporting Act** requires that, if a loan is denied, the lender or mortgage broker must provide a statement of:

- the specific reasons for the denial
- the name of the federal agency that the applicant can contact if the applicant feels that he/she has been discriminated against by the lender or mortgage broker
- if the denial is based on the contents of a credit report, the fact that the applicant is entitled to a copy of the report and how one can be obtained

The **Truth in Lending Act** was passed by Congress and became effective on July 1, 1969. It was amended in 1982 and 1991. **Regulation Z** of the **Federal Reserve Board** carries out the provisions of the Truth in Lending Act.

The law applies to creditors (lenders) involved in either one of the following:

- more than 25 consumer credit transactions per year
- more than five transactions per year with a dwelling used as security

Unless they involve property that is the borrower's principal residence, the law exempts either one of the following:

- loans for business, commercial, or agricultural uses
- loans for more than $25,000

In general, loans to acquire owner-occupied rental property of two of more units, or to improve or maintain owner-occupied rental property of four or more units, fall within the business purpose classification and thus are exempt from the law. All loans on rental properties that are not owner-occupied also are exempt from the law.

The required truth-in-lending disclosures must be made in a disclosure statement that highlights certain information in a box or by using boldface type, a different type style or a different background color. The disclosure statement must be presented to the borrower before the transaction is completed. Information to be disclosed includes (in addition to other items) the

- amount financed
- **finance charge**
- **annual percentage rate (APR)**
- total amount that will be paid over the life of the loan
- prepayment penalties
- late-payment charges

There is no **right to rescind** when a loan involving a consumer's principal dwelling is either one of the following:

- purchase money first mortgage or trust deed loan
- a refinancing of a purchase money loan in which no new funds are received by the borrower

On all other transactions involving a consumer's principal dwelling, the consumer has a three-day right to rescind the transaction. This right may be waived in writing by the consumer if compliance would delay funding. Unless waived in writing, the rescission period ends at midnight of the third business day following the latest to occur of:

- delivery of the **truth in lending disclosure statement**
- delivery of notice of the right to rescind
- completion of the transaction

Advertisements for covered loans must give the APR and provide other payment terms.

Loan Brokerage

The components of the typical transaction can be put together efficiently with the **Computerized Loan Origination (CLO)** available at many real estate or mortgage brokerage offices.

The **Federal National Mortgage Association** (**FNMA** or **Fannie Mae**) is the largest purchaser of all types of home loans. FNMA was originally a government agency, then was converted to entirely private ownership and control. FNMA sells stock, bonds, and notes.

The **Government National Mortgage Association** (**GNMA** or **Ginnie Mae**), originally part of FNMA but now a division of HUD, is a major purchaser of government-backed mortgage loans. GNMA sells pass-through certificates that pass on mortgage payments of principal and interest (less servicing fees).

The **Federal Home Loan Mortgage Corporation** (**FHLMC** or **Freddie Mac**) is a subsidiary of the **Federal Home Loan Bank** and primarily purchases conventional loans. FHLMC sells bonds and participation certificates.

The **Federal Agricultural Mortgage Corporation** (**FAMC** or **Farmer Mac**) is a part of the **Farm Credit System** and helps expand the availability of funds for agricultural lending. **FAMC** serves as a co-insurer (with the original lender) of pools of such loans.

Privately formed companies also buy pools of loans; ownership of the loans ultimately belongs to holders of the company's stock.

When real estate is used as security for a loan, it is said to be **hypothecated** (it remains in possession of the borrower). When personal property is used as security, it is **pledged** (it is held by the lender until the debt is repaid).

The states differ in how they view the effect of using real estate to secure a loan.

In **title theory** states, a debt secured by real estate is considered to constructively transfer title (termed **bare legal title**, because it does not include the right of possession) to the lender.

California is a **lien theory** state. In this state, a debt secured by real estate is considered to impose a lien on the real estate. But because the most frequently used security instrument in California is the deed of trust, bare legal title is actually held by the trustee.

A **bridge loan** (**gap loan** or **swing loan**) is a temporary, short-term, relatively high-interest loan used before a longer-term loan can be made. Typical use of a bridge loan is to finance construction of improvements.

A **hard money loan** is one that is made by a **private** (**noninstitutional**) **lender**, usually for a term of no more than three to five years, and usually at an interest rate that is higher than the market rate. Real property is used as security, but the borrower receives cash instead of using the loan money to purchase the property. It is usually a second or junior loan, meaning that it is subject to the security interest of another lender.

A **soft-money** loan includes charges financed as part of the purchase price that are not part of the cost of the real estate, such as closing costs.

Concerns about **seller financing** (**creative financing**) can arise at any time, but particularly when the supply of properties available is much greater than the number of qualified purchasers, or (as is often the case in California) when rising prices make it more difficult for borrowers to qualify for conventional loans.

California's Creative Financing Disclosure Law provides protection to homebuyers when seller financing is used, including preparation of a seller financing disclosure form, to be given to the buyer by the seller, in which all terms and conditions of the financing are stated. The law applies to all seller carry-back loans on one-to four-unit residential properties. The disclosures include:

- credit report
- warning of any balloon payment due

- negative amortization, if any
- status and details of any senior loans, and buyer's need to file a request for copy of **Notice of Default** on any senior loans
- warning on problems that may arise with an **all-inclusive deed of trust** (**wrap-around deed of trust**) in which the buyer makes payments to the seller, who is responsible for repaying senior lien(s)

Federal tax requirements for creation and reporting of an installment sale may apply. In California, mortgage loan foreclosure consultants are strictly regulated to prevent consumer fraud.

A California real estate broker is permitted to solicit borrowers or lenders or negotiate real property loans. The **Real Property Loan Law** (found in the **Business and Professions Code** as part of the Real estate Law) applies to loans in which real property or a business opportunity is used as **security**. The borrower must be informed if the source of the loan is the broker's own funds, or those of a member of the broker's family.

A **Mortgage Loan Disclosure Statement** providing details of the loan, including term, interest rate, payment schedule, and fees charged, must be presented to and signed by the borrower before the loan can be made.

The **Department of Real Estate** can provide a **Mortgage Loan Disclosure Statement/Good Faith Estimate** (**Form MLDS/GFE**) that meets both federal and state loan disclosure requirements.

The maximum commission that can be charged depends upon the length of the loan term and whether the security for the loan will be a first deed of trust or second deed of trust.

On a **first deed of trust** with a loan of less than $30,000 and a term of three years or more, the maximum commission is 10% of the loan amount. If the term is less than three years, the maximum commission is 5%. If the loan amount is $30,000 or more, there is no limit on the commission no matter what the loan term.

On a **second deed of trust** with a loan of less than $20,000 and a term of three years or more, the maximum commission is 15% of the loan amount. If the term is two to less than three years, the maximum commission is 10% and if the term is less than two years, the maximum commission is 5%. If the loan amount is $20,000 or more, there is no limit on the commission no matter what the loan term.

In addition to the broker's commission or fee, the maximum amount that a mortgage loan broker may charge for **expenses** (appraisal, **credit report**, **notary**, and so on) depends on the loan amount.

If the loan is more than $14,000, the broker can charge actual costs, but not more than $700.

If the loan amount is from $7,800 to $14,000, the broker can charge actual costs or 5% of the loan amount, whichever is less.

If the loan amount is less than $7,800, the broker can charge actual costs or $390, whichever is less.

Separate requirements apply to loans made to private and small **pension trust lenders/investor** (as opposed to banks, S&Ls, credit unions, and other institutional investors). In the case of a private lender, a **Lender/Purchaser Disclosure Statement** (**Form LPDS**) is required. There are separate versions for:

- loan origination
- sale of an existing note
- collateralized loan

The **California Residential Mortgage Lending Act** covers persons licensed by the **Commissioner of Corporations** to make or service loans that are secured by one- to four-unit dwellings. The law exempts:

- California real estate brokers
- California finance lenders licensed under the **California Finance Lenders Law**, who make personal or business loans backed by personal property
- lenders (including banks, savings and loans, and insurance companies) already licensed by the state or federal government
- court-appointed representatives
- government and pension plan employees
- the trustee under a deed of trust

▶ Transfer of Property

Title Insurance

The primary responsibility of the property seller is to convey **marketable title**—an ownership interest that a well-informed buyer can reasonably be expected to accept and that the buyer can transfer in a future transaction. There are several ways in which the buyer is assured of acceptable title.

A **certificate of title** is an opinion of the condition of the title as of the date specified. An **abstract of title**, accompanied by an attorney's **opinion of title**, is a cumbersome method. It provides a complete history of the recorded documents affecting the title, called the **chain of title**. Although once used for all types of transactions, today it is used mainly for large commercial properties.

Title insurance has become the most common method of protecting the buyer. A **title company** issues a **preliminary title report** or **title commitment**. It will indicate the present condition of the title based on examination of the documents maintained by the title company as well as any exceptions to the coverage that the title company is willing to provide. The title company will defend the purchaser's title in a title dispute covered by the policy. If an insured claim is paid out by the title company to the policy holder, the title company will be entitled by its **right of subrogation** to take the policy holder's place in seeking compensation from the party who caused the loss.

Standard policy of title insurance (**owner's policy**) does not protect the purchaser against defects actually known to the purchaser, claims of parties in possession of the property, defects in the survey or any other item noted as an exception. The **California Land Title Association** (**CLTA**) provides a standard form policy for its members. The standard policy does protect against monetary loss due to:

- forged documents
- mistakes in the public records
- incapacity of the grantor(s)
- improperly delivered deeds

Extended coverage policy of title insurance (lender's policy) does not protect against defects actually known to the purchaser or any other item noted as an exception. The **American Land Title Association (ALTA)** provides an extended coverage policy to its members. The extended coverage policy does protect against monetary loss stemming from any of the four categories noted above for the standard policy, plus:

- defects revealed by examination of the property survey
- encumbrances or unrecorded claims that would be revealed by an inspection of the property
- unrecorded liens that were not known to the purchaser

Title insurance does not cover property damage. If there is material damage to the property while a sale is pending, the **Uniform Vendor and Purchaser Risk Act** (adopted by California) provides two alternatives. If the buyer is not at fault and has neither title nor possession, the seller cannot enforce the contract and any funds the buyer has already paid must be returned. If the seller is not at fault and the buyer has already received either legal title or possession, the buyer is required to fulfill the contract terms.

Deeds

A **deed** is a written document that conveys property from the **grantor** (owner) to the **grantee**. The requirements for a valid deed are as follows.

- It must be in writing.
- The grantor(s) must be of sound mind (legally capable).
- It must identify the parties, preferably by full name and marital status (single, married, widow, and so on).
- It must identify the property adequately, preferably by full legal description.
- It must contain a **granting clause** that contains the appropriate words ("I hereby grant and convey").
- It must be signed by the grantor(s).
- It must be delivered to the grantee and accepted by the grantee. A deed held by a third party until the grantor dies, for instance, will have no effect during the grantor's life and on the grantor's death will be invalid. Even after a valid delivery, the fact that the deed is in the hands of the grantee does not mean that it is accepted. Many charitable donations **of real estate** have ultimately been rejected because of the high cost of their **maintenance** or **remediation** (as in the case of contaminated property).

A deed must be **acknowledged** (signed before a notary public or other official) in order to be **recorded** (made a part of the public records of the county in which the property is located). Deeds due not have to be dated or recorded to be valid.

A recorded deed provides **constructive notice** (assumed notice) of the conveyance.

There are different types of deeds.

A **bargain and sale deed** states the consideration paid by the grantee. There may or may not be a warranty that the grantor actually has an interest in the described property.

A **gift deed** requires no consideration to be paid by the grantee.

A **grant deed** (using the words "I grant and convey" or similar) carries two implied promises of the grantor:

- The grantor has not previously conveyed title.
- The grantor has not created any encumbrances other than those stated on the deed.
- The grantor will convey any after-acquired title (ownership interest received after the grant deed is delivered) to the grantee.

A **quitclaim deed** conveys whatever interest the grantor may own, but does not warrant that the grantor actually has any interest in the described property.

A **sheriff's deed** conveys title to property sold at public auction following a foreclosure or other court action.

A **tax deed** conveys title to property sold at public auction to cover unpaid taxes.

A **trust deed** (**deed of trust**) is used to make real estate security for the repayment of a debt. The trust deed conveys title from the **trustor** (property owner) to the **trustee** to be held for the benefit of the named **beneficiary** (the lender). In the event of default by the trustor, and in conformance with state law, the trustee will sell the property at public auction in order to repay the underlying debt. After the sale, a trustee's deed is used to convey title from the trustee to the purchaser. In the event the debt is repaid, the trustee returns title to the trustor by a reconveyance deed.

A **general warranty deed** (typically not used in California) carries the grantor's **express or implied assurances** (called **warranties** or **covenants**).

The **covenant of seizing** and **right to convey** promises that the grantor is the rightful owner of the property as described in the deed.

The **covenant against encumbrances** promises that there is no encumbrance (cloud on the title) other than what may be stated in the document.

The **covenant of quiet enjoyment** promises that no one will object to the conveyance and that the grantee's possession will not be interfered with in the future.

The **covenant of further assurance** promises that the grantor will take whatever action is necessary in the future to correct any title defect.

The **covenant of warranty forever** promises that the grantor will **defend the grantee's title** (pay for legal expenses) in any dispute brought by a third party.

A **special warranty deed** (**limited warranty deed**) carries the grantor's assurances only as to the state of the title after the grantor acquired ownership.

Alienation is the **conveyance** (transfer) of all or part of the ownership interests in real property.

Voluntary and Involuntary

A **property transfer** is **voluntary** when it is made with the consent of the owner.

A deed from the present owner is the principal method of voluntary transfer of title to real property.

A **will** can identify the recipient of property to be transferred on the death of the owner, who is said to die **testate**. To be valid, a will must comply with state law. In California a will must comply with the following.

- A **formal** or **statutory will** must be signed by the **testator** and at least two witnesses.
- A **codicil** that contains an addition or change can be added to a will at a later date, but it must also be signed and witnessed.
- A **holographic will**—one that is entirely handwritten by the testator—does not need to be witnessed.
- A **new will** cancels any prior will.
- A transfer of personal property by will is called a **bequest** or **legacy** (money).
- A transfer of real estate by will is called a **devise**.

Transfer of title to all or part of a parcel of real estate without the consent or action of the owner is considered **involuntary**. Remember the types of involuntary transfer by **INAFEE**. **Intestate succession** is the manner of distribution of property by state law when the property owner has died **intestate**; that is, without leaving a valid will.

Natural forces may diminish property boundaries or destroy improvements. **Avulsion** is the sudden and violent action of a body of water that washes away part of a parcel of land. (Soil added to land by the action of a body of water is called **alluvion** or **alluvium**. An increase in land caused by a body of water that recedes permanently is called **reliction**.) **Erosion** is the gradual wearing away of surface soil by action of rain or wind.

Adverse possession may be used to acquire title to property by someone who occupies it for the five-year period required by state law. The occupancy must be **open, notorious** (not secretive), **continuous, hostile** (without permission), **under claim of right or color of title** (a belief that you own or have a right to the property) and **adverse** to the interests of the true owner. The **adverse possessor** must pay all property taxes during the period of occupancy. The required period of possession may be accomplished by **tacking** (adding together) the occupancy periods of successive adverse possessors. An **adverse possessor** can claim title by **virtue of occupancy** or by occupancy accompanied by **color of title**—a deed that appears on its face to be valid. **Clear title** may be established by the adverse possessor by bringing a quiet title action in court.

Foreclosure is the loss of secured property following default on the underlying debt.

California provides **homestead protection** that prohibits sale of a residence for the benefit of nonsecured creditors unless the homeowner's equity is greater than the amount of the **homestead exemption**.

The home can be sold and the amount of the exemption protected from creditors provided that a new residence is purchased within six months.

The definition of a **homestead** includes a house and land, boat, **manufactured home and land, planned development, stock cooperative**, community apartment project, and other forms of housing.

The amount of the exemption varies, as listed below.

- Homeowner's exemption is $50,000.
- Exemption for a homeowner who is a member of a family unit (as defined by the law) is $75,000.
- Exemption when a homeowner (or homeowner's spouse who lives with the homeowner) is 65 years of age or older is $100,000.
- Exemption when a homeowner or spouse is physically or mentally disabled and cannot engage in gainful employment is $125,000.

- Exemption when a homeowner is 55 years of age or older, has income no greater than that specified by the law, and the homestead is the subject of a forced sale, is $100,000.

Eminent domain is the right of the government (federal or state) to take private property for a public purpose.

Condemnation is the action taken by the government. If necessary, there is a trial in which the right to take the property is established and the fair market value of the property is determined in order to provide just compensation to the owner.

In an **inverse condemnation** action, a property owner brings suit for compensation against the government, claiming that a public **regulation** (i.e. excessive zoning) has, in effect, diminished the right to the owner's full use of affected property.

Escheat is the state's right to claim ownership of property for which no heirs can be found.

Escrow

The culmination of the real estate sale is the **closing**, when the purchase funds are transferred to the seller and title is transferred to the buyer. A closing is also used for an exchange, refinancing, lease, or other type of transaction. Typically, the parties will execute documents at separate times for transfer at a stipulated future date.

Settlement procedures vary throughout the state. The details of the closing may be handled by any one of the following:

- an attorney for either the buyer or seller
- a real estate agent who was the listing or selling agent, or a party in the transaction
- an agent of a title company (more common in Northern California)
- an agent of a state-licensed **escrow** company (more common in Southern California)

Throughout the rest of this section we refer to the **escrow agent**, who can be any of the above individuals.

An **escrow** is the possession by a third party of the funds and documents necessary to close a transaction. Although the escrow agent should be a disinterested third party, a real estate agent or attorney for one of the parties can act as the escrow. The escrow agent is not allowed to carry out the terms of the underlying agreement (such as the transfer of funds and title in a sales transaction) until all of the contract requirements of all of the parties have been met.

The legal requirements for a valid escrow include both of the following:

- a binding contract between the parties to the transaction
- conditional delivery of the necessary documentation and funds

The escrow agent is given **escrow instructions** (including a copy of the transaction agreement) to know what is to be accomplished.

- In Northern California, a real estate transaction typically will involve **unilateral escrow instructions**. Each party prepares its own instructions, which are given to the escrow agent a short time before the closing.
- In Southern California, a real estate transaction typically will involve **bilateral escrow instructions**. One set of instructions is signed by both parties and given to the escrow agent at the time the escrow is opened.

When all of the **requirements** (conditions) of the transaction have been met, the transaction can be closed. If there is any disagreement of the parties or other impediment to a closing, the escrow agent may bring a legal action called **interpleader** against the parties to the transaction. The escrow agent asks the court to determine the action that should be taken. It is not a function of the escrow agent to settle disputes or determine the rights of the parties, but merely to carry out the escrow instructions.

Settlement Documents

The escrow agent makes sure that all of the necessary paperwork is on hand before the closing takes place. The number of documents will vary depending on the nature of the transaction, state and federal law, and unique requirements of the agreement. A residential sales transaction will include most of the following:

- escrow instructions
- transaction agreement
- agency relationship disclosure statement and confirmation
- preliminary title report (discussed below)
- seller's **Real Estate Transfer Disclosure Statement**
- other disclosures required by federal or state law, such as the **Lead Paint Disclosure Statement**
- **property inspection reports**—pest control (termite), well, septic system, and other reports
- statement from each of the present lenders

    Demand for payoff will indicate the remaining balance to be paid at closing in order to satisfy the seller's debt and release the lender's lien on the property.

    Beneficiary statement will indicate loan balance as of the date of closing, if the buyer will assume the existing loan.

- paperwork from the new lender(s)—if the source of funds for the purchase is a new lender, there will be a new note and security instrument to be executed before the funds will be released at closing.
- fire, flood, and other insurance policies—the new lender will require necessary insurance in order to protect the value of the **collateral**.
- property tax and assessment statements—depending on the date of the transaction and the date that taxes and assessments are due: the seller may owe taxes that will be a debit to the seller and credit to the buyer or the seller may have prepaid taxes, in which case there will be a credit to the seller and debit to the buyer.

- settlement statement prepared by the escrow agent indicating how funds are to be **disbursed**
- other documents required by the sales contract, such as **notes** and **deeds**

The **Real Estate Settlement and Procedures Act** (**RESPA**) is the federal law that requires disclosures by lenders or mortgage brokers in federally related transactions involving the sale or transfer of a dwelling of one to four units. As noted earlier, in the section on financing, a federally related transaction involves either one of the following:

- a federally chartered or insured lender
- a loan made with funds or with insurance or guarantees of any federal agency
- a loan to be sold on the secondary mortgage market

The **Real Estate Settlement Procedures Act** (**RESPA**) took effect on June 30, 1976; amendments were effective on December 2, 1992.

- The lender or mortgage broker must provide the borrower with a copy of the **Special Information Booklet** prepared by HUD.
- The lender or mortgage broker must provide the borrower with a good-faith estimate of closing costs, which must disclose any lender-paid mortgage broker fees.
- If there are two or more loan applicants, the information needs to be given to only one of them.
- A **Uniform Settlement Statement** (**form HUD-1** or **HUD 1-A**) must be given to the borrower and seller by at least the day of closing.

The borrower can waive the right to receive the **Uniform Settlement Statement** by the day of closing. If the borrower does so, the information must be delivered as soon as possible after the closing.

The statement must disclose any lender-paid mortgage broker fees.

- The lender or mortgage broker is not allowed to charge a fee for preparing any of the documents required by RESPA or by the **Truth-in-Lending Act**.
- Fees, **kickbacks**, or other such payments to persons who do not actually provide loan services are strictly prohibited.
- Any affiliated business arrangement with an individual or entity offering settlement services must be disclosed.
- A fee may be charged by someone who counsels a borrower or who assists the buyer in entering information into a **Computerized Loan Origination** (**CLO**) **program**.

Reports

Buyers will frequently hire inspectors to investigate the condition of the property either before making an offer or during escrow. The **purchase agreement** will typically have an **inspection period** for these inspections.

Inspections cover property condition and defects, mold, geologic conditions, soil stability, earthquake dangers and wood destroying pests.

Tax Aspects

Throughout the United States, taxation of real property is the primary method of financing schools, police and fire departments, and other amenities and services provided by state and local governments. Real property taxes are ***ad valorem*** taxes, which means that they are based on the value of the property taxed.

California law, as directed by the voter initiative known as **Proposition 13,** specifies when and how often real property is to be assessed or reassessed to determine its value for tax purposes. A property owner who disagrees with an assessed valuation can present an independent appraisal as the basis for an appeal to the **Board of Equalization**.

The base value of property for property tax purposes is its **full cash value** (market value) as of February 28, 1975, or a subsequent reassessment event. A **reassessment event** is a sale or other change of ownership. A yearly increase by the taxing jurisdiction of up to 2% of assessed value is permitted.

Subsequent voter action resulted in the following changes to the basic rules.

- A transfer of title between spouses is not considered a reassessment event.
- The transfer of a principal residence and the first $1 million of other real property between parents and children are not considered reassessment events.
- Homeowners over age 55 or severely disabled can transfer their old base value to a new residence in the same county if the new property is of the same or less value.
- Homeowners over age 55 or severely disabled may transfer their old assessed valuation to a new residence in a different county, if the new county permits such transfers.
- A severely disabled homeowner can make property improvements necessitated by the disability with no reassessment.

Homeowners are entitled to a homeowner's exemption, which reduces the assessed valuation by $7,000.

- There is a $4,000 veteran's exemption for property of qualified veterans to which the homeowner's exemption does not apply.
- A veteran who is totally disabled is entitled to an exemption of $100,000 on the principal residence. The exemption can also be used by the veteran's surviving spouse until he or she remarries.

The tax rate is set at 1% of assessed value.

The property tax year contains the following deadlines:

- On January 1, a lien is placed on property for the next fiscal year's taxes.
- July 1 through June 30 is the tax fiscal year.
- On November 1, the first installment of property tax is due.
- After 5 P.M. on December 10, the first installment of property tax becomes delinquent if unpaid.

- On February 1, the second installment of property tax is due.
- After 5 P.M. on April 10, the second installment of property tax becomes delinquent if unpaid.

When property is transferred, one or more **supplemental assessments** insure that property tax is based on the new market value starting on the first day of the reassessment event.

California provides relief for older residents with low incomes who face high property tax bills.

The **Property Tax Postponement Law** allows low-income persons aged 62 or older to postpone payment of property taxes until the principal residence is sold or no longer occupied.

The **Homeowner Assistance Program** provides a rebate of property tax paid to qualified low-income persons aged 62 or older.

Some property payments are not considered taxes.

Local improvements, such as street and sewer repair, can be paid by means of **bonds** that are then paid by a special assessment of the affected property. Such payments are not considered tax-deductible property tax payments.

A **benefit assessment** (which can also be called a **local assessment** or **special assessment**) is applied only to properties that are benefitted from a specific improvement. A benefit assessment is not tax-deductible. The **Mello-Roos Community Facilities Act** of 1982 allowed the assessment to be spread over a greater number of properties, but payments are still not considered tax-deductible property taxes. The existence of a Mello-Roos assessment on a one-to four-unit dwelling must be disclosed to a prospective purchaser.

A **tax lien** is placed on all property taxed and is enforced if taxes remain unpaid for five years.

Net proceeds from the sale of real estate in excess of the property's **tax basis** (book value) are subject to both federal and state income tax, with the exceptions noted below. Corporations that are incorporated in California (or doing business in the state) must pay California franchise tax.

The basis of real estate for purposes of calculating income tax owed (or deductible loss) is the following:

- the acquisition cost of the property (or market value at the time title passes if acquired by inheritance, exchange, or other nonsale transaction)
- property acquired by gift assumes the basis of the givor, not the value at the time title passes
- plus any amount spent on capital improvements (additions to the property, such as a new room, but not maintenance expenses, such as a new furnace)
- minus any depreciation taken on the property

In order to encourage homeownership and home affordability, Congress has provided several important benefits for homeowners. For purposes of the tax law, a residence is any habitation that has living space as well as cooking and toilet facilities. Thus, a motor home or houseboat can qualify as a residence.

The **mortgage interest deduction** is available for interest paid on loans secured by the principal residence and one other residence and in an amount no greater than a total of $1,000,000 of acquisition indebtedness (loan amount at the time of purchase) and $100,000 of other indebtedness (the home equity loan).

It is important to note that, if a home mortgage loan is refinanced, only the interest paid on the loan balance remaining from the original loan will be deductible. Additional loan amounts may be designated as home equity indebtedness, to take advantage of the $100,000 home equity loan mortgage interest deduction.

The mortgage interest deduction is also allowed for interest paid at the time of financing in the form of **points** (**discount points**).

- Points paid at the time of purchase are deductible from that year's income.
- Points paid in a refinancing are deductible on a **pro rata basis** over the life of the loan.

For example, on a 20-year loan refinancing, 5% of the amount paid in points is deductible in each full year.

The **Taxpayers Relief Act** of 1997 established the exclusion rule for gain on sale of the principal residence. Previously, gain on the sale of the principal residence could be deferred as long as a new residence of equal or greater value was purchased within two years before or after the sale; persons aged 55 or over were allowed a once-in-a-lifetime exclusion of up to $125,000 of gain.

The new rule allows single individuals to exclude up to $250,000 of gain on the sale of the principal residence. A married couple filing a joint return is allowed to exclude up to $500,000 of gain on the sale of the principal residence.

The principal residence usually is the home in which the taxpayer lives most often and from which the taxpayer works, votes, and pays taxes. But each spouse is allowed to have a different principal residence (for instance, when they work in two different cities), in which case each will be entitled to a separate $250,000 exclusion.

The home must have been occupied as the principal residence for at least two of the five years preceding the sale.

The new rule applies to sales on or after May 7, 1997.

There is no limit to the number of times that the exclusion may be taken, but it may be taken only once every two years. A portion of a residence used for business (say, a home office) will be considered part of the residence for the purpose of the exclusion if that portion of the home is converted back to residential use for at least two years prior to the sale.

If the property is used as the principal residence for less than two of the five years preceding a sale, the exclusion may be claimed if the sale is due to "unforseen circumstances," but only up to the percentage of two years that the taxpayer used the home as the principal residence. For example, if a home has been occupied for 18 months by a single taxpayer, and all other conditions are met, the percentage of the exclusion to which the taxpayer is entitled is $\frac{18}{24}$, or 75% of $250,000, which is $187,500. For a married couple in the same circumstance, the exclusion would be $375,000.

Use of the exclusion is optional; that is, the taxpayer may elect to pay tax on the gain.

The **residence replacement rollover rule** is no longer in effect. Whether or not they take advantage of the exclusion, homeowners can no longer defer taxation on any gain by purchasing a new home of equal or greater value.

The **once-in-a-lifetime exclusion** of up to $125,000 of gain for a home seller aged 55 or older is no longer in effect. If a homeowner has already taken advantage of that exclusion, it is no impediment to taking advantage of the new $250,000/$500,000 exclusion on the sale of a subsequent principal residence.

There is no longer any deduction for fixing-up expenses incurred in the sale of a home. But the homeowner may still increase the property's cost basis by the amount of any capital improvements (the cost of a new room, for example, but not the cost of a new roof or water heater).

As in the past, the amount paid for property taxes is a deduction from income. The amount paid for **special assessments** (for improvements such as sewers) is not deductible from income, but can be added to the cost basis of the property.

In California, a real estate broker who sells manufactured (mobile) homes as a retailer must have a **seller's (dealer's) permit**.

New manufactured homes are taxed on 75% of selling price and are also assessed property tax. Used manufactured homes assessed for property tax do not require payment of sales tax. Sales tax is also charged on transfer of manufactured homes subject to license fees. Sales or use tax paid on the sale must be reported by the broker.

Owning real estate as an investment has several important tax consequences.

In general, **active management** of real estate provides greater tax benefits than does passive ownership. Active management involves regular participation on a continuous basis in the operation of the investment; the level of involvement required will vary depending on the demands of the property.

Passive losses (losses from rental real estate are typically deductible only from **passive income** (such as income received as a limited partner or other rental real estate).

Adjusted gross income is the total potential income that could be received from a property, less an allowance for expected vacancy and collection losses. Net income is what remains after deducting actual expenses of ownership, including estimated annual depreciation of buildings and other depreciable assets.

Depreciation is computed at the time of property acquisition by the straight-line method. The cost attributable to an improvement is divided by the number of years of its economic life (remaining useful life). The **Tax Reform Act** of 1986, which took effect on January 1, 1987, increased the minimum period of years over which depreciation may be taken from 19 years to $27\frac{1}{2}$ years for residential property and from 19 years to $31\frac{1}{2}$ years for commercial (non-residential) property; the period for non-residential property was increased to 39 years on August 10, 1993.

Prior to January 1, 1987, investors had the option of using various forms of accelerated depreciation in which a greater amount of depreciation could be claimed in the early years of the investment. This method is no longer available, but may continue to be used for properties acquired before January 1, 1987.

At-risk rules limit the amount that an investor may deduct from any investment to the amount of the investment plus any recourse financing (loan amount for which the investment is liable).

As of May 28, 2003, the maximum tax rate on long-term capital gains (profits from the sale of real estate held for one year or longer) is between 5–15% depending on the taxpayer's bracket.

An **installment sale** can be used by an investor to spread out the receipt of taxable income from a sale; the income is taxed in the year received under an installment sale.

A **land contract** (**contract for sale**) is an installment sale in which the seller retains title for at least one year following the date of sale, even though the buyer takes possession of the property. The parties to a **tax-deferred exchange** under **Internal Revenue Code Section 1031** trade like-kind properties. Taxation is avoided at the time of the trade unless boot (cash or equivalent) is received in addition to title to the traded property. The party receiving the boot must pay tax on that amount to the extent that it represents a profit on the value of the property traded.

A tax lien is available to federal, state, and local taxing authorities. Enforcement usually is by tax sale following which the purchaser receives a tax deed. Tax liens take precedence over all other liens.

The **Foreign Investment in Real Property Tax Act** (**FIRPTA**) is the federal law that requires that a buyer of real property withhold and send to the IRS 10% of the gross sales price, if the seller is a foreign person. In general, the law does not apply if one of the following is true:

- the seller provides an affidavit of nonforeign status and a U.S. taxpayer I.D. number
- the seller provides a qualifying statement obtained through the IRS specifying other arrangements for collection of, or exemption from, the tax
- the sales price is less than $300,000 and the property will qualify as an owner-occupied residence

State law requires that, in certain transactions, the buyer must withhold $3\frac{1}{3}$% of the sales price as state income tax and send it to the **State Franchise Tax Board**. It is up to the escrow agent to notify the buyer of this requirement in applicable transactions. Applicable transactions include the following:

- The seller provides an out-of-state address, or sale proceeds are to be disbursed to a financial intermediary of the seller
- The sales price is more than $100,000 and the seller does not certify that the property being conveyed is his/her personal residence. A corporation's certification would be that the corporation has a permanent place of business in California.

Special Processes

Transfer by Will

A person who makes a will is called a testator; to die with a will is to die testate, to die without a will is to die intestate. There are three types of wills: a formal will is typically typed by an attorney and requires two witnesses to the testator's signature. A statutory will has blanks, which are filled in by the testator, it too requires two witnesses. A holographic will is entirely in the testator's handwriting and requires no witnesses. A codicil is an amendment to a will and follows the same requirements as a will.

If someone dies without a will, the **rule of intestate succession** controls the distribution of the estate. Community property goes to the surviving spouse. Separate property will go to the spouse if no children exist. If one child exists, the separate property is divided equally between spouse and child. If two or more children exist, one-third goes to the spouse and two-thirds is divided between the children.

Accession, Erosion, Reliction, and Avulsion

Accession refers to property lost by natural forces. **Erosion** is the gradually wearing away of the land. **Reliction** is when water recedes from the property; the newly exposed land belongs to the adjoining property. **Avulsion** is the violent tearing away of land, the owner of the lost property has one year to reclaim the lost land.

▶ Practice of Real Estate and Mandated Disclosures

Trust Account Management

Another important area concerns the handling of client and customer funds. In fact, the most frequent cause of license suspension or revocation is mishandling of trust funds. While it is the employing broker's responsibility to establish a trust fund account, every salesperson must comply with the applicable regulations.

In general, funds made payable to the broker are held as stipulated in written instructions, deposited into the broker's trust account, or endorsed and turned over to the specified party. A check may be held uncashed per the contract while an offer is pending. Once the offer is accepted, the check must be deposited with the specified escrow or trust fund account or given to the party for which it was collected within three business days. The check can be held undeposited for a longer time, if there is written permission from the buyer, tenant, or other person from whom the funds have been received.

Normally, trust fund accounts are not interest-bearing unless at the request of the owner of the funds or the parties to a transaction.

The broker's own funds must not be kept in the trust fund account, although a minimal amount (not more than $200) may be deposited by the broker to cover depository expenses. Any other deposit of the broker's own funds into the trust fund account, or deposit of trust funds into the broker's personal or business account, is considered **commingling** and is prohibited. Funds in the trust account that are payable to the broker as commissions or fees must be removed no later than 25 days after authorization.

Personal property (coins, jewelry) received by the broker should be kept in a safe or safety deposit box. Records of trust funds and other accounts must be maintained in accordance with generally accepted accounting practices. Trust fund and other brokerage accounts are subject to audit by the Department of Real Estate. All trust records, as well as listing agreements, deposit receipts, canceled checks, and other documents must be retained by the broker for at least three years following closing of a transaction or the date of listing if no transaction resulted.

Fair Housing Laws

Federal **fair housing laws** are supplemented by state regulations in many states, including California. If the two cover the same subject, the more stringent will apply. In other words, it is not possible to ignore a federal provision if the state law is more lenient, and vice versa.

Federal Law

The **Civil Rights Act of 1866** prohibits discrimination on the basis of race in the sale, lease, or other transfer of real or personal property. The Civil Rights Act of 1866 has no exceptions. It applies to individual home sellers as well as to agencies that represent sellers and/or buyers. The law was upheld by the U.S. Supreme Court in **Jones v. Mayer** (1968).

The **Civil Rights Act of 1964** prohibits housing discrimination in transactions involving loans insured by the **Federal Housing Administration** (**FHA**) or guaranteed by the **Department of Veterans Affairs** (**VA**).

The **Federal Fair Housing Act** (**Title VIII of the Civil Rights Act of 1968**) broadened the prohibitions against discrimination in housing to include national origin, race, color, and religion. With the **Housing and Community Development Act** of 1974, Congress increased the range of protected classes to include sex (gender). The law was amended in 1988 to include protection against discrimination on the basis of handicap and familial status. There is to be no discrimination against:

- children (those under age 18)
- families with children (whether headed by a parent or guardian)
- persons who are in the process of obtaining custody of a child
- pregnant women

Families with children may not be limited to only certain units in an apartment complex and must be allowed full access to facilities unless rules limiting or prohibiting access to children are nondiscriminatory.

An exception to compliance with the law regarding familial status is allowed if one of the following is true:

- the housing is intended for and solely occupied by persons age 62 or older
- at least 80% of units are occupied by at least one person age 55 or older

A complaint alleging a violation of the law may be filed with HUD or the office of the U.S. Attorney General.

A real estate agent should display an **Equal Housing Opportunity** poster in the agent's principal place of business.

The **Americans with Disabilities Act** of 1988 (**ADA**) prohibits discrimination by employers and businesses against persons with a physical and/or mental disability.

An individual with a **disability** is defined as:

- anyone with a physical or mental impairment that substantially limits a major life activity (walking, seeing, hearing, speaking, performing manual tasks, caring for one's self, and so on)
- anyone who has had such an impairment
- anyone who is perceived as having such an impairment

ADA covers both temporary and chronic conditions, including vision loss, mental retardation, AIDS, HIV infection, cancer, heart disease, and others. ADA does not cover such categories as homosexuality or bisexuality, gender identity disorders, compulsive gambling, kleptomania, pyromania, and psychoactive substance use disorders stemming from illegal use of drugs.

An employer must make reasonable accommodation for known impairments, but the employer is not expected to accept an undue hardship to the business in doing so.

Businesses involved in public facilities, goods, and services must make those sites, products, or services accessible to customers with disabilities. Responsibility for compliance rests with any person who owns, leases, leases to, or operates a place of public accommodation. **Architectural barriers** must be removed whenever **readily achievable** (possible without undue expense or difficulty). Company policies, practices, or standards must be changed to provide equal access to persons with disabilities, provided the changes are reasonable and would not:

- impose an undue burden on the business
- make a fundamental change in the goods and services of the business
- cause a direct threat to the health or safety of others

State Law

The **Fair Employment and Housing Act** applies to the sale, lease, rental, or financing of housing. The law forbids discrimination based on race, color, religion, sex, marital status, national origin, or ancestry.

The **California Civil Code** (**Sections 54-55.1**) forbids discrimination in the sale, lease, or rental of housing to persons who are physically disabled, including persons who are blind, visually handicapped, or deaf.

The **Unruh Civil Rights Act** applies to accommodations as well as business establishments. It forbids discrimination based on age, sex, race, color, religion, ancestry, or national origin.

The **Housing Financial Discrimination Act** applies to all loans (including financing, refinancing, construction, repair, and remodeling) on residences of one to four units. The law forbids discrimination by financial institutions on the basis of a property's geographic location, neighborhood or other characteristic, unless a decision based on one of those factors can be proven to be based on sound business practice. Factors such as race, color, religion, sex, marital status, national origin, and ancestry of residents in the neighborhood are not to be considered. **Steering,** showing one type of neighborhood and refusing to tell about the availability of other neighborhoods, **blockbusting,** and **panic selling,** suggesting that prices will fall because people of a different race or religion are buying in the area, are prohibited by both federal and state law.

Truth in Advertising

No misrepresentation about the property's condition may be made by the agent or seller, either in person or through advertising.

The **Truth in Lending Act** requires that the true percentage rate be given if any financial terms are mentioned in an advertisement. The term "**nothing down**" violates Regulation Z under the Truth in Lending Act. An agent can avoid this situation by merely stating, "100% financing." The Federal Trade Commission enforces regulation Z.

The Truth in Lending Act requires that the borrower be told how much they are paying for credit so they can make comparisons between lenders. The most important financial disclosures, according to Regulation Z, are the **Annual Percentage Rate** (**APR**) and the amount financed. Additional disclosures include the **finance charges,** the total number of payments, and the total sales price.

Record Keeping Requirements

Agents are required to give a copy of all documents signed by a party to a transaction. Agents are required to keep documents for at least three years.

Copies of loan documents typically need to be kept for at least four years.

Agent Supervision

In California, a real estate broker is someone licensed to act as a real estate agent, representing one of the parties to a **real estate transaction** (sale, lease, exchange, and so on).

A **real estate brokerage** can be a corporation provided there is an individual who serves as the designated broker and who is responsible for the supervision of all sales associates employed by the firm. A real estate brokerage can be a partnership provided that all the partners who perform activities requiring a license are licensed as **real estate brokers**.

A **real estate salesperson** can be licensed to perform the activities of a **real estate agent**, but only under the supervision of an employing **broker**. The real estate salesperson can be hired by the real estate broker as an employee or as an **independent contractor** for tax and some liability purposes. A written agreement between real estate broker and salesperson is required and will list the responsibilities and obligations of each.

A real estate broker's license must be available for inspection at the broker's principal place of business. A fictitious business name may be used by a brokerage, and must be recorded in the county where the broker's principal business address is located.

Permitted Activities of Unlicensed Sales Assistants

An **unlicensed assistant** may not make any representations about a property, including its features and condition. An unlicensed assistant may host an **open house**, but they must limit their conduct to passing out flyers and refrain from making any statements about the features of the property. For this reason, it is difficult for an unlicensed assistant to hold an open house.

Unlicensed assistants may perform tasks for an agent, but may not accept deposits from clients nor can they make statements regarding the features, condition, or availability of listings held by the agent.

DRE Jurisdiction and Disciplinary Actions

The Real Estate Commissioner appointed by the Governor heads the **Department of Real Estate** (**DRE**) and enforces the **Real Estate Law** found in the **Business and Professions Code**. The Real Estate Commissioner appoints a 10-member **Real Estate Advisory Commission**, which makes recommendations on matters affecting the public and the practice of real estate.

A **real estate license** will not be issued to, or renewed for, anyone who is listed by the Department of Social Services as being delinquent in payment of court-ordered child support. A current licensee who is listed will have 150 days to pay all amounts owed or the license will be suspended.

Actions that may result in license suspension or revocation, a restricted license, or a requirement that the license be bonded include the following:

- misusing a trade name, such as REALTOR®
- commingling a licensee's own funds with those of a client or customer
- making a substantial misrepresentation or a false promise
- any conduct that is fraud or dishonest dealing
- not providing a definite termination date in an exclusive listing agreement
- acting as a **dual agent** without the knowledge and consent of both parties (termed **divided agency**)

The **Real Estate Education and Research Fund** is portion of licensee fees used to improve the quality of real estate training and support research that will ultimately benefit the real estate industry.

The Real Estate Commissioner, by means of the Regulations that are contained in the Business and Professions Code, places great importance on the ethical conduct of real estate licensees. Certain activities are prohibited and can be sanctioned by suspension or loss of the real estate license. Court cases have also enlarged the responsibilities of the real estate agent, as shown by the **Easton v. Strassberger** case that resulted in property inspection requirements that are now part of the Civil Code.

The increasing reliance on computerized listing and lending practices also means that agents must be up-to-date on the technology of real estate practice. One of the best ways to stay informed on changes in the industry is to join a **trade group**, such as the **California Association of REALTORs®**.

Licensing, Continuing Education Requirements, and Procedures

A real estate license is not needed by the following:

- someone (individual or company) dealing only with their own property
- an attorney acting in that capacity
- someone acting under a power of attorney
- court-appointed representatives
- escrow agents
- employees of lending institutions
- licensed securities brokers or dealers dealing with the sale or exchange of a business opportunity

The role of the real estate salesperson is undergoing discussion and legal redefinition in many states. The increasing number of legal requirements that must be met to protect the licensee's clients and customers, as well as the licensee, have resulted in ever greater emphasis on pre-licensing education and training, as well as increasing continuing education requirements.

California Real Estate Recovery Fund

The **Real Estate Recovery Account** has been established from licensee fees to serve as a source of reimbursement when a court judgment against a real estate licensee cannot be collected.

Recovery amounts are limited to $20,000 for each claimant and a maximum recovery of $100,000 total against any one licensee.

General Ethics

The Real Estate Commissioner has issued standards for **ethical conduct**, **Regulation 2785** which real estate licensees are to abide by in the listing, sale of real estate, and in the negotiation or arranging of a loan secured by real estate. In addition, the Commissioner has also provided suggestions for ethical conduct by licensees.

The **National Association of REALTORs®** adopted a **Code of Ethics and Standards of Practice** in 1913. Presently it consists of **17 Articles**, the first five being aspirational, which it requires it members to follow.

Technology

Agents typically utilize technology in maintaining their client base, communications, and **prospecting**. Laptop computers, contact management software, cellular telephones, facsimile machines, personal digital assistants, and global positioning systems are now common in the real estate profession.

Property Management/Landlord-Tenant Rights

A real estate license is required to manage real property for an owner, except for an on site property manager, which is required for apartments containing 16 units or more.

Landlords have an **implied obligation** to provide residential premises in a habitable condition; that the property must conform to all building, health, and safety codes. It must have heat, electricity, functional plumbing and appliances, locking doors, and windows. A landlord's failure to maintain the property in a habitable condition may cause the tenant to remain in the premises without payment of rent, or vacate the premises without any penalty. More information on landlord/tenant obligations is found under Contracts.

Tenants must pay rent on time, maintain the interior of their unit, occupy the premises in a legal and lawful manner and not interfere with the tenancies of other tenants.

Further discussions on this area can be found under Leases in the Contracts section.

Commercial/Industrial/Income Properties

In a **commercial lease**, the lessor owes fewer obligations to the lessee unless specifically set out in the lease. In general, the commercial tenant will bear a greater responsibility for maintenance and repair of the property.

Specialty Areas

A real estate brokerage can engage in transactions involving business inspection, or to remove the hazardous material. The appropriate documentation of compliance with the law must be retained by the seller/lessor and agents for three years from completion of the sale or the date the rental period begins.

The seller of a newly constructed home must disclose in every sales contract the type, thickness, and **R-value** of the insulation that has been or will be installed in the house.

Material Facts Affecting Property Value

While residential property is typically sold in "**as is**" condition, sellers and their agents are required to disclose all material facts regarding a property. This is interpeted to mean any item that affects the value of the propery, unless the disclosure is against the law, i.e. fair housing laws. There are a number of disclosure forms that are used to make such disclosures.

The Real Estate Transfer Disclosure Statement

This statement is given by the seller of residential property of one to four units to a prospective buyer must include environmental hazards known to the seller. Both listing and selling agents must inspect the property and disclose any material facts that may affect the value or desirability of the property. If either seller or agent gives the buyer a copy of the California pamphlet, "Environmental Hazards: A Guide for Homeowners, Buyers, Landlords, and Tenants," no further information need be provided unless there is a known hazard.

Hazardous substances include (but are not limited to) asbestos, formaldehyde, radon gas, lead-based paint, hazardous wastes, fuel, or chemical storage tanks and contaminated soil or water.

Natural Hazards Disclosure

Emergency legislation effective June 1, 1998, requires that a seller of any real property (whether residential or non-residential) must disclose to a buyer property location in a special flood hazard area, dam failure inundation area, earthquake fault zone, seismic hazard zone, high fire severity area, or wildland fire area.

The seller's agent has primary responsibility for disclosure if a property is located in an earthquake fault zone, seismic hazard zone, FEMA Zone A or V, or dam failure inundation area. If there is no agent, the seller is responsible for the disclosure.

The seller has primary responsibility for disclosure that property is located in a high fire severity zone or wildland fire area. Location in an area identified by the **Department of Forestry and Fire Protection** as posing the possibility of substantial fire risk must be disclosed.

Location in an area that may contain **ordnance** (live ammunition), if known to the seller, must be revealed to the buyer of residential property.

Need for a Property Inspection and Obtaining/Verifying Information

Since most property is sold in as is condition and sellers may not have disclosed all items wrong with the property, it is important for a buyer to inspect the property prior to purchasing. A prudent buyer will also hire professional inspectors to make inspections and review the reports of others.

The **Alquist-Priolo Earthquake Fault Zoning Act,** described earlier in **Property Ownership and Land Use Controls and Regulations**, requires that the seller of property located in an earthquake fault zone must disclose that fact to a buyer. The **"Homeowner's Guide to Earthquake Safety,"** prepared by the **Seismic Safety Commission,** is sufficient to fulfill the general requirement of the law if provided to a buyer. Specific known hazards affecting the property must still be indicated by the seller and agent, however. There is a **"Commercial Property Owner's Guide"** for affected nonresidential property.

The Homeowner's Guide must be provided in any transfer of real property improved with a wood frame residential dwelling of one to four units that was built prior to January 1, 1960. Both guides must be provided in the transfer of any masonry residential building of one to four units that has wood-frame floors or roof and was built before January 1, 1975. The Commercial Guide must be provided in the transfer of commercial masonry buildings with wood-frame floors or roofs built before January 1, 1975.

Factors that must be disclosed in the transfer of residential property of one to four units as potential hazards, if known to the seller, include:

- absence of foundation anchor bolts
- unbraced or inadequately braced perimeter cripple walls or first story walls
- unreinforced masonry perimeter foundation or dwelling walls
- habitable room or rooms above a garage
- water heater not anchored, strapped, or braced

State law imposes minimum requirements for thermal insulation and other methods of energy conservation in newly constructed homes. **Local ordinances** may require energy retrofitting as a condition of sale of an existing home.

Local ordinances may require special fire and natural hazard protections, such as sprinkler systems in areas of high fire danger.

Failure to make a required disclosure will not invalidate a transaction, but may result in actual damages being imposed on the seller and/or agent.

▶ Contracts

General

In the practice of real estate, there are many contracts and other documents used to initiate various steps in the transaction process and bring a transaction to a successful conclusion.

Many **contract clauses** discussed earlier in this course, such as **property condition disclosures**, are mandated by state or federal law. There are other contract provisions that have become widely accepted practice because of their appearance on contract forms produced by trade associations as well as commercial publishers.

Contract Elements

A **contract** is a promise between two or more legally competent parties to do or refrain from doing some legal act. In exchange for the promise, each party gives the other something of value, called **consideration**. Consideration can be money, goods, or services. In the case of a real estate transaction, it can also be another parcel of real estate, as in an exchange.

The elements of a valid contract are:

- **legal capacity** by both parties
- an offer by one party that is accepted by the other party
- a lawful activity or subject

- payment of consideration
- a written agreement, as the parties choose or as required by law

Persons without **legal capacity** include a minor (usually, anyone under the age of 18) and a person who is judged incompetent by a court. A minor can be emancipated and gain the ability to enter into a contract by doing one of the following:

- marrying
- joining the armed forces
- successfully petitioning the court

A **legal representative** (attorney, guardian, or estate executor or administrator) can act on behalf of a minor, a person who is judged incompetent, or the estate of a deceased individual.

An offer can be revoked before acceptance, unless there has been some form of **consideration** (payment) given for it (such as payment for an option).

An offer is not made until it is received by the **offeree** (the person to whom the offer is made).

According to the **mailbox rule**, an offer is accepted when it is given over for delivery via the mail. Most residential contracts require actual notice of acceptance to be given. Any change to the terms of an offer is a **counteroffer** and has the effect of rejecting the initial offer and making a new offer. The offer and acceptance must both be made **voluntarily** (without coercion) and **without misrepresentation**.

Actual fraud can be an act or omission with the intent to deceive. **Constructive fraud** is an act or omission made without intent to deceive, but with a disregard for the truth of the action or omission that goes beyond mere negligence.

The obligation of both parties to pay consideration as part of the agreement is termed mutuality of contract.

The **Statute of Frauds** that is part of state law requires most contracts dealing with real estate to be in writing. An exception is a lease that will terminate one year or less from the date of agreement. Even then, it is in the best interests of both landlord and tenant to have a written agreement.

To be **enforceable** in court, all expressed contracts should be in writing.

If a written agreement is required, the **parol evidence rule** will prevent oral testimony or previously written documents as to the contract terms (from discussions in the period before the writing was signed) from being admitted in any future contract dispute.

A contract is **executory** when it has not yet been fully performed. A contract is **executed** when all contract terms have been met and the transaction is completed. (The word *executed* also refers to the signing of a contract, deed or other document by the necessary parties.)

A contract is **express** when its terms are stated in a written or oral agreement. A contract is **implied** when its terms are understood by the conduct of the parties (acting as if a contract exists).

A **bilateral contract** is one in which both parties exchange promises to do or refrain from doing something. A real estate sales contract is bilateral because both sides have an obligation to perform—the turning over of title to the property in exchange for money or other consideration. A **unilateral contract** is one in which one party makes a promise and the other party does not promise, but can make the contract a binding agreement by taking some action.

A **voidable contract** is one that appears valid but is subject to cancellation by one of the parties.

If one of the parties is acting under a fraudulent misrepresentation by the other party, the misrepresentation will give the deceived party the option to perform the contract or to cancel it. A **void contract** is one that fails to meet all of the requirements for a valid contract. An **unenforceable contract** is one that cannot be sued upon by either party, for example a contract that violates the statute of frauds.

When all the terms of a contract have been fulfilled, the contract is **discharged**.

A **novation** is a redrafting of the agreement, substituting the new one for the old one.

A **rescission** is a mutual agreement to cancel the agreement.

A **reformation** is a mutually agreed change to some contract term to remove an ambiguity or to correct a mistake.

An **assignment** is a transfer of the contract rights and obligations of one of the parties to another person. Some contracts, by the nature of the obligation imposed, cannot be assigned. Examples are contracts offering a **personal service** (a listing agreement). A **breach of contract** is a failure by one of the parties to fulfill the agreed-upon terms. Because every parcel of real estate is considered unique, if a seller refuses to complete a sale of real estate, the buyer may bring a suit for specific performance requesting that the court enforce the contract. The same remedy may be available in an exchange, lease, or option agreement, if the property owner refuses to complete the transaction.

Listing Agreements

Note: Some information about listing agreements is found in Laws of Agency.

The listing agreement will include:

- identity of the parties
- description of the property
- object of the agreement (property sale, exchange, lease)
- **term** (length of time) of the agreement (optional for an open listing)
- definition of the agent's role and list of agent's obligations
- statement of compensation to which agent is entitled on fulfilling the agent's obligations
- **safety clause** stipulating that agent's compensation is to be paid if a sale is transacted with a buyer who was introduced to the property owner by the agent, within a stated period after termination of the listing agreement
- authorization for the agent to use the local **multiple listing system**, Internet listing system, or other marketing forum
- authorization for the use of subagents
- authorization to hold key or to use lock box or other means of property entry in owner's absence

- authorization to receive deposit or other funds on behalf of the buyer, and stipulation as to how those funds are to be handled
- **arbitration** or **mediation** provision to be enforced in the event of a contract dispute
- statement of compliance with all applicable fair housing laws
- any other provision required by law
- signature of seller and signature of agent

Buyer Broker Agreements

In increasing numbers, real estate agents are asking buyers to sign exclusive buyer-broker agreements. These agreements create an obligation for the buyer to go through the agent in making offers on listed and unlisted properties. The agreements also allow for the buyer to pay a commission to the agent if the seller is not offering compensation to the selling agent.

These agreements demand loyalty of the buyer to the agent as the buyer could be obligated to paying two commissions if the buyer entered into a purchase contract with a second agent.

Offers/Purchase Contracts

The **real estate sales contract** begins as an offer from buyer to seller and typically will include the following:

- identity of all parties to the transaction
- full legal description of the real estate as well as a listing of any personal property to be included
- sales price, including amount of down payment and indication of how the remainder of the price will be paid at closing
- **financing contingency** giving details of the type of financing the buyer hopes to obtain and stipulating a deadline for release of the contingency
- statement that the transaction is contingent on a sale of other property of the buyer. (The seller will want a deadline for release of the contingency, particularly if a noncontingent offer is made while the transaction is pending.)
- escrow agent for the transaction and by whom the fee for this service will be paid
- property inspections to be made and by whom, including deadlines for the inspections as well as the appropriate notifications to buyer and/or seller. (The seller will want a limit on expenditures for any pest control treatment or necessary repairs.)
- list of applicable categories of disclosure required by state and federal law, which may include location in a flood, earthquake, or other zone, and the presence of hazardous materials, such as lead-based paint
- arbitration or mediation of disputes
- **liquidated damages** in the event of breach by one of the parties
- compliance with the federal Foreign Investment in Real Property Tax Act (FIRPTA)
- statement of compliance with all applicable fair housing laws
- compliance with any other state or federal law not already mentioned

- final walk-through by the buyer to insure that the property has been adequately maintained before closing
- statement of who will bear the risk of loss in the event of property damage or destruction between the time the contract is signed and the transaction is closed
- statement of the agency representation
- statement of how long the offer will be left open
- signature of the buyer(s) and space for signature of the seller(s)
- statement that the agent has received the indicated deposit, and signature of **the agent**

An offer will **expire** (end) if it is not accepted by the deadline specified in its terms. If no deadline is specified, a reasonable time period will be implied.

The purchase offer can be terminated by one of the following:

- revocation of the **offeror** (buyer) before acceptance
- rejection by the **offeree** (seller)
- counteroffer by the offeree

If it is accepted by the seller, a real estate sales contract can be terminated by one of the following:

- completion of the terms of the contract
- **mutual consent** of the parties (**rescission**)
- **breach** by one of the parties
- destruction of the property

Counteroffers/Multiple Counteroffers

A **counteroffer** constitutes a rejection of the previous offer. Typically a counteroffer will incorporate the majority of the initial offer, making a few changes, usually in the purchase price, amount of deposit and term of escrow. Should more than one offer be received by a seller, that seller may want to individually counter each offer, or counter all of the offers at the same time.

If a multiple counteroffer situation occurs, then the seller should make sure that the counteroffer has to be signed a second time by the seller upon acceptance by the buyer so to avoid entering into two contracts with two buyers on the same property.

Leases

Leasehold Estates, Leases, Lease Clauses, and Rental Agreements

The **lessor** (owner of the leased fee) permits the **lessee** (holder of the leasehold interest) to use the property for the period and under the terms specified in the lease.

An **estate for years** (**tenancy for years**) is a leasehold with a specified termination date. A **periodic tenancy** specifies a lease term that is renewed automatically. A **tenancy at will** has no definite termination date and may be terminated by notice of either lessor or lessee. A **tenancy at sufferance** is created when a tenant remains in the premises after the termination date. If the lessor accepts rent from the holdover tenant, a new lease term is created; otherwise, the tenant at sufferance may be evicted.

The **Statute of Frauds** requires that a lease that will terminate more than one year from the date of its signing must be in writing.

A **lease option** can allow a prospective purchaser to occupy the property before making a purchase decision.

State law governs many of the provisions in a residential lease. The typical lease will include the following:

- identity of the lessor (**landlord**) and lessee (**tenant**)
- description of the premises to be leased
- term of the lease, including beginning and ending times
- rent to be paid and when payment is due—a grace period is usually specified, as well as the penalty for late payment due after that time
- obligations of the lessor, which will include compliance with an express or implied warranty of habitability
- obligations of the lessee, which will include payment of the stated rent as well as maintenance of the premises
- arbitration or mediation clause to be enforced in the event of a dispute in the terms of the agreement
- signature of the lessee and signature of the lessor (or agent)—if a lessee moves in and does not sign the lease, acceptance of the lease is presumed.

Other terms are used to refer to commercial leases.

With a **percentage lease** (participation lease), the lessee pays part of the proceeds from operation of the business on the leased premises. The terms of the percentage lease may indicate a base rent as well as a percentage that varies depending on the level of income achieved, usually per month.

With a **gross lease**, the lessor is responsible for paying all expenses of property ownership, such as property taxes.

With a **net lease**, the lessee pays rent but is also responsible for paying some or all of the expenses of ownership. Under the terms of a **triple net** (net, net, net) lease, the lessee pays all of the **expenses of ownership** (taxes, insurance, and maintanence) in addition to the required rent.

A **sale and leaseback** may be used by a company that wants the advantages of receiving the proceeds of a sale, while still retaining the use of the property under the terms of a lease.

A **ground lease** can allow building and land ownership to be separate. The lease agreement may allow the right of possession to be assigned to someone else. In an assignment the original tenant is relieved of further responsibility under the lease. If the property is sublet, the original tenant remains liable.

Lessor and Lessee Rights, Responsibilities, and Recourse

The **lessor** (property owner, or landlord) of residential property will have certain obligations imposed by the terms of the lease, or by state law. The lessor's obligations can also be termed the **lessee's** (tenant's) **rights**.

In residential situations, the maximum security deposit that can be collected is the equivalent of:

- two months rent for an unfurnished unit
- three months rent for a furnished unit

The landlord will not be allowed to interfere with the tenant's quiet enjoyment of the leased property. This means that the landlord must recognize the tenant's right of possession of the property. The landlord cannot enter the property without the tenant's permission, except in these circumstances:

- in an emergency
- to provide services or make repairs that were agreed to, or that are necessary to maintain the habitability of the property (after giving reasonable notice to the tenant)
- to show the property to prospective tenants, purchasers, or service providers (after giving reasonable notice to the tenant)
- if the tenant has abandoned or surrendered the property
- if a court orders or permits an entry

An **express** or **implied warranty of habitability** will require the landlord to keep the property in livable condition. This includes:

- structural integrity of the building, including weatherproofing of roof, walls, windows, and doors
- provision of utilities, including water (hot and cold), sewage disposal, electricity and gas or other source of heat, all in compliance with state and local laws
- maintenance and cleanup of common areas, such as halls and stairways
- federally mandated disclosure of the possible presence of lead-based paint in new and renewal leases on property built before 1978
- other state and local requirements, such as installation of a smoke detector, deadbolt lock, or sprinkler system

If the landlord fails to meet these obligations, the tenant usually can do any of the following:

- withhold rent up to a certain amount (although the repair and deduct remedy can only be used twice in any 12-month period)
- abandon the property with no further obligation under the lease

In turn, the tenant is obliged to:

- keep the leased property clean and dispose of trash in a sanitary manner
- use fixtures and appliances in a safe and sanitary manner, and in the rooms designated for their use
- not damage, deface, or otherwise destroy the property, or permit anyone else to do so

Liability for injuries on leased property may belong to lessor, lessee, or both.

In general, if a dangerous condition or property defect is due to the negligence or deliberate act of the lessee, the lessee will be liable to an injured party. If the property is residential, and the lessor was negligent (the lessor knew or should have known of the condition or defect, and did not act to correct it), the lessor will be liable, as well.

Termination of a lease can be accomplished in the following ways:

- notice as required by the lease agreement or by law:

    three days if in breach of a provision of the lease or rental agreement (including nonpayment of rent)
    thirty days without cause if the periodic tenant has been in the premises for less than one year
    sixty days without cause if the periodic tenant has been in the premises for one year or longer

- destruction or condemnation of the leased property
- breach of an express or implied condition or covenant
- illegal use of the property
- in a tenancy at will or tenancy at sufferance, death of the lessor or lessee
- merger of property rights, which occurs if the lessor acquires the leasehold interest, or the lessee acquires the leased fee
- bankruptcy of the lessee, at the court's discretion, or, in some cases, bankruptcy of the lessor

Unlawful detainer is the legal action that is the usual method of ousting a defaulting lessee. **Statutory notice** and other procedural requirements must be met by the lessor. An **action in ejectment** is a holdover from the common law, and is a lengthier court proceeding used by a lessor to evict a lessee.

Management Contracts and Obligations of Parties

Management of **investment (rental) property** increasingly is placed in the hands of professional property managers. California law requires that a **property manager** (individual or firm) have a real estate license.

The agreement between the property owner and property manager usually will provide the following:

- identity of the parties
- description of the property to be managed

- term (time period) during which the agreement will be in effect, including specified beginning and ending times
- responsibilities of the agent, including the agent's authority to arrange for building maintenance, market vacancies, execute leases, serve notice on tenants when necessary, and hire an attorney for necessary legal services
- financial limitation on agent's authority to order repairs, materials, or services on behalf of the property owner
- agent's authority to use rents and other property income to make authorized payments
- responsibilities of the property owner, including payment of specified compensation to the agent
- signature of owner and signature of agent

A licensed property manager can employ nonlicensed individuals to:

- show units to prospective tenants
- accept deposits, fees, security deposits, and rents
- provide information on rental rates and lease provisions
- accept signed leases and rental agreements from prospective tenants

In California, residential rental property of 16 or more units must have a resident property manager on the premises. A resident property manager does not need a real estate license.

There is a special two-year license for an individual or corporation who wants to operate a **Prepaid Rental Listing Service** (**PRLS**). A licensed real estate broker can also conduct this activity.

Whether it will be under authority of a Prepaid Rental Listing Service license or real estate broker's license, any contract to be entered into between the licensee and client/prospective tenant must be approved in advance by the Department of Real Estate.

Agreements

Express agreements are either in writing or oral, as long as words are used to create the agreement; implied agreements are created with actions, not words.

A **valid agreement** will occur when an offer is accepted by the **offeree** (or a **counteroffer** is accepted by the **counterofferee**) and **communication of the acceptance** is delivered to the other party. The other party can revoke their offer (or counteroffer) at any time prior to the delivery of the acceptance. The delivery may be in any form, the contract itself must conform to the requirements of the Statute of Frauds.

Promissory Notes/Securities

The **promissory note** from borrower to lender records the amount borrowed and the terms of payment.

When it meets legal requirements, a promissory note can qualify as a negotiable instrument. This means that it is as acceptable as a check to a future buyer. To qualify as a negotiable instrument, a promissory note must be an unconditional promise to pay a specified amount of money (**sum certain**) at a definite time or **on demand** (whenever payment is requested) to the identified party or the bearer of the note and be signed by the maker of the note.

Someone who buys a negotiable instrument will be termed a **holder in due course** (**HDC**) if that party takes the note as an innocent transferee who has no business relationship with the party from whom the document was received. A holder in due course is one who takes a negotiable instrument:

- for value
- in good faith
- without notice that it has been dishonored, is overdue, or that there is any defense against it or claim to it by anyone else

5 ▶ Real Estate Math Review

CHAPTER SUMMARY
Even if math is not your favorite subject, this chapter will help you do your best on math questions you may encounter. It not only covers arithmetic, algebra, geometry, and word problems, but also has practice problems for each of the real estate math topics.

ERE ARE SOME types of math questions you may encounter on an exam.

- Percents
- Areas
- Property Tax
- Loan-to-Value Ratios
- Points
- Equity
- Qualifying Buyers
- Prorations
- Commissions
- Sale Proceeds

- Transfer Tax/Conveyance Tax/Revenue Stamps
- Competitive Market Analyses (CMA)
- Income Properties
- Depreciation

Keep in mind that although the math topics are varied, you will be using the same math skills to complete each question. But before you review your math skills, take a look at some helpful strategies for doing your best.

► Strategies for Math Questions

Answer Every Question

You should answer every single question, even if you don't know the answer. There is usually no penalty for a wrong answer, and, if there are four answer choices, you have a 25% chance of guessing correctly. If one or two answers are obviously wrong, the odds may be even higher on selecting the correct one.

Bring a Calculator

You must check with your exam center to find out exactly what type of calculator is permitted. In general, permissible calculators are battery-operated, do not print, are not programmable, and do not have a keypad with letters. As a precaution, you should bring an extra battery with you to your exam. Try not to rely entirely on the calculator. Although using one can prevent simple adding and subtracting errors, it may take longer for you to use the calculator than to figure it out yourself.

Use Scratch Paper

Resist the temptation to "save time" by doing all your work on your calculator. The main pitfall with calculators is the temptation to work the problem all the way through to the end on the calculator. At this point, if none of the answers provided is correct, there is no way to know where the mistake lies. Use scratch paper to avoid this problem.

Check Your Work

Checking your work is always good practice, and it's usually quite simple. Even if you come up with an answer that is one of the answer choices, you should check your work. Test writers often include answer choices that are the results of common errors, which is what you may have.

▶ Real Estate Math Review

Here's a quick review of some basic arithmetic, algebra, geometry, and word problem skills you will need for your exam.

Arithmetic Review

Symbols of Multiplication

When two or more numbers are being multiplied, they are called **factors**. The answer that results is called the **product**.

> *Example:*
> $5 \times 6 = 30$ 5 and 6 are **factors** and 30 is the **product**.

There are several ways to represent multiplication in the above mathematical statement.

- A dot between factors indicates multiplication:

  $5 \cdot 6 = 30$

- Parentheses around any part of the one or more factors indicates multiplication:

  $(5)6 = 30, 5(6) = 30,$ and $(5)(6) = 30$

- Multiplication is also indicated when a number is placed next to a variable:

  $5a = 30$ In this equation, 5 is being multiplied by a.

Divisibility

Like multiplication, division can be represented in a few different ways:

$8 \div 3$ $3\overline{)8}$ $\frac{8}{3}$

In each of the above, 3 is the divisor and 8 is the dividend.

If the number after the one you need to round to is 5 or more, make the preceding number one higher. If it is less than 5, drop it and leave the preceding number the same. (Information about rounding is usually provided in the exam instructions or in the exam bulletin.)

Example:
0.0135 = .014 or .01

Decimals

The most important thing to remember about decimals is that the first place value to the right begins with tenths. The place values are as follows:

1	2	6	8	•	3	4	5	7
THOUSANDS	HUNDREDS	TENS	ONES	DECIMAL POINT	TENTHS	HUNDREDTHS	THOUSANDTHS	TEN THOUSANDTHS

In expanded form, this number can also be expressed as . . .

$1268.3457 = (1 \times 1{,}000) + (2 \times 100) + (6 \times 10) + (8 \times 1) + (3 \times .01) + (4 \times .01) + (5 \times .001) + (7 \times .0001)$

Fractions

To do well when working with fractions, it is necessary to understand some basic concepts. Here are some math rules for fractions using variables:

$$\frac{a}{b} \times \frac{c}{d} = \frac{a \times c}{b \times d}$$

$$\frac{a}{b} + \frac{c}{b} = \frac{a + c}{b}$$

$$\frac{a}{b} \div \frac{c}{d} = \frac{a}{b} \times \frac{d}{c} = \frac{a \times d}{b \times c}$$

$$\frac{a}{b} + \frac{c}{d} = \frac{ad + bc}{bd}$$

Multiplication of Fractions

Multiplying fractions is one of the easiest operations to perform. To multiply fractions, simply multiply the numerators and the denominators, writing each in the respective place over or under the fraction bar.

Example:

$\frac{4}{5} \times \frac{6}{7} = \frac{24}{35}$

Dividing of Fractions

Dividing fractions is the same thing as multiplying fractions by their **reciprocals**. To find the reciprocal of any number, switch its numerator and denominator. For example, the reciprocals of the following numbers are:

$\frac{1}{3} \rightarrow \frac{3}{1} = 3$

$x \rightarrow \frac{1}{x}$

$\frac{4}{5} \rightarrow \frac{5}{4}$

$5 \rightarrow \frac{1}{5}$

When dividing fractions, simply multiply the dividend (what is being divided) by the divisor's (what is doing the dividing) reciprocal to get the answer.

Example:

$\frac{12}{21} \div \frac{3}{4} = \frac{12}{21} \times \frac{4}{3} = \frac{48}{63} = \frac{16}{21}$

Adding and Subtracting Fractions

To add or subtract fractions with like denominators, just add or subtract the numerators and leave the denominator as it is. For example,

$\frac{1}{7} + \frac{5}{7} = \frac{6}{7}$ and $\frac{5}{8} - \frac{2}{8} = \frac{3}{8}$

To add or subtract fractions with unlike denominators, you must find the **Least Common Denominator**, or LCD.

For example, if given the denominators 8 and 12, 24 would be the LCD because $8 \times 3 = 24$, and $12 \times 2 = 24$. In other words, the LCD is the smallest number divisible by each of the denominators.

Once you know the LCD, convert each fraction to its new form by multiplying both the numerator and denominator by the necessary number to get the LCD, and then add or subtract the new numerators.

Example:

$\frac{1}{3} + \frac{2}{5} = \frac{5(1)}{5(3)} + \frac{3(2)}{3(5)} = \frac{5}{15} + \frac{6}{15} = \frac{11}{15}$

Percent

A **percent** is a measure of a part to a whole, with the whole being equal to 100.

- To change a decimal to a percentage, move the decimal point two units to the right and add a percentage symbol.

    Example:
    .45 = 45%   .07 = 7%   .9 = 90%

- To change a fraction to a percentage, first change the fraction to a decimal. To do this, divide the numerator by the denominator. Then change the decimal to a percentage.

    Example:
    $\frac{4}{5} = .80 = 80\%$

    $\frac{2}{5} = .4 = 40\%$

    $\frac{1}{8} = .125 = 12.5\%$

- To change a decimal to a percentage, move the decimal point two units to the right and add a percentage symbol.
- To change a percentage to a decimal, simply move the decimal point two places to the left and eliminate the percentage symbol.

    Example:
    64% = .64   87% = .87   7% = .07

- To change a percentage to a fraction, divide by 100 and reduce.

    Example:
    $64\% = \frac{64}{100} = \frac{16}{25}$

    $75\% = \frac{75}{100} = \frac{3}{4}$

    $82\% = \frac{82}{100} = \frac{41}{50}$

- Keep in mind that any percentage that is 100 or greater will need to reflect a whole number or mixed number when converted.

    Example:
    $125\% = 1.25$ or $1\frac{1}{4}$
    $350\% = 3.5$ or $3\frac{1}{2}$

Here are some conversions you should be familiar with:

Fraction	Decimal	Percentage
$\frac{1}{2}$	.5	50%
$\frac{1}{4}$	.25	25%
$\frac{1}{3}$	.333 . . .	33.$\overline{3}$%
$\frac{2}{3}$	.666 . . .	66.$\overline{6}$%
$\frac{1}{10}$	.1	10%
$\frac{1}{8}$	.125	12.5%
$\frac{1}{6}$	.1666 . . .	16.$\overline{6}$%
$\frac{1}{5}$	.2	20%

Algebra Review

Equations

An **equation** is solved by finding a number that is equal to an unknown variable.

Simple Rules for Working with Equations

1. The equal sign separates an equation into two sides.
2. Whenever an operation is performed on one side, the same operation must be performed on the other side.
3. Your first goal is to get all of the variables on one side and all of the numbers on the other.
4. The final step often will be to divide each side by the coefficient, leaving the variable equal to a number.

Checking Equations

To check an equation, substitute the number equal to the variable in the original equation.

Example:

To check the equation below, substitute the number 10 for the variable *x*.

$$\frac{x}{6} = \frac{x+10}{12}$$

$$\frac{10}{6} = \frac{10+10}{12} = \frac{10}{6} = \frac{20}{12}$$

$$1\frac{2}{3} = 1\frac{2}{3} \quad \frac{10}{6} = \frac{10}{6}$$

Because this statement is true, you know the answer *x* = 10 must be correct.

Special Tips for Checking Equations

1. If time permits, be sure to check all equations.
2. Be careful to answer the question that is being asked. Sometimes, this involves solving for a variable and then performing an operation.

Example:

If the question asks the value of $x - 2$, and you find $x = 2$, the answer is not 2, but $2 - 2$. Thus, the answer is 0.

Algebraic Fractions

Algebraic fractions are very similar to fractions in arithmetic.

Example:

Write $\frac{x}{5} - \frac{x}{10}$ as a single fraction.

Solution:

Just like in arithmetic, you need to find the LCD of 5 and 10, which is 10. Then change each fraction into an equivalent fraction that has 10 as a denominator.

$$\frac{x}{5} - \frac{x}{10} = \frac{x(2)}{5(2)} - \frac{x}{10}$$
$$= \frac{2x}{10} - \frac{x}{10}$$
$$= \frac{x}{10}$$

Geometry Review

Area	the space inside a two-dimensional figure
Circumference	the distance around a circle
Perimeter	the distance around a figure
Radius	the distance from the center point of a circle to any point on the circle

Area

Area is the space inside of the lines defining the shape.

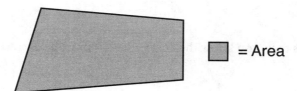

= Area

This geometry review will focus on the area formula for three main shapes: circles, rectangles/squares, and triangles.

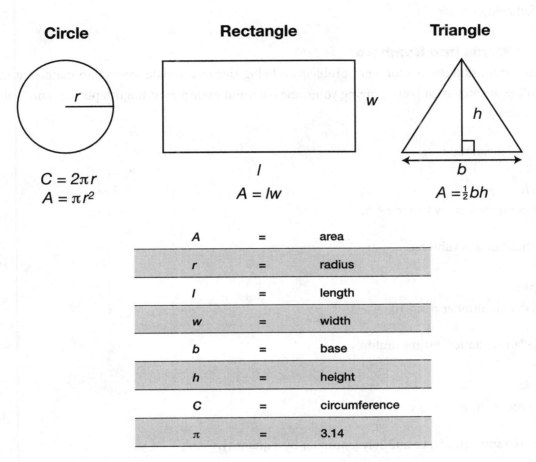

Circle

$C = 2\pi r$
$A = \pi r^2$

Rectangle

$A = lw$

Triangle

$A = \frac{1}{2}bh$

A	=	area
r	=	radius
l	=	length
w	=	width
b	=	base
h	=	height
C	=	circumference
π	=	3.14

Perimeter

The perimeter of an object is simply the sum of all of its sides.

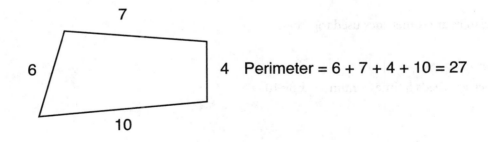

Perimeter = 6 + 7 + 4 + 10 = 27

The circumference is the perimeter of a circle.

$C = 2\pi r$

Word Problem Review

Since many of the math problems the California real estate sales exam will be word problems, pay extra attention to the following review.

Translating Words into Numbers

The most important skill needed for word problems is being able to translate words into mathematical operations. The following will assist you by giving you some common examples of English phrases and their mathematical equivalents.

- "Increase" means add

    Example:
    A number increased by five $= x + 5$.

- "Less than" means subtract.

    Example:
    10 less than a number $= x - 10$.

- "Times" or "product" means multiply

    Example:
    Three times a number $= 3x$.

- "Times the sum" means to multiply a number by a quantity.

    Example:
    Five times the sum of a number and three $= 5(x + 3)$.

- Two variables are sometimes used together.

    Example:
    A number y exceeds 5 times a number x by 10.
    $y = 5x + 10$

- "Of" means multiply.

    Example:
    10% of 100 is 10 $= 10\% \times 100 = 10$

- "Is" means equals.

Example:

15 is 14 plus 1 becomes $15 = 14 + 1$.

Assigning Variables in Word Problems

It may be necessary to create and assign variables in a word problem. To do this, first identify an unknown and a known. You may not actually know the exact value of the "known," but you will know at least something about its value.

Examples:

Max is three years older than Ricky

Unknown = Ricky's age = x

Known = Max's age is three years older.

Therefore,

Ricky's age = x and Max's age = $x + 3$.

Heidi made twice as many cookies as Rebecca.

Unknown = number of cookies Rebecca made = x

Known = number of cookies Heidi made = $2x$

Jessica has five more than three times the number of books that Becky has.

Unknown = the number of books Becky has = x

Known = the number of books Jessica has = $3x + 5$

Percentage Problems

There is one formula that is useful for solving the three types of percentage problems:

$$\frac{\#}{\text{whole}}\ \frac{\text{part}}{} = \frac{\%}{100}$$

When reading a percentage problem, substitute the necessary information into the above formula based on the following:

- 100 is always written in the denominator of the percentage sign column.
- If given a percentage, write it in the numerator position of the number column. If you are not given a percentage, then the variable should be placed there.
- The denominator of the number column represents the number that is equal to the whole, or 100%. This number always follows the word "of" in a word problem.

- The numerator of the number column represents the number that is the percent.
- In the formula, the equal sign can be interchanged with the word "is."

Examples:

- Finding a percentage of a given number.

  What number is equal to 40% of 50?

$$\frac{\overset{\#}{x}}{50} = \frac{\overset{\%}{40}}{100}$$

Cross multiply:

$100(x) = (40)(50)$

$100x = 2{,}000$

$\frac{100x}{100} = \frac{2{,}000}{100}$

$x = 20$ Therefore, 20 is 40% of 50.

- Finding a number when a percentage is given:

  40% of what number is 24?

$$\frac{\overset{\#}{24}}{x} = \frac{\overset{\%}{40}}{100}$$

Cross multiply:

$(24)(100) = (40)(x)$

$2{,}400 = 40x$

$\frac{2{,}400}{40} = \frac{40x}{40}$

$60 = x$ Therefore, 40% of 60 is 24.

- Finding what percentage one number is of another:

  What percentage of 75 is 15?

$$\frac{\overset{\#}{15}}{75} = \frac{\overset{\%}{x}}{100}$$

$$\textbf{Rate} = \frac{x \text{ units}}{y \text{ units}}$$

A percentage problem simply means that y units is equal to 100. It is important to remember that a percentage problem may be worded using the word *rate*.

Cross multiply:

$15(100) = (75)(x)$

$1,500 = 75x$

$\frac{1,500}{75} = \frac{75x}{75}$

$20 = x$ Therefore, 20% of 75 is 15.

Rate Problems

You may encounter a couple of different types of rate problems on your state's real estate sales exam: cost per unit, interest rate, and tax rate. Rate is defined as a comparison of two quantities with different units of measure.

$$\textbf{Rate} = \frac{x \text{ units}}{y \text{ units}}$$

Examples: $\frac{\text{dollars}}{\text{square foot}}, \frac{\text{interest}}{\text{year}}$

Cost Per Unit

Some problems on your exam may require that you calculate the cost per unit.

Example:

If 100 square feet cost $1,000, how much does 1 square foot cost?

Solution:

$\frac{\text{Total Cost}}{\text{\# of square feet}} = \frac{1,000}{100} = \$10/\text{square foot}$

Interest Rate

The formula for simple interest is Interest = Principal × Rate × Time or $I = PRT$. If you know certain values, but not others, you can still find the answer using algebra. In simple interest problems, the value of T is usually 1, as in 1 year. There are three basic kinds of interest problems, depending on which number is missing.

▶ Practice

Now that you have reviewed some of the math skills you will need, it's time to practice real estate math questions. Below you will find practice problems and thorough answer explanations for the real estate math topics listed.

Here are some equivalencies you may need to use to complete some questions. Generally, any equivalencies you will need to know for your exam are provided to you.

> **Equivalencies**
> 12 inches (in. or ″) = 1 foot (ft. or ′)
> 3 feet or 36 inches = 1 yard (yd.)
> 1,760 yards = 1 mile (mi.)
> 5,280 feet = 1 mile
> 144 square inches (sq. in. or in^2) = 1 square foot (sq. ft or $ft.^2$)
> 9 square feet = 1 square yard
> 43,560 feet = 1 acre
> 640 acres = 1 square mile

Percents

You may be asked a basic percentage problem.

Example:

What is 86% of 1,750?

Solution:

Start by translating words into math terms.

$x = (86\%)(1,750)$

Change the percent into a decimal by moving the decimal point 2 spaces to the LEFT.

$86\% = .86$

Now you can solve.

$x = (.86)(1,750)$

$x = 1,505$

Other percentage problems you may find on your real estate sales exam will come in the form of rate problems. Keep reading for more examples of these problems.

Interest Problems

Let's take a look at a problem in which you have calculate the interest rate (R). Remember, the rate is the same as the percentage.

Example:

Mary Valencia borrowed $5,000, for which she is paying $600 interest per year. What is the rate of interest being charged?

Solution:

Start with the values you know.

Principal = $5,000

Interest = $600

Rate = x

Time = 1 year

Using the formula $I = PRT$, insert the values you know, and solve for x.

$600 = 5,000(x)(1)$

$600 = 5,000x$

$\frac{600}{5,000} = \frac{x}{5,000}$

$.12 = x$

To convert .12 to a percent, move the decimal point two places to the RIGHT.

$.12 = 12\%$

Area

Some of the problems on your exam may ask you to figure the area of a piece of land, a building, or some other figure. Here are some formulas and how to use them.

Rectangles

Remember the formula: Area = (length)(width)

Example:

A man purchased a lot that is 50 feet by 10 feet for a garden. How many square feet of land does he have?

Solution:

Using the formula, Area = (length)(width), you have:

$A = (50)(10) = 500$ square feet

Example:

The Meyers family bought a piece of land for a summer home that was 2.75 acres. The lake frontage was 150 feet. What was the length of the lot?

Solution:

When you take your salesperson exam, you may be provided with certain equivalencies. You will need to refer to the "Equivalencies" list on the previous page to answer this question. First, find the area of the land in square feet.

$(2.75)(43,560) = 119,790$ square feet

In the previous example, you were given the length and the width. In this example, you are given the area and the width, so you are solving for the length. Since you know the area and the width of the lot, use the formula to solve.

Area = (length)(width)

$119{,}790 = (x)(150)$

Divide both sides by 150.

$\frac{119{,}790}{150} = \frac{(x)(150)}{150}$

$x = \frac{119{,}790}{150}$

$x = 798.6$ feet

Triangles

Although it may not be as common, you may be asked to find the area of a triangle. If you don't remember the formula, see page 143.

Example:

The Baron family is buying a triangular piece of land for a gas station. It is 200 feet at the base, and the side perpendicular to the base is 200 feet. They are paying $2.00 per square foot for the property. What will it cost?

Solution:

Start with the formula Area = $\frac{1}{2}$(base)(height).

Now, write down the values you know.

Area = x

Base = 200

Height = 200

If it's easier, you can change $\frac{1}{2}$ to a decimal.

$\frac{1}{2} = .5$

Now you can plug these values into the formula.

$x = (.5)(200)(200)$

$x = (.5)(40{,}000)$

$x = 20{,}000$ square feet

Don't forget that the question is not asking for the number of square feet, but of the *cost* of the property per square foot. This is a rate problem, so you need to complete one more step. (20,000 square feet)($2 per square foot) = $40,000

Example:

Victor and Evelyn Robinson have an outlot that a neighbor wants to buy. The side of the outlot next to their property is 86 feet. The rear line is perpendicular to their side lot, and the road frontage is 111 feet. Their plat shows they own 3,000 square feet in the outlot. What is the length of the rear line of the outlot? Round your answer to the nearest whole number.

Solution:

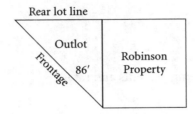

It helps to draw the figure to conceive shapes. The rear lot line is perpendicular to the side lot line. This makes the side lot line the base and the rear lot line the height (altitude).

Area = $\frac{1}{2}$(base)(height)

Area = 3,000 square feet

Base = 86 feet

Height = x

If it's easier, you can change $\frac{1}{2}$ to a decimal.

$\frac{1}{2} = .5$

Now you can plug these values into the formula.

$3,000 = (.5)(86)(x)$

$3,000 = (43)(x)$

Divide both sides by 43.

$\frac{3,000}{43} = \frac{(43)(x)}{43}$

$x = 69.767$ feet

Don't forget the question says to round your answer to the nearest whole number. The answer is 70 feet.

Circles

Remember the formula Area = πr^2.

Example:

Murray Brodman, a contractor, has been awarded the job to put up a circular bandstand in the town square. The radius of the circular area for the bandstand is 15 feet. What is the area of the bandstand? Use 3.14 for π.

Solution:

Area $= \pi r^2$

Start with the values you know.

Area $= x$

$\pi = 3.14$

Radius $= 15$

Now plug these values into the formula.

Area $= (3.14)(15)(15) = 706.5$ sq ft.

Property Tax

To solve property tax questions, you will be using percents and rates.

Example:

The tax rate in your county is $4.17 per hundred of assessed valuation, and Mr. Brown, a possible client, has told you his taxes are $1,100. What is his property assessment? (Round your answer to the nearest 10 cents.)

Solution:

Start off with the values you know.

Taxes $= \$1,100$

Assessment $= x$

Tax rate $= \$4.17$ per hundred (%)

If you remember the definition of percent as being an amount per hundred, then $4.17 per hundred is actually 4.17%. To make this equation more manageable, convert this percent to a decimal by moving the decimal point two spaces to the LEFT. Now the tax rate is .0417.

.0417 of the assessed value of the house is $1,100. Translate the words into math terms. This means:

$(.0417)(x) = 1,100$

To solve the equation, divide both sides by .0417.

$\frac{.0417x}{.0417} = \frac{1,100}{.0417}$

$x = \$26,378.896$

Remember, the question asks you to round to the nearest 10 cents. That means that .896 needs to be rounded up to 90. So the answer is $26,378.90

Example:

Mr. Smith knew his own taxes were $975 and his property assessment was $17,000 for the house and $6,000 for the land. He wanted to know the tax rate (%).

Tip

Note that you may be asked for monthly amounts in certain problems. Most calculations are on an annual basis—unless you divide by 12.

Solution:

Start with the values you know.

Tax = $975

Assessment for house = $17,000 plus assessment for land = $6,000. Therefore, total = $23,000

Rate (%) = x

According to the question, $23,000 at a rate of x is $975. Convert this statement into an equation.

($23,000)($x$) = 975

Solve the equation by dividing both sides by 23,000.

$$\frac{23,000x}{23,000} = \frac{975}{23,000}$$

$x = .0423913$

To make this equation more simple, round the answer to .0424.

Remember that you are looking for the rate. Therefore, you need to convert this decimal to a percent by moving the decimal point two places to the RIGHT. The rate is 4.24%. (This can also be expressed as $4.24 per hundred.)

Loan-to-Value Ratios

These problems often deal with percentages.

Example:

A mortgage loan for 10% is at a 75% loan-to-value ratio. The interest on the original balance for the first year is $6,590. What is the value of the property securing the loan? Round to the nearest one cent.

Solution:

First, find out the loan amount.

$6,590 is 10% of the loan amount. Let x equal the loan amount. Now, translate these words into math terms.

$6,590 = (10%)($x$)

Change 10% into a decimal by moving the decimal point two places to the LEFT.

10% = .1

Now you have

$6,590 = (.1)($x$)

Divide both sides by (.1)

x = $65,900

Now that you know the loan amount ($65,900), use this information to find the value of the property.

Write down the values you know.

Loan amount = $65,900

Loan-to-value ratio = 75%

Value = x

We know that 75% of the value is $65,900.

Translate this into math terms.

$(75\%)(x) = \$65,900$

Change the percent into a decimal (75% = .75) and solve.

$(.75)(x) = 65,900$

Divide both sides by .75.

$$\frac{(.75)(x)}{(.75)} = \frac{65,900}{(.75)}$$

$x = 87,866.66666$

When rounded to the nearest one cent, the answer is $87,866.67

Points

Loan discounts are often called *points*, or loan placement fees, *one point* meaning one percent of the face amount of the loan. The service fee of one percent paid by buyers of government backed loans is called a *loan origination fee*.

Example:

A homebuyer may obtain a $50,000 FHA mortgage loan, provided the seller pays a discount of five points. What is the amount of the discount?

Solution:

The definition of one point is one percent of the face amount of the loan.

Therefore, 5 points = 5% of face of loan. First, change the percent to a decimal.

5% = .05

Now you can use these values to solve.

Amount of discount = x

Points = .05

Amount of loan = $50,000

So, $x = (.05)(50,000)$

$x = \$2,500$

Example:

A property is listed at $74,000. An offer is made for $72,000, provided the seller pays 3 points on a loan for 80% of the purchase price. The brokerage commission rate is 7%. How much less will the seller receive if he accepts the offer than he would have received if he sold at all cash at the original terms?

Solution:
Here are the values you know:

Sold for original terms—price	$74,000	
Less 7% commission	– 5,180	(.07)(74,000) = 5,180
Seller's net	$68,820	

This question becomes more difficult, because in order to find the seller's net on the offered price, you must calculate the discount. The provision is that the seller pays 3 points (or .03) on a loan for 80% (or .8) of the price.

Start by finding 80% of the price.

(.8)(72,000) = $57,600

Now, the points are applied to this amount. This means .03 of $57,600 is the discount.

So, (.03)(57,600) = discount = 1,728.

You know these values:

Sold at offered terms—price	$72,000	
Less 7% Commission	– 5,040	(.07)(72,000) = 5,040
Less discount	1,728	
Seller's net	$65,232	

$72,000	Sales price		Net at original	$68,820
× .80	Loan-to-value ratio		Net at offered	–65,232
$57,600	Loan amount		Difference	$ 3,588
× .03	Points			
$ 1,728	Discount			

Equity

Example:
If a homeowner has a first mortgage loan balance of $48,350, a second mortgage loan balance of $18,200, and $26,300 equity, what is the value of her home?

Solution:
In this case, the value of the home is determined by the total loan balance plus the equity. Add the three numbers to find the value of the home.

$48,350 loan balance + $18,200 loan balance + $26,300 = value of the home

$92,850 = value of the home.

Qualifying Buyers

Example:

A buyer is obtaining a conventional loan that requires 29/33 ratios. He earns $66,000 a year, and has a $1,350 car payment. What is his maximum PITI payment?

   a. $1,612.50
   b. $1,812.50
   c. $21,750.00
   d. $2,475.00

Solution:

$66,000 divided by 12 = $5,500 monthly income

($5,500)(.29) = $1,595 front end qualifier

($5,500)(.33) = $1,850 − $1,350 debt = $500 back end qualifier

Maximum PITI (Principal, Interest, Taxes, and Insurance) is the lower of these two qualifiers, $500.

Prorations

At the time of settlement, there must be a reconciliation or adjustment of any monies owed by either party as of that date. The important fact to bear in mind is that *the party who used the service pays for it.* If you will keep this firmly in mind you will not have any difficulty deciding who to credit and who to debit.

Example:

Mr. Seller's taxes are $1,200 a year paid in advance on a calendar year. He is settling on the sale of his house to Mr. Buyer on August 1. Which of them owes how much to the other?

Solution:

Ask yourself some questions:

How many months has the seller paid for?	12	($1,200)
How many months has the seller used?	7	($700)
How many months should the seller be reimbursed for?	5	($500)
How many months will the buyer use?	5	($500)
How many months has he paid for?	0	($0)
How many months should he reimburse the seller for?	5	($500)

Credit Mr. Seller $500

Debit Mr. Buyer $500

What would the answer be if the taxes were paid in arrears? In other words, the seller has used the service for seven months but hasn't paid anything. The buyer will have to pay it all at the end of the year. In that case, the seller owes the buyer for seven months, or $700.

In working proration problems, be sure you have the right dates when you subtract. Sometimes the termination date for the policy is not given, and the tendency is to subtract the date the policy was written from the date of settlement. This will not give you the unused portion. You must subtract the date of settlement from the date of termination of the policy, which will be exactly the same date, one, three, or five years after written, depending on the term of the policy. Most problems use either a one- or three-year term.

Remember!
Use a 30-day month and a 360-day year in all calculations unless you are told otherwise. Assume a calendar year, unless a fiscal or school year is specified.

Commissions

Let's look at a commission problem. They are typically rate (percentage) problems.

Example:
Broker Jones sold the Smith house for $65,000. The total commission came to $4,000. What was Jones's commission rate? Round to the nearest whole percent.

Solution:
You see the word *rate* and decide this is solved using percentages.
Start with the values you know.
Price of house = 65,000
Commission Rate = x
Commission = 4,000

Now, translate the word problem into an equation.
$65,000x = 4,000$

Divide both sides by 65,000
$x = \frac{4,000}{65,000}$
$x = 0.061$
Convert the decimal to a percent by moving the decimal two places to the RIGHT. 0.061 becomes 6.1%.

Example:
An agent received a 3% commission on $\frac{1}{4}$ of her total sales. On the remainder, she received a 6% commission. What was her average commission for all of her sales?

Solution:

Start off by asking yourself: How many fourths (parts) were there? Four, naturally.

3%   6%   6%   6%

To find the average, you add up all the numbers, and divide by the number of items you add together. In this case, there are four numbers.

So, 3 + 6 + 6 + 6 = 21

And 21% ÷ 4 = 5.25%

Sale Proceeds

Example:

Salesman Garcia was trying to list a house. The owner said he wanted to clear (net) $12,000 from the sale of the house. The balance of the mortgage was $37,000. It would cost about $1,200 to fix the house up to sell. How much would the owner have to sell the house for if the 7% commission was included? (Round your answer to the nearest cent.)

Solution:

Use a chart to clarify the problem.

Expenses	In Dollars	In Percents
Seller's net	12,000	
Loan balance	37,000	
Repairs	1,200	
Commission		7%
	50,200	7%

If the sales price is 100% and the commission is 7% of the sales price, all the remaining items added together must make 93% of the sales price. The place where most people go wrong is in not including the seller's net when they add the expenses. The seller's net has to come out of the sales price. (Where else would it come from?) Therefore, it is part of the remaining 93%. You now have a percentage problem. As always, convert your percents to decimals.

Start with the values you know:

Expenses = $50,200

Sales price = x

Seller's net, loan balance, repairs = .93 of sales price

.93 of the sales price is $50,200.

Convert this statement into an equation.

$(.93)(x) = \$50,200$

Divide both sides by .93.

$\frac{(.93)(x)}{.93} = \frac{\$50,200}{.93}$

$x = \frac{\$50,200}{.93}$

$x = \$53,978.4945$

Don't forget to round to the nearest cent!

$x = \$53,978.49$

Transfer Tax/Conveyance Tax/Revenue Stamps

Here is a transfer tax question.

Example:

A property is sold for $135,800 in cash. The transfer tax is $441.35. If transfer taxes are calculated per $200 of value, what was the rate (per $200) of the transfer tax?

Solution:

Start with the values you know.

Selling price = $135,800

Transfer tax rate = x per $200

Transfer tax = $441.35

It's probably easiest to begin by dividing $200 since the rate is calculated per $200 of value.

So, $\frac{\$135,800}{\$200} = \$679$

You know that $441.35 is some rate of $679. Translate this into math terms.

$\$441.35 = (x)(\$679)$

Divide both sides by $679 to get

$\frac{\$441.35}{(\$679)} = \frac{(x)(\$679)}{(\$679)}$

$.65 = x$

Therefore, the transfer tax rate is $.65 per $200.

Competitive Market Analyses (CMA)

To solve these problems you will use measurements and other hypothetical features of the comparable property to arrive at a value. Remember, a CMA is not an appraisal.

Example:

If Building A measures 52′ by 106′ and Building B measures 75′ by 85′, how much will B cost if A costs $140,000 and both cost the same per square foot to build?

Solution:

Area = (length)(width)

Area of Building A = (52)(106) = 5,512 square feet

Area of Building B = (75)(85) = 6,375 square feet

Cost of Building A per square foot = $\frac{140,000}{5,512}$ = $25.40

Cost of Building B = (6,375)($25.40) = $161,925

Example:

Carson's house (B), which is being appraised, is an exact twin of the houses on either side of it, built by the same builder at the same time. House A was appraised for $45,000, but it has a 14 × 20 foot garage which was added at a cost of about $18 per square foot. House C was recently sold for $43,000, with central air valued at $3,000. What would be a fair estimate of the value of Carson's house?

Solution:

Comparable C	$43,000
– Air Conditioning	−3,000
	40,000

Comparable A	$45,000	Garage: 14′ × 20′ = 280 sq. ft.
– Cost of Garage	− 5,040	280 sq. ft. × $18 = $5,040
	$39,960	

Answer: $40,000

Income Properties

Example:

An investor is considering the purchase of an income property generating a gross income of $350,000. Operating expenses constitute 70% of gross income. If the investor wants a return of 14%, what is the maximum he can pay?

Solution:

Gross income = $350,000

Expenses = 70% of gross income

Net income = Gross income – Expenses

Desired return = 14%

Maximum buyer can pay = x

This is a multi-step problem. Start by calculating the expenses, but remember you will need to stop to calculate the net income. First, change the percent to a decimal.

70% = .70

Now, you know that expenses are 70% of the gross income of $350,000. Change the words to mathematical terms.

Expenses = (.7)(350,000) = $245,000

Gross income − Expenses = Net income

$350,000 − $245,000 = $105,000

The buyer wants the net income ($105,000) to be 14% of what he pays for the property.

Change the percent to a decimal (14% = .14) and then convert this statement to an equation.

$150,000 = (.14)(x)

Divide both sides by .14.

$$\frac{\$150,000}{.14} = \frac{(.14)(x)}{.14}$$

$150,000 ÷ .14 = x

$750,000 = x

Depreciation

There are several methods of depreciation, but the only one you are likely to meet on your exam is the straight-line method. This method spreads the total depreciation over the useful life of the building in equal annual amounts. It is calculated by dividing the replacement cost by the years of useful life left.

$$\frac{\text{replacement cost}}{\text{years of useful life}} = \text{annual depreciation}$$

The depreciation rate may be given or may have to be calculated by the straight-line method. This means dividing the total depreciation (100%) by the estimated useful life given for the building.

$$\frac{100\%}{\text{years of useful life}} = \text{depreciated rate}$$

If a building has 50 years of useful life left, the depreciation rate would be computed as follows:

$$\frac{100\%}{50} = 2\%$$

In other words, it has a 2% depreciation rate annually.

Example:

The replacement cost of a building has been estimated at $80,000. The building is 12 years old and has an estimated 40 years of useful life left. What can be charged to annual depreciation? What is the total depreciation for 12 years? What is the present value of this building?

Solution:

Calculate the annual depreciation.

$$\frac{\text{replacement cost}}{\text{years of useful life}} = \text{annual depreciation}$$

$$\frac{\$80,000}{40} = \$2,000$$

Find the total depreciation over the 12 years.

Annual depreciation of $\$2,000 \times 12$ years $= \$24,000$

Find the current value: replacement – depreciation = current value

$\$80,000 - \$24,000 = \$56,000$

▶ Summary

Hopefully, with this review you have realized that real estate math is not as bad as it seems. If you feel you need more practice, check out LearningExpress's *Practical Math Success in 20 Minutes a Day* or *1,001 Math Problems*. Use the exams in the books to practice even more real estate math.

6▶ Real Estate Glossary

CHAPTER SUMMARY
One of the most basic components in preparing for your California real estate exam is making sure you know all the terminology. This glossary provides a list of the most commonly used real estate terms and their definitions.

THESE TERMS WILL help you not only as you study for your real estate exam, but also after you pass your exam and are practicing in the field. The terms are listed in alphabetical order for easy reference.

▶ A

abandonment the voluntary surrender of a right, claim, or interest in a piece of property without naming a successor as owner or tenant.

abstract of title a certified summary of the history of a title to a particular parcel of real estate that includes the original grant and all subsequent transfers, encumbrances, and releases.

abutting sharing a common boundary; adjoining.

acceleration clause a clause in a note, mortgage, or deed of trust that permits the lender to declare the entire amount of principal and accrued interest due and payable immediately in the event of default.

acceptance the indication by a party receiving an offer that they agree to the terms of the offer. In most states the offer and acceptance must be reduced to writing when real property is involved.

accretion the increase or addition of land resulting from the natural deposit of sand or soil by streams, lakes, or rivers.

accrued depreciation (1) the amount of depreciation, or loss in value, that has accumulated since initial construction; (2) the difference between the current appraised value and the cost to replace the building new.

accrued items a list of expenses that have been incurred but have not yet been paid, such as interest on a mortgage loan, that are included on a closing statement.

acknowledgment a formal declaration before a public official, usually a notary public, by a person who has signed a deed, contract, or other document that the execution was a voluntary act.

acre a measure of land equal to 43,560 square feet or 4,840 square yards.

actual eviction the result of legal action brought by a landlord against a defaulted tenant, whereby the tenant is physically removed from rented or leased property by a court order.

actual notice the actual knowledge that a person has of a particular fact.

addendum any provision added to a contract, or an addition to a contract that expands, modifies, or enhances the clarity of the agreement. To be a part of the contract and legally enforceable, an addendum must be referenced within the contract.

adjacent lying near to but not necessarily in actual contact with.

adjoining contiguous or attached; in actual contact with.

adjustable-rate mortgage (ARM) a mortgage in which the interest changes periodically, according to corresponding fluctuations in an index. All ARMs are tied to indexes. For example, a seven-year, adjustable-rate mortgage is a loan where the rate remains fixed for the first seven years, then fluctuates according to the index to which it is tied.

adjusted basis the original cost of a property, plus acquisition costs, plus the value of added improvements to the property, minus accrued depreciation.

adjustment date the date the interest rate changes on an adjustable-rate mortgage.

administrator a person appointed by a court to settle the estate of a person who has died without leaving a will.

ad valorem tax tax in proportion to the value of a property.

adverse possession a method of acquiring title to another person's property through court action after taking actual, open, hostile, and continuous possession for a statutory period of time; may require payment of property taxes during the period of possession.

affidavit a written statement made under oath and signed before a licensed public official, usually a notary public.

agency the legal relationship between principal and agent that arises out of a contract wherein an agent is employed to do certain acts on behalf of the principal who has retained the agent to deal with a third party.

agent one who has been granted the authority to act on behalf of another.

agreement of sale a written agreement between a seller and a purchaser whereby the purchaser agrees to buy a certain piece of property from the seller for a specified price.

air rights the right to use the open space above a particular property.

alienation the transfer of ownership of a property to another, either voluntarily or involuntarily.

alienation clause the clause in a mortgage or deed of trust that permits the lender to declare all unpaid principal and accrued interest due and payable if the borrower transfers title to the property.

allodial system in the United States, a system of land ownership in which land is held free and clear of any rent or services due to the government; commonly contrasted with the feudal system, in which ownership is held by a monarch.

amenities features or benefits of a particular property that enhance the property's desirability and value, such as a scenic view or a pool.

amortization the method of repaying a loan or debt by making periodic installment payments composed of both principal and interest. When all principal has been repaid, it is considered fully amortized.

amortization schedule a table that shows how much of each loan payment will be applied toward principal and how much toward interest over the lifespan of the loan. It also shows the gradual decrease of the outstanding loan balance until it reaches zero.

amortize to repay a loan through regular payments that are comprised of principal and interest.

annual percentage rate (APR) the total or effective amount of interest charged on a loan, expressed as a percentage, on a yearly basis. This value is created according to a government formula intended to reflect the true annual cost of borrowing.

anti-deficiency law laws used in some states to limit the claim of a lender on default on payment of a purchase money mortgage on owner-occupied residential property to the value of the collateral.

anti-trust laws laws designed to protect free enterprise and the open marketplace by prohibiting certain business practices that restrict competition. In reference to real estate, these laws would prevent such practices as price-fixing or agreements by brokers to limit their areas of trade.

apportionments adjustment of income, expenses, or carrying charges related to real estate, usually computed to the date of closing so that the seller pays all expenses to date, then the buyer pays all expenses beginning on the closing date.

appraisal an estimate or opinion of the value of an adequately described property, as of a specific date.

appraised value an opinion of a property's fair market value, based on an appraiser's knowledge, experience, and analysis of the property, based on comparable sales.

appraiser an individual qualified by education, training, and experience to estimate the value of real property. Appraisers may work directly for mortgage lenders, or they may be independent contractors.

appreciation an increase in the market value of a property.

appurtenance something that transfers with the title to land even if not an actual part of the property, such as an easement.

arbitration the process of settling a dispute in which the parties submit their differences to an impartial third party, on whose decision on the matter is binding.

ARELLO the Association of Real Estate License Law Officials.

assessed value the value of a property used to calculate real estate taxes.

assessor a public official who establishes the value of a property for taxation purposes.

assessment the process of assigning value on property for taxation purposes.

asset items of value owned by an individual. Assets that can be quickly converted into cash are considered "liquid assets," such as bank accounts and stock portfolios. Other assets include real estate, personal property, and debts owed.

assignment the transfer of rights or interest from one person to another.

assumption of mortgage the act of acquiring the title to a property that has an existing mortgage and agreeing to be liable for the payment of any debt still existing on that mortgage. However, the lender must accept the transfer of liability for the original borrower to be relieved of the debt.

attachment the process whereby a court takes custody of a debtor's property until the creditor's debt is satisfied.

attest to bear witness by providing a signature.

attorney-in-fact a person who is authorized under a power of attorney to act on behalf of another.

avulsion the removal of land from one owner to another when a stream or other body of water suddenly changes its channel.

▶ B

balloon mortgage a loan in which the periodic payments do not fully amortize the loan, so that a final payment (a balloon payment) is substantially larger than the amount of the periodic payments that must be made to satisfy the debt.

balloon payment the final, lump-sum payment that is due at the termination of a balloon mortgage.

bankruptcy an individual or individuals can restructure or relieve themselves of debts and liabilities by filing in federal bankruptcy court. There are many types of bankruptcies, and the most common for an individual is "Chapter 7 No Asset," which relieves the borrower of most types of debts.

bargain and sale deed a deed which conveys title, but does not necessarily carry warranties against liens or encumbrances.

base line one of the imaginary East-West lines used as a reference point when describing property with the rectangular or government survey method of property description.

bench mark a permanently marked point with a known elevation, used as a reference by surveyors to measure elevations.

beneficiary (1) one who benefits from the acts of another; (2) the lender in a deed of trust.

bequest personal property given by provision of a will.

betterment an improvement to property that increases its value.

bilateral contract a contract in which each party promises to perform an act in exchange for the other party's promise also to perform an act.

bill of sale a written instrument that transfers ownership of personal property. A bill of sale cannot be used to transfer ownership of real property, which is passed by deed.

binder an agreement, accompanied by an earnest money deposit, for the purchase of a piece of real estate to show the purchaser's good faith intent to complete a transaction.

biweekly mortgage a mortgage in which payments are made every two weeks instead of once a month. Therefore, instead of making 12 monthly payments during the year, the borrower makes the equivalent of 13 monthly payments. The extra payment reduces the principal, thereby reducing the time it takes to pay off a 30-year mortgage.

blanket mortgage a mortgage in which more than one parcel of real estate is pledged to cover a single debt.

blockbusting the illegal and discriminatory practice of inducing homeowners to sell their properties by suggesting or implying the introduction of members of a protected class into the neighborhood.

bona fide in good faith, honest.

bond evidence of personal debt secured by a mortgage or other lien on real estate.

boot money or property provided to make up a difference in value or equity between two properties in an exchange.

branch office a place of business secondary to a principal office. The branch office is a satellite office generally run by a licensed broker, for the benefit of the broker running the principal office, as well as the associate broker's convenience.

breach of contract violation of any conditions or terms in a contract without legal excuse.

broker the term "broker" can mean many things, but in terms of real estate, it is the owner-manager of a business that brings together the parties to a real estate transaction for a fee. The roles of brokers and brokers' associates are defined by state law. In the mortgage industry, broker usually refers to a company or individual that does not lend the money for the loans directly, but that brokers loans to larger lenders or investors.

brokerage the business of bringing together buyers and sellers or other participants in a real estate transaction.

broker's price opinion (BPO) a broker's opinion of value based on a comparative market analysis, rather than a certified appraisal.

building code local regulations that control construction, design, and materials used in construction that are based on health and safety regulations.

building line the distance from the front, rear, or sides of a building lot beyond which no structures may extend.

building restrictions limitations listed in zoning ordinances or deed restrictions on the size and type of improvements allowed on a property.

bundle of rights the concept that ownership of a property includes certain rights regarding the property, such as possession, enjoyment, control of use, and disposition.

buydown usually refers to a fixed-rate mortgage where the interest rate is "bought down" for a temporary period, usually one to three years. After that time and for the remainder of the term, the borrower's payment is calculated at the note rate. In order to buy down the initial rate for the temporary payment, a lump sum is paid and held in an account used to supplement the borrower's monthly payment. These funds usually come from the seller as a financial incentive to induce someone to buy their property.

buyer's broker real estate broker retained by a prospective buyer; this buyer becomes the broker's client to whom fiduciary duties are owed.

bylaws rules and regulations adopted by an association—for example, a condominium.

▶ C

cancellation clause a provision in a lease that confers on one or all parties to the lease the right to terminate the parties' obligations, should the occurrence of the condition or contingency set forth in the clause happen.

canvassing the practice of searching for prospective clients by making unsolicited phone calls and/or visiting homes door-to-door.

cap the limit on fluctuation rates regarding adjustable rate mortgages. Limitations, or caps, may apply to how much the loan may adjust over a six-month period, an annual period, and over the life of the loan. There is also a limit on how much that payment can change each year.

capital money used to create income, or the net worth of a business as represented by the amount by which its assets exceed its liabilities.

capital expenditure the cost of a betterment to a property.

capital gains tax a tax charged on the profit gained from the sale of a capital asset.

capitalization the process of estimating the present value of an income-producing piece of property by dividing anticipated future income by a capitalization rate.

capitalization rate the rate of return a property will generate on an owner's investment.

cash flow the net income produced by an investment property, calculated by deducting operating and fixed expenses from gross income.

caveat emptor a phrase meaning "let the buyer beware."

CC&R covenants, conditions, and restrictions of a cooperative or condominium development.

certificate of discharge a document used when the security instrument is a mortgage.

certificate of eligibility a document issued by the Veterans Administration that certifies a veteran's eligibility for a VA loan.

certificate of reasonable value (CRV) once the appraisal has been performed on a property being bought with a VA loan, the Veterans Administration issues a CRV.

certificate of sale the document given to a purchaser of real estate that is sold at a tax foreclosure sale.

certificate of title a report stating an opinion on the status of a title, based on the examination of public records.

chain of title the recorded history of conveyances and encumbrances that affect the title to a parcel of land.

chattel personal property, as opposed to real property.

chattel mortgage a loan in which personal property is pledged to secure the debt.

city a large municipality governed under a charter and granted by the state.

clear title a title that is free of liens and legal questions as to ownership of a property that is a requirement for the sale of real estate; sometimes referred to as just title, good title, or free and clear.

closing the point in a real estate transaction when the purchase price is paid to the seller and the deed to the property is transferred from the seller to the buyer.

closing costs there are two kinds: (1) "non-recurring closing costs" and (2) "pre-paid items." "Non-recurring closing costs" are any items paid once as a result of buying the property or obtaining a loan. "Pre-paid items" are items that recur over time, such as property taxes and homeowners insurance. A lender makes an attempt to estimate the amount of non-recurring closing costs and pre-paid items on the good faith estimate, which is issued to the borrower within three days of receiving a home loan application.

closing date the date on which the buyer takes over the property.

closing statement a written accounting of funds received and disbursed during a real estate transaction. The buyer and seller receive separate closing statements.

cloud on the title an outstanding claim or encumbrance that can affect or impair the owner's title.

clustering the grouping of home sites within a subdivision on smaller lots than normal, with the remaining land slated for use as common areas.

codicil a supplement or addition to a will that modifies the original instrument.

coinsurance clause a clause in an insurance policy that requires the insured to pay a portion of any loss experienced.

collateral something of value hypothecated (real property) or pledged (personal property) by a borrower as security for a debt.

collection when a borrower falls behind, the lender contacts the borrower in an effort to bring the loan current. The loan goes to "collection."

color of title an instrument that gives evidence of title, but may not be legally adequate to actually convey title.

commercial property property used to produce income, such as an office building or a restaurant.

commingling the illegal act of an agent mixing a client's monies, which should be held in a separate escrow account, with the agent's personal monies; in some states, it means placing funds that are separate property in an account containing funds that are community property.

commission the fee paid to a broker for services rendered in a real estate transaction.

commitment letter a pledge in writing affirming an agreement.

common law the body of laws derived from local custom and judicial precedent.

common areas portions of a building, land, and amenities owned (or managed) by a planned unit development or condominium project's homeowners' association or a cooperative project's cooperative corporation. These areas are used by all of the unit owners, who share in the common expenses of their operation and maintenance. Common areas may include swimming pools, tennis courts, and other recreational facilities, as well as common corridors of buildings, parking areas, and lobbies.

community property a system of property ownership in which each spouse has equal interest in property acquired during the marriage; recognized in nine states.

comparable sales recent sales of similar properties in nearby areas that are used to help estimate the current market value of a property.

competent parties people who are legally qualified to enter a contract, usually meaning that they are of legal age, of sound mind, and not under the influence of drugs or other mind-altering substances.

competitive market analysis (CMA) an analysis intended to assist a seller or buyer in determining a property's range of value.

condemnation the judicial process by which the government exercises its power of eminent domain.

condominium a form of ownership in which an individual owns a specific unit in a multi-unit building and shares ownership of common areas with other unit owners.

condominium conversion changing the ownership of an existing building (usually a multi-dwelling rental unit) from single ownership to condominium ownership.

conformity an appraisal principle that asserts that property achieves its maximum value when a neighborhood is homogeneous in its use of land; the basis for zoning ordinances.

consideration something of value that induces parties to enter into a contract, such as money or services.

construction mortgage a short-term loan used to finance the building of improvements to real estate.

constructive eviction action or inaction by a landlord that renders a property uninhabitable, forcing a tenant to move out with no further liability for rent.

constructive notice notice of a fact given by making the fact part of the public record. All persons are responsible for knowing the information, whether or not they have actually seen the record.

contingency a condition that must be met before a contract is legally binding. A satisfactory home inspection report from a qualified home inspector is an example of a common type of contingency.

contract an agreement between two or more legally competent parties to do or to refrain from doing some legal act in exchange for a consideration.

contract for deed a contract for the sale of a parcel of real estate in which the buyer makes periodic payments to the seller and receives title to the property only after all, or a substantial part, of the purchase price has been paid, or regular payments have been made for one year or longer.

conventional loan a loan that is neither insured nor guaranteed by an agency of government.

conversion option an option in an adjustable-rate mortgage to convert it to a fixed-rate mortgage.

convertible ARM an adjustable-rate mortgage that allows the borrower to change the ARM to a fixed-rate mortgage at a specific time.

conveyance the transfer of title from the grantor to the grantee.

cooperative a form of property ownership in which a corporation owns a multi-unit building and stockholders of the corporation may lease and occupy individual units of the building through a proprietary lease.

corporation a legal entity with potentially perpetual existence that is created and owned by shareholders who appoint a board of directors to direct the business affairs of the corporation.

cost approach an appraisal method whereby the value of a property is calculated by estimating the cost of constructing a comparable building, subtracting depreciation, and adding land value.

counteroffer an offer submitted in response to an offer. It has the effect of overriding the original offer.

credit an agreement in which a borrower receives something of value in exchange for a promise to repay the lender.

credit history a record of an individual's repayment of debt.

cul-de-sac a dead-end street that widens at the end, creating a circular turnaround area.

curtesy the statutory or common law right of a husband to all or part of real estate owned by his deceased wife, regardless of will provisions, recognized in some states.

curtilage area of land occupied by a building, its outbuildings, and yard, either actually enclosed or considered enclosed.

▶ D

damages the amount of money recoverable by a person who has been injured by the actions of another.

datum a specific point used in surveying.

DBA the abbreviation for "doing business as."

debt an amount owed to another.

decedent a person who dies.

dedication the donation of private property by its owner to a governmental body for public use.

deed a written document that, when properly signed and delivered, conveys title to real property from the grantor to the grantee.

deed-in-lieu a foreclosure instrument used to convey title to the lender when the borrower is in default and wants to avoid foreclosure.

deed of trust a deed in which the title to property is transferred to a third party trustee to secure repayment of a loan; three-party mortgage arrangement.

deed restriction an imposed restriction for the purpose of limiting the use of land, such as the size or type of improvements to be allowed. Also called a restrictive covenant.

default the failure to perform a contractual duty.

defeasance clause a clause in a mortgage that renders it void where all obligations have been fulfilled.

deficiency judgment a personal claim against a borrower when mortgaged property is foreclosed and sale of the property does not produce sufficient funds to pay off the mortgage. Deficiency judgments may be prohibited in some circumstances by anti-deficiency protection.

delinquency failure to make mortgage or loan payments when payments are due.

density zoning a zoning ordinance that restricts the number of houses or dwelling units that can be built per acre in a particular area, such as a subdivision.

depreciation a loss in value due to physical deterioration, functional, or external obsolescence.

descent the transfer of property to an owner's heirs when the owner dies intestate.

devise the transfer of title to real estate by will.

devisee one who receives a bequest of real estate by will.

devisor one who grants real estate by will.

directional growth the direction toward which certain residential sections of a city are expected to grow.

discount point one percent of the loan amount charged by a lender at closing to increase a loan's effective yield and lower the fare rate to the borrower.

discount rate the rate that lenders pay for mortgage funds—a higher rate is passed on to the borrower.

dispossess to remove a tenant from property by legal process.

dominant estate (tenement) property that includes the right to use an easement on adjoining property.

dower the right of a widow in the property of her husband upon his death in non-community property states.

down payment the part of the purchase price that the buyer pays in cash and is not financed with a mortgage or loan.

dual agency an agent who represents both parties in a transaction.

due-on-sale clause a provision in a mortgage that allows the lender to demand repayment in full if the borrower sells the property that serves as security for the mortgage.

duress the use of unlawful means to force a person to act or to refrain from an action against his or her will.

▶ E

earnest money down payment made by a buyer of real estate as evidence of good faith.

easement the right of one party to use the land of another for a particular purpose, such as to lay utility lines.

easement by necessity an easement, granted by law and requiring court action that is deemed necessary for the full enjoyment of a parcel of land. An example would be an easement allowing access from land-locked property to a road.

easement by prescription a means of acquiring an easement by continued, open, and hostile use of someone else's property for a statutorily defined period of time.

easement in gross a personal right granted by an owner with no requirement that the easement holder own adjoining land.

economic life the period of time over which an improved property will generate sufficient income to justify its continued existence.

effective age an appraiser's estimate of the physical condition of a building. The actual age of a building may be different than its effective age.

emblements cultivated crops; generally considered to be personal property.

eminent domain the right of a government to take private property for public use upon payment of its fair market value. Eminent domain is the basis for condemnation proceedings.

encroachment a trespass caused when a structure, such as a wall or fence, invades another person's land or air space.

encumbrance anything that affects or limits the title to a property, such as easements, leases, mortgages, or restrictions.

equitable title the interest in a piece of real estate held by a buyer who has agreed to purchase the property, but has not yet completed the transaction; the interest of a buyer under a contract for deed.

equity the difference between the current market value of a property and the outstanding indebtedness due on it.

equity of redemption the right of a borrower to stop the foreclosure process.

erosion the gradual wearing away of land by wind, water, and other natural processes.

escalation clause a clause in a lease allowing the lessor to charge more rent based on an increase in costs; sometimes called a pass-through clause.

escheat the claim to property by the state when the owner dies intestate and no heirs can be found.

escrow the deposit of funds and/or documents with a disinterested third party for safekeeping until the terms of the escrow agreement have been met.

escrow account a trust account established to hold escrow funds for safekeeping until disbursement.

escrow analysis annual report to disclose escrow receipts, payments, and current balances.

escrow disbursements money paid from an escrow account.

estate an interest in real property. The sum total of all the real property and personal property owned by an individual.

estate for years a leasehold estate granting possession for a definite period of time.

estate tax federal tax levied on property transferred upon death.

estoppel certificate a document that certifies the outstanding amount owed on a mortgage loan, as well as the rate of interest.

et al. abbreviation for the Latin phrase *et alius,* meaning "and another."

et ux. abbreviation for Latin term *et uxor,* meaning "and wife."

et vir Latin term meaning "and husband."

eviction the lawful expulsion of an occupant from real property.

evidence of title a document that identifies ownership of property.

examination of title a review of an abstract to determine current condition of title.

exchange a transaction in which property is traded for another property, rather than sold for money or other consideration.

exclusive agency listing a contract between a property owner and one broker that only gives the broker the right to sell the property for a fee within a specified period of time but does not obligate the owner to pay the broker a fee if the owner produces his own buyer without the broker's assistance. The owner is barred only from appointing another broker within this time period.

exclusive right to sell a contract between a property owner and a broker that gives the broker the right to collect a commission regardless of who sells the property during the specified period of time of the agreement.

execution the signing of a contract.

executor/executrix a person named in a will to administer an estate. The court will appoint an administrator if no executor is named. "Executrix" is the feminine form.

executory contract a contract in which one or more of the obligations have yet to be performed.

executed contract a contract in which all obligations have been fully performed.

express contract an oral or written contract in which the terms are expressed in words.

extension agreement an agreement between mortgagor and mortgagee to extend the maturity date of the mortgage after it is due.

external obsolescence a loss in value of a property due to factors outside the property, such as a change in surrounding land use.

▶ F

fair housing law a term used to refer to federal and state laws prohibiting discrimination in the sale or rental of residential property.

fair market value the highest price that a buyer, willing but not compelled to buy, would pay, and the lowest a seller, willing but not compelled to sell, would accept.

Federal Housing Administration (FHA) an agency within the U.S. Department of Housing and Urban Development (HUD) that insures mortgage loans by FHA-approved lenders to make loans available to buyers with limited cash.

Federal National Mortgage Association (Fannie Mae) a privately-owned corporation that buys existing government-backed and conventional mortgages.

Federal Reserve System the central banking system of the United States, which controls the monetary policy and, therefore, the money supply, interest rates, and availability of credit.

fee simple the most complete form of ownership of real estate.

FHA-insured loan a loan insured by the Federal Housing Administration.

fiduciary relationship a legal relationship with an obligation of trust, as that of agent and principal.

finder's fee a fee or commission paid to a mortgage broker for finding a mortgage loan for a prospective borrower.

first mortgage a mortgage that has priority to be satisfied over all other mortgages.

fixed-rate loan a loan with an interest rate that does not change during the entire term of the loan.

fixture an article of personal property that has been permanently attached to the real estate so as to become an integral part of the real estate.

foreclosure the legal process by which a borrower in default of a mortgage is deprived of interest in the mortgaged property. Usually, this involves a forced sale of the property at public auction, where the proceeds of the sale are applied to the mortgage debt.

forfeiture the loss of money, property, rights, or privileges due to a breach of legal obligation.

franchise in real estate, an organization that lends a standardized trade name, operating procedures, referral services, and supplies to member brokerages.

fraud a deliberate misstatement of material fact or an act or omission made with deliberate intent to deceive (active fraud) or gross disregard for the truth (constructive fraud).

freehold estate an estate of ownership in real property.

front foot a measurement of property taken by measuring the frontage of the property along the street line.

functional obsolescence a loss in value of a property due to causes within the property, such as faulty design, outdated structural style, or inadequacy to function properly.

future interest ownership interest in property that cannot be enjoyed until the occurrence of some event; sometimes referred to as a household or equitable interest.

▶ G

general agent an agent who is authorized to act for and obligate a principal in a specific range of matters, as specified by their mutual agreement.

general lien a claim on all property, real and personal, owned by a debtor.

general warranty deed an instrument in which the grantor guarantees the grantee that the title being conveyed is good and free of other claims or encumbrances.

government backed mortgage a mortgage that is insured by the Federal Housing Administration (FHA) or guaranteed by the Department of Veterans Affairs (VA) or the Rural Housing Service (RHS). Mortgages that are not government loans are identified as conventional loans.

Government National Mortgage Association (Ginnie Mae) a government-owned corporation within the U.S. Department of Housing and Urban Development (HUD). Ginnie Mae manages and liquidates government-backed loans and assists HUD in special lending projects.

government survey system a method of land description in which meridians (lines of longitude) and base lines (lines of latitude) are used to divide land into townships and sections.

graduated lease a lease that calls for periodic, stated changes in rent during the term of the lease.

grant the transfer of title to real property by deed.

grant deed a deed that includes three warranties: (1) that the owner has the right to convey title to the property, (2) that there are no encumbrances other than those noted specifically in the deed, and (3) that the owner will convey any future interest that he or she may acquire in the property.

grantee one who receives title to real property.

grantor one who conveys title to real property; the present owner.

gross income the total income received from a property before deducting expenses.

gross income multiplier a rough method of estimating the market value of an income property by multiplying its gross annual rent by a multiplier discovered by dividing the sales price of comparable properties by their annual gross rent.

gross lease a lease in which a tenant pays only a fixed amount for rental and the landlord pays all operating expenses and taxes.

gross rent multiplier similar to *gross income multiplier,* except that it looks at the relationship between sales price and monthly gross rent.

ground lease a lease of land only, on which a tenant already owns a building or will construct improvements.

guaranteed sale plan an agreement between a broker and a seller that the broker will buy the seller's property if it does not sell within a specified period of time.

guardian one who is legally responsible for the care of another person's rights and/or property.

▶ H

habendum clause the clause in a deed, beginning with the words "to have and to hold," that defines or limits the exact interest in the estate granted by the deed.

hamlet a small village.

heir one who is legally entitled to receive property when the owner dies intestate.

highest and best use the legally permitted use of a parcel of land that will yield the greatest return to the owner in terms of money or amenities.

holdover tenancy a tenancy where a lessee retains possession of the property after the lease has expired, and the landlord, by continuing to accept rent, agrees to the tenant's continued occupancy.

holographic will a will that is entirely handwritten, dated, and signed by the testator.

home equity conversion mortgage (HECM) often called a reverse-annuity mortgage; instead of making payments to a lender, the lender makes payments to you. It enables older homeowners to convert the equity they have in their homes into cash, usually in the form of monthly payments. Unlike traditional home equity loans, a borrower does not qualify on the basis of income but on the value of his or her home. In addition, the loan does not have to be repaid until the borrower no longer occupies the property.

home equity line of credit a mortgage loan that allows the borrower to obtain cash drawn against the equity of his or her home, up to a predetermined amount.

home inspection a thorough inspection by a professional that evaluates the structural and mechanical condition of a property. A satisfactory home inspection is often included as a contingency by the purchaser.

homeowner's insurance an insurance policy specifically designed to protect residential property owners against financial loss from common risks such as fire, theft, and liability.

homeowner's warranty an insurance policy that protects purchasers of newly-constructed or pre-owned homes against certain structural and mechanical defects.

homestead the parcel of land and improvements legally qualifying as the owner's principal residence.

HUD an acronym for the Department of Housing and Urban Development, a federal agency that enforces federal fair housing laws and oversees agencies such as FHA and GNMA.

▶ I

implied contract a contract where the agreement of the parties is created by their conduct.

improvement human-made addition to real estate.

income capitalization approach a method of estimating the value of income-producing property by dividing its expected annual net operating income of the property by a capitalization rate.

income property real estate developed or improved to produce income.

incorporeal right intangible, non-possessory rights in real estate, such as an easement or right of way.

independent contractor one who is retained by another to perform a certain task and is not subject to the control and direction of the hiring person with regard to the end result of the task. Individual contractors receive a fee for their services but pay their own expenses and taxes and receive no employee benefits.

index a number used to compute the interest rate for an adjustable-rate mortgage (ARM). The index is a published number or percentage, such as the average yield on Treasury bills. A margin is added to the index to determine the interest rate to be charged on the ARM. This interest rate is subject to any caps that are associated with the mortgage.

industrial property buildings and land used for the manufacture and distribution of goods, such as a factory.

inflation an increase in the amount of money or credit available in relation to the amount of goods or services available, which causes an increase in the general price level of goods and services.

initial interest rate the beginning interest rate of the mortgage at the time of closing. This rate changes for an adjustable-rate mortgage (ARM).

installment the regular, periodic payment that a borrower agrees to make to a lender, usually related to a loan.

installment contract see *contract for deed.*

installment loan borrowed money that is repaid in periodic payments, known as installments.

installment sale a transaction in which the sales price is paid to the seller in two or more installments over more than one calendar year.

insurance a contract that provides indemnification from specific losses in exchange for a periodic payment. The individual contract is known as an insurance policy, and the periodic payment is known as an insurance premium.

insurance binder a document that states that temporary insurance is in effect until a permanent insurance policy is issued.

insured mortgage a mortgage that is protected by the Federal Housing Administration (FHA) or by private mortgage insurance (PMI). If the borrower defaults on the loan, the insurer must pay the lender the insured amount.

interest a fee charged by a lender for the use of the money loaned; or a share of ownership in real estate.

interest accrual rate the percentage rate at which interest accrues on the mortgage.

interest rate the rent or rate charged to use funds belonging to another.

interest rate buydown plan an arrangement where the property seller (or any other party) deposits money to an account so that it can be released each month to reduce the mortgagor's monthly payments during the early years of a mortgage. During the specified period, the mortgagor's effective interest rate is "bought down" below the actual interest rate.

interest rate ceiling the maximum interest rate that may be charged for an adjustable-rate mortgage (ARM), as specified in the mortgage note.

interest rate floor the minimum interest rate for an adjustable-rate mortgage (ARM), as specified in the mortgage note.

interim financing a short-term loan made during the building phase of a project; also known as a construction loan.

intestate to die without having authored a valid will.

invalid not legally binding or enforceable.

investment property a property not occupied by the owner.

▶ J

joint tenancy co-ownership that gives each tenant equal interest and equal rights in the property, including the right of survivorship.

joint venture an agreement between two or more parties to engage in a specific business enterprise.

judgment a decision rendered by a court determining the rights and obligations of parties to an action or lawsuit.

judgment lien a lien on the property of a debtor resulting from a court judgment.

judicial foreclosure a proceeding that is handled as a civil lawsuit and conducted through court; used in some states.

jumbo loan a loan that exceeds Fannie Mae's mortgage amount limits. Also called a nonconforming loan.

junior mortgage any mortgage that is inferior to a first lien and that will be satisfied only after the first mortgage; also called a secondary mortgage.

▶ L

laches a doctrine used by a court to bar the assertion of a legal claim or right, based on the failure to assert the claim in a timely manner.

land the Earth from its surface to its center, and the air space above it.

landlocked property surrounded on all sides by property belonging to another.

lease a contract between a landlord and a tenant wherein the landlord grants the tenant possession and use of the property for a specified period of time and for a consideration.

leased fee the landlord's interest in a parcel of leased property.

lease option a financing option that allows homebuyers to lease a home with an option to buy. Each month's rent payment may consist of rent, plus an additional amount that can be applied toward the down payment on an already specified price.

leasehold a tenant's right to occupy a parcel of real estate for the term of a lease.

legal description a description of a parcel of real estate specific and complete enough for an independent surveyor to locate and identify it.

lessee the one who receives that right to use and occupy the property during the term of the leasehold estate.

lessor the owner of the property who grants the right of possession to the lessee.

leverage the use of borrowed funds to purchase an asset.

levy to assess or collect a tax.

license (1) a revocable authorization to perform a particular act on another's property, (2) authorization granted by a state to act as a real estate broker or salesperson.

lien a legal claim against a property to secure payment of a financial obligation.

life estate a freehold estate in real property limited in duration to the lifetime of the holder of the life estate or another specified person.

life tenant one who holds a life estate.

liquidity the ability to convert an asset into cash.

lis pendens a Latin phrase meaning "suit pending;" a public notice that a lawsuit has been filed that may affect the title to a particular piece of property.

listing agreement a contract between the owner and a licensed real estate broker where the broker is employed to sell real estate on the owner's terms within a given time, for which service the owner agrees to pay the broker an agreed-upon fee.

listing broker a broker who contracts with a property owner to sell or lease the described property; the listing agreement typically may provide for the broker to make property available through a multiple listing system.

littoral rights landowner's claim to use water in large, navigable lakes and oceans adjacent to property; ownership rights to land-bordering bodies of water up to the high-water mark.

loan a sum of borrowed money, or principal, that is generally repaid with interest.

loan officer or lender, serves several functions and has various responsibilities, such as soliciting loans; a loan officer both represents the lending institution and represents the borrower to the lending institution.

lock-in an agreement in which the lender guarantees a specified interest rate for a certain amount of time.

lock-in period the time period during which the lender has guaranteed an interest rate to a borrower.

lot and block description a method of describing a particular property by referring to a lot and block number within a subdivision recorded in the public record.

▶ **M**

management agreement a contract between the owner of an income property and a firm or individual who agrees to manage the property.

margin the difference between the interest rate and the index on an adjustable rate mortgage. The margin remains stable over the life of the loan, while the index fluctuates.

market data approach a method of estimating the value of a property by comparing it to similar properties recently sold and making monetary adjustments for the differences between the subject property and the comparable property.

market value the amount that a seller may expect to obtain for merchandise, services, or securities in the open market.

marketable title title to property that is free from encumbrances and reasonable doubts and that a court would compel a buyer to accept.

mechanic's lien a statutory lien created to secure payment for those who supply labor or materials for the construction of an improvement to land.

metes and bounds a method of describing a parcel of land using direction and distance.

mil one-tenth of one cent; used by some states to express or calculate property tax rates.

minor a person who has not attained the legal age of majority.

misrepresentation a misstatement of fact, either deliberate or unintentional.

modification the act of changing any of the terms of the mortgage.

money judgment a court order to settle a claim with a monetary payment, rather than specific performance.

month-to-month tenancy tenancy in which the tenant rents for only one month at a time.

monument a fixed, visible marker used to establish boundaries for a survey.

mortgage a written instrument that pledges property to secure payment of a debt obligation as evidenced by a promissory note. When duly recorded in the public record, a mortgage creates a lien against the title to a property.

mortgage banker an entity that originates, funds, and services loans to be sold into the secondary money market.

mortgage broker an entity that, for a fee, brings borrowers together with lenders.

mortgage lien an encumbrance created by recording a mortgage.

mortgagee the lender who benefits from the mortgage.

mortgagor the borrower who pledges the property as collateral.

multi-dwelling units properties that provide separate housing units for more than one family that secure only a single mortgage. Apartment buildings are also considered multi-dwelling units.

multiple listing system (MLS—also multiple listing service) the method of marketing a property listing to all participants in the MLS.

mutual rescission an agreement by all parties to a contract to release one another from the obligations of the contract.

▶ **N**

negative amortization occurs when an adjustable rate mortgage is allowed to fluctuate independently of a required minimum payment. A gradual increase in mortgage debt happens when the monthly payment is not large enough to cover the entire principal and interest due. The amount of the shortfall is added to the remaining balance to create negative amortization.

net income the income produced by a property, calculated by deducting operating expenses from gross income.

net lease a lease that requires the tenant to pay maintenance and operating expenses, as well as rent.

net listing a listing in which the broker's fee is established as anything above a specified amount to be received by the seller from the sale of the property.

net worth the value of all of a person's assets.

no cash-out refinance a refinance transaction in which the new mortgage amount is limited to the sum of the remaining balance of the existing first mortgage.

nonconforming use a use of land that is permitted to continue, or grandfathered, even after a zoning ordinance is passed that prohibits the use.

non-liquid asset an asset that cannot easily be converted into cash.

notarize to attest or certify by a notary public.

notary public a person who is authorized to administer oaths and take acknowledgments.

note a written instrument acknowledging a debt, with a promise to repay, including an outline of the terms of repayment.

note rate the interest rate on a promissory note.

notice of default a formal written notice to a borrower that a default has occurred on a loan and that legal action may be taken.

novation the substitution of a new contract for an existing one; the new contract must reference the first and indicate that the first is being replaced and no longer has any force and effect.

▶ O

obligee person on whose favor an obligation is entered.

obligor person who is bound to another by an obligation.

obsolescence a loss in the value of a property due to functional or external factors.

offer to propose as payment; bid on property.

offer and acceptance two of the necessary elements for the creation of a contract.

open-end mortgage a loan containing a clause that allows the mortgagor to borrow additional funds from the lender, up to a specified amount, without rewriting the mortgage.

open listing a listing contract given to one or more brokers in which a commission is paid only to the broker who procures a sale. If the owner sells the house without the assistance of one of the brokers, no commission is due.

opinion of title an opinion, usually given by an attorney, regarding the status of a title to property.

option an agreement that gives a prospective buyer the right to purchase a seller's property within a specified period of time for a specified price.

optionee one who receives or holds an option.

optionor one who grants an option; the property owner.

ordinance a municipal regulation.

original principal balance the total amount of principal owed on a loan before any payments are made; the amount borrowed.

origination fee the amount charged by a lender to cover the cost of assembling the loan package and originating the loan.

owner financing a real estate transaction in which the property seller provides all or part of the financing.

ownership the exclusive right to use, possess, control, and dispose of property.

▶ **P**

package mortgage a mortgage that pledges both real and personal property as collateral to secure repayment of a loan.

parcel a lot or specific portion of a large tract of real estate.

participation mortgage a type of mortgage in which the lender receives a certain percentage of the income or resale proceeds from a property, as well as interest on the loan.

partition the division of property held by co-owners into individual shares.

partnership an agreement between two parties to conduct business for profit. In a partnership, property is owned by the partnership, not the individual partners, so partners cannot sell their interest in the property without the consent of the other partners.

party wall a common wall used to separate two adjoining properties.

payee one who receives payment from another.

payor one who makes payment to another.

percentage lease a lease in which the rental rate is based on a percentage of the tenant's gross sales. This type of lease is most often used for retail space.

periodic estate tenancy that automatically renews itself until either the landlord or tenant gives notice to terminate it.

personal property (hereditaments) all items that are not permanently attached to real estate; also known as chattels.

physical deterioration a loss in the value of a property due to impairment of its physical condition.

PITI principal, interest, taxes, and insurance—components of a regular mortgage payment.

planned unit development (PUD) a type of zoning that provides for residential and commercial uses within a specified area.

plat a map of subdivided land showing the boundaries of individual parcels or lots.

plat book a group of maps located in the public record showing the division of land into subdivisions, blocks, and individual parcels or lots.

plat number a number that identifies a parcel of real estate for which a plat has been recorded in the public record.

PMI private mortgage insurance.

point a point is one percent of the loan.

point of beginning the starting point for a survey using the "metes and bounds" method of description.

police power the right of the government to enact laws, ordinances, and regulations to protect the public health, safety, welfare, and morals.

power of attorney a legal document that authorizes someone to act on another's behalf. A power of attorney can grant complete authority or can be limited to certain acts and/or certain periods of time.

pre-approval condition where a borrower has completed a loan application and provided debt, income, and savings documentation that an underwriter has reviewed and approved. A pre-approval is usually done at a certain loan amount, making assumptions about what the interest rate will actually be at the time the loan is actually made, as well as estimates for the amount that will be paid for property taxes, insurance, and so on.

prepayment amount paid to reduce the outstanding principal balance of a loan before the due date.

prepayment penalty a fee charged to a borrower by a lender for paying off a debt before the term of the loan expires.

prequalification a lender's opinion on the ability of a borrower to qualify for a loan, based on furnished information regarding debt, income, and available capital for down payment, closing costs, and prepaids. Prequalification is less formal than pre-approval.

prescription a method of acquiring an easement to property by prolonged, unauthorized use.

primary mortgage market the financial market in which loans are originated, funded, and serviced.

prime rate the short-term interest rate that banks charge to their preferred customers. Changes in prime rate are used as the indexes in some adjustable rate mortgages, such as home equity lines of credit.

principal (1) one who authorizes another to act on his or her behalf, (2) one of the contracting parties to a transaction, (3) the amount of money borrowed in a loan, separate from the interest charged on it.

principal meridian one of the 36 longitudinal lines used in the rectangular survey system method of land description.

probate the judicial procedure of proving the validity of a will.

procuring cause the action that brings about the desired result. For example, if a broker takes actions that result in a sale, the broker is the procuring cause of the sale.

promissory note details the terms of the loan and is the debt instrument.

property management the operating of an income property for another.

property tax a tax levied by the government on property, real or personal.

prorate to divide ongoing property costs such as taxes or maintenance fees proportionately between buyer and seller at closing.

pur autre vie a phrase meaning "for the life of another." In a life estate *pur autre vie*, the term of the estate is measured by the life of a person other than the person who holds the life estate.

purchase agreement a written contract signed by the buyer and seller stating the terms and conditions under which a property will be sold.

purchase money mortgage a mortgage given by a buyer to a seller to secure repayment of any loan used to pay part or all of the purchase price.

► **Q**

qualifying ratios calculations to determine whether a borrower can qualify for a mortgage. There are two ratios. The "top" ratio is a calculation of the borrower's monthly housing costs (principle, taxes, insurance, mortgage insurance, homeowner's association fees) as a percentage of monthly income. The "bottom" ratio includes housing costs as well as all other monthly debt.

quitclaim deed a conveyance where the grantor transfers without warranty or obligations whatever interest or title he/she may have.

► **R**

range an area of land six miles wide, numbered East or West from a principal meridian in the rectangular survey system.

ready, willing, and able one who is able to pay the asking price for a property and is prepared to complete the transaction.

real estate land, the earth below it, the air above it, and anything permanently attached to it.

real estate agent a real estate broker who has been appointed to market a property for and represent the property owner (listing agent), or a broker who has been appointed to represent the interest of the buyer (buyer's agent).

real estate board an organization whose members are primarily comprised of real estate sales agents, brokers, and administrators.

real estate broker a licensed person, association, partnership, or corporation who negotiates real estate transactions for others for a fee.

Real Estate Settlement Procedures Act (RESPA) a consumer protection law that requires lenders to give borrowers advance notice of closing costs and prohibits certain abusive practices against buyers using federally related loans to purchase their homes.

real property the rights of ownership to land and its improvements.

REALTOR® a registered trademark for use by members of the National Association of REALTORS® and affiliated state and local associations.

recording entering documents, such as deeds and mortgages, into the public record to give constructive notice.

rectangular survey system a method of land description based on principal meridians (lines of longitude) and base lines (lines of latitude). Also called the government survey system.

redemption period the statutory period of time during which an owner can reclaim foreclosed property by paying the debt owed plus court costs and other charges established by statute.

redlining the illegal practice of lending institutions refusing to provide certain financial services, such as mortgage loans, to property owners in certain areas.

refinance transaction the process of paying off one loan with the proceeds from a new loan using the same property as security or collateral.

Regulation Z a Federal Reserve regulation that implements the federal Truth-in-Lending Act.

release clause a clause in a mortgage that releases a portion of the property upon payment of a portion of the loan.

remainder estate a future interest in an estate that takes effect upon the termination of a life estate.

remaining balance in a mortgage, the amount of principal that has not yet been repaid.

remaining term the original amortization term minus the number of payments that have been applied to it.

rent a periodic payment paid by a lessee to a landlord for the use and possession of leased property.

replacement cost the estimated current cost to replace an asset similar or equivalent to the one being appraised.

reproduction cost the cost of building an exact duplicate of a building at current prices.

rescission canceling or terminating a contract by mutual consent or by the action of one party on default by the other party.

restriction (restrict covenant) a limitation on the way a property can be used.

reversion the return of interest or title to the grantor of a life estate.

reverse annuity mortgage when a homeowner receives monthly checks or a lump sum with no repayment until property is sold, usually an agreement between mortgagor and elderly homeowners.

revision a revised or new version, as in a contract.

right of egress (or ingress) the right to enter or leave designated premises.

right of first refusal the right of a person to have the first opportunity to purchase property before it is offered to anyone else.

right of redemption the statutory right to reclaim ownership of property after a foreclosure sale.

right of survivorship in joint tenancy, the right of survivors to acquire the interest of a deceased joint tenant.

riparian rights the rights of a landowner whose property is adjacent to a flowing waterway, such as a river, to access and use the water.

▶ S

safety clause a contract provision that provides a time period following expiration of a listing agreement, during which the agent will be compensated if there is a transaction with a buyer who was initially introduced to the property by the agent.

sale-leaseback a transaction where the owner sells improved property and, as part of the same transaction, signs a long-term lease to remain in possession of its premises, thus becoming the tenant of the new owner.

sales contract a contract between a buyer and a seller outlining the terms of the sale.

salesperson one who is licensed to sell real estate in a given territory.

salvage value the value of a property at the end of its economic life.

satisfaction an instrument acknowledging that a debt has been paid in full.

second mortgage a mortgage that is in less than first lien position; see *junior mortgage*.

section as used in the rectangular survey system, an area of land measuring one square mile, or 640 acres.

secured loan a loan that is backed by property or collateral.

security property that is offered as collateral for a loan.

selling broker the broker who secures a buyer for a listed property; the selling broker may be the listing agent, a subagent, or a buyer's agent.

separate property property owned individually by a spouse, as opposed to community property.

servient tenement a property on which an easement or right-of-way for an adjacent (dominant) property passes.

setback the amount of space between the lot line and the building line, usually established by a local zoning ordinance or restrictive covenants; see *deed restrictions*.

settlement statement (HUD-1) the form used to itemize all costs related to closing of a residential transaction covered by RESPA regulations.

severalty the ownership of a property by only one legal entity.

special assessment a tax levied against only the specific properties that will benefit from a public improvement, such as a street or sewer; an assessment by a homeowners' association for a capital improvement to the common areas for which no budgeted funds are available.

special warranty deed a deed in which the grantor guarantees the title only against the defects that may have occurred during the grantor's ownership and not against any defects that occurred prior to that time.

specific lien a lien, such as a mortgage, that attaches to one defined parcel of real estate.

specific performance a legal action in which a court compels a defaulted party to a contract to perform according to the terms of the contract, rather than awarding damages.

standard payment calculation the method used to calculate the monthly payment required to repay the remaining balance of a mortgage in equal installments over the remaining term of the mortgage at the current interest rate.

statute of frauds the state law that requires certain contracts to be in writing to be enforceable.

statute of limitations the state law that requires that certain actions be brought to court within a specified period of time.

statutory lien a lien imposed on property by statute, such as a tax lien.

steering the illegal practice of directing prospective homebuyers to or away from particular areas.

straight-line depreciation a method of computing depreciation by decreasing value by an equal amount each year during the useful life of the property.

subdivision a tract of land divided into lots as defined in a publicly recorded plat that complies with state and local regulations.

sublet the act of a lessee transferring part or all of his or her lease to a third party while maintaining responsibility for all duties and obligations of the lease contract.

subordinate to voluntarily accept a lower priority lien position than that to which one would normally be entitled.

substitution the principle in appraising that a buyer will be willing to pay no more for the property being appraised than the cost of purchasing an equally desirable property.

subrogation the substitution of one party into another's legal role as the creditor for a particular debt.

suit for possession a lawsuit filed by a landlord to evict a tenant who has violated the terms of the lease or retained possession of the property after the lease expired.

suit for specific performance a lawsuit filed for the purpose of compelling a party to perform particular acts to settle a dispute, rather than pay monetary damages.

survey a map that shows the exact legal boundaries of a property, the location of easements, encroachments, improvements, rights of way, and other physical features.

syndicate a group formed by a syndicator to combine funds for real estate investment.

▶ T

tax deed in some states, an instrument given to the purchaser at the time of sale.

tax lien a charge against a property created by law or statue. Tax liens take priority over all other types of liens.

tax rate the rate applied to the assessed value of a property to determine the property taxes.

tax sale the court-ordered sale of a property after the owner fails to pay *ad valorem* taxes owed on the property.

tenancy at sufferance the tenancy of a party who unlawfully retains possession of a landlord's property after the term of the lease has expired.

tenancy at will an indefinite tenancy that can be terminated by either the landlord or the tenant at any time by giving notice to the other party one rental period in advance of the desired termination date.

tenancy by the entirety ownership by a married couple of property acquired during the marriage with right of survivorship; not recognized by community property states.

tenancy in common a form of co-ownership in which two or more persons hold an undivided interest in property without the right of survivorship.

tenant one who holds or possesses the right of occupancy title.

tenement the space that may be occupied by a tenant under the terms of a lease.

testate to die having created a valid will directing the testator's desires with regard to the disposition of the estate.

"time is of the essence" a phrase in a contract that requires strict adherence to the dates listed in the contract as deadlines for the performance of specific acts.

timesharing undivided ownership of real estate for only an allotted portion of a year.

title a legal document that demonstrates a person's right to, or ownership of, a property. **Note:** title is *not* an instrument. The instrument, such as a deed, gives evidence of title or ownership.

title insurance an insurance policy that protects the holder from defects in a title, subject to the exceptions noted in the policy.

title search a check of public records to ensure that the seller is the legal owner of the property and that there are no liens or other outstanding claims.

Torrens System a system of registering titles to land with a public authority, who is usually called a registrar.

township a division of land, measuring 36 square miles, in the government survey system.

trade fixtures an item of personal property installed by a commercial tenant and removable upon expiration of the lease.

transfer tax a state or municipal tax payable when the conveyancing instrument is recorded.

trust an arrangement in which title to property is transferred from a grantor to a trustee, who holds title but not the right of possession for a third party, the beneficiary.

trustee a person who holds title to property for another person designated as the beneficiary.

Truth-in-Lending Law also known as Regulation Z; requires lenders to make full disclosure regarding the terms of a loan.

▶ U

underwriting the process of evaluating a loan application to determine the risk involved for the lender.

undivided interest the interest of co-owners to use of an entire property despite the fractional interest owned.

unilateral contract a one-sided contract in which one party is obligated to perform a particular act completely, before the other party has any obligation to perform.

unsecured loan a loan that is not backed by collateral or security.

useful life the period of time a property is expected to have economic utility.

usury the practice of charging interest at a rate higher than that allowed by law.

► V

VA-guaranteed loan a mortgage loan made to a qualified veteran that is guaranteed by the Department of Veterans Affairs.

valid contract an agreement that is legally enforceable and binding on all parties.

valuation estimated worth.

variance permission obtained from zoning authorities to build a structure that is not in complete compliance with current zoning laws. A variance does not permit a non-conforming use of a property.

vendee a buyer.

vendor a seller; the property owner.

village an incorporated minor municipality usually larger than a hamlet and smaller than a town.

void contract a contract that is not legally enforceable; the absence of a valid contract.

voidable contract a contract that appears to be valid but is subject to cancellation by one or both of the parties.

► W

waiver the surrender of a known right or claim.

warranty deed a deed in which the grantor fully warrants a good clear title to the property.

waste the improper use of a property by a party with the right to possession, such as the holder of a life estate.

will a written document that directs the distribution of a deceased person's property, real and personal.

wraparound mortgage a mortgage that includes the remaining balance on an existing first mortgage plus an additional amount. Full payments on both mortgages are made to the wraparound mortgagee who then forwards the payments on the first mortgage to the first mortgagee.

writ of execution a court order to the sheriff or other officer to sell the property of a debtor to satisfy a previously rendered judgment.

► Z

zone an area reserved by authorities for specific use that is subject to certain restrictions.

zoning ordinance the exercise of regulating and controlling the use of a property in a municipality.

7 ▶ California Real Estate Sales Exam 2

CHAPTER SUMMARY

This is the second of the four practice tests in this book. Since you have taken one practice test already, you should feel more confident with your test-taking skills. Use this test to see how knowing what to expect can make you feel better prepared.

LIKE THE FIRST exam in this book, this test is based on the California Real Estate Sales Exam. If you are following the advice in this book, you have done some studying between the first exam and this one. This second exam will give you a chance to see how much you've improved. The answer sheet follows this page, and the test is followed by the answer key and explanations.

▶ California Real Estate Sales Exam 2 Answer Sheet

1.	ⓐ ⓑ ⓒ ⓓ		51.	ⓐ ⓑ ⓒ ⓓ		101.	ⓐ ⓑ ⓒ ⓓ
2.	ⓐ ⓑ ⓒ ⓓ		52.	ⓐ ⓑ ⓒ ⓓ		102.	ⓐ ⓑ ⓒ ⓓ
3.	ⓐ ⓑ ⓒ ⓓ		53.	ⓐ ⓑ ⓒ ⓓ		103.	ⓐ ⓑ ⓒ ⓓ
4.	ⓐ ⓑ ⓒ ⓓ		54.	ⓐ ⓑ ⓒ ⓓ		104.	ⓐ ⓑ ⓒ ⓓ
5.	ⓐ ⓑ ⓒ ⓓ		55.	ⓐ ⓑ ⓒ ⓓ		105.	ⓐ ⓑ ⓒ ⓓ
6.	ⓐ ⓑ ⓒ ⓓ		56.	ⓐ ⓑ ⓒ ⓓ		106.	ⓐ ⓑ ⓒ ⓓ
7.	ⓐ ⓑ ⓒ ⓓ		57.	ⓐ ⓑ ⓒ ⓓ		107.	ⓐ ⓑ ⓒ ⓓ
8.	ⓐ ⓑ ⓒ ⓓ		58.	ⓐ ⓑ ⓒ ⓓ		108.	ⓐ ⓑ ⓒ ⓓ
9.	ⓐ ⓑ ⓒ ⓓ		59.	ⓐ ⓑ ⓒ ⓓ		109.	ⓐ ⓑ ⓒ ⓓ
10.	ⓐ ⓑ ⓒ ⓓ		60.	ⓐ ⓑ ⓒ ⓓ		110.	ⓐ ⓑ ⓒ ⓓ
11.	ⓐ ⓑ ⓒ ⓓ		61.	ⓐ ⓑ ⓒ ⓓ		111.	ⓐ ⓑ ⓒ ⓓ
12.	ⓐ ⓑ ⓒ ⓓ		62.	ⓐ ⓑ ⓒ ⓓ		112.	ⓐ ⓑ ⓒ ⓓ
13.	ⓐ ⓑ ⓒ ⓓ		63.	ⓐ ⓑ ⓒ ⓓ		113.	ⓐ ⓑ ⓒ ⓓ
14.	ⓐ ⓑ ⓒ ⓓ		64.	ⓐ ⓑ ⓒ ⓓ		114.	ⓐ ⓑ ⓒ ⓓ
15.	ⓐ ⓑ ⓒ ⓓ		65.	ⓐ ⓑ ⓒ ⓓ		115.	ⓐ ⓑ ⓒ ⓓ
16.	ⓐ ⓑ ⓒ ⓓ		66.	ⓐ ⓑ ⓒ ⓓ		116.	ⓐ ⓑ ⓒ ⓓ
17.	ⓐ ⓑ ⓒ ⓓ		67.	ⓐ ⓑ ⓒ ⓓ		117.	ⓐ ⓑ ⓒ ⓓ
18.	ⓐ ⓑ ⓒ ⓓ		68.	ⓐ ⓑ ⓒ ⓓ		118.	ⓐ ⓑ ⓒ ⓓ
19.	ⓐ ⓑ ⓒ ⓓ		69.	ⓐ ⓑ ⓒ ⓓ		119.	ⓐ ⓑ ⓒ ⓓ
20.	ⓐ ⓑ ⓒ ⓓ		70.	ⓐ ⓑ ⓒ ⓓ		120.	ⓐ ⓑ ⓒ ⓓ
21.	ⓐ ⓑ ⓒ ⓓ		71.	ⓐ ⓑ ⓒ ⓓ		121.	ⓐ ⓑ ⓒ ⓓ
22.	ⓐ ⓑ ⓒ ⓓ		72.	ⓐ ⓑ ⓒ ⓓ		122.	ⓐ ⓑ ⓒ ⓓ
23.	ⓐ ⓑ ⓒ ⓓ		73.	ⓐ ⓑ ⓒ ⓓ		123.	ⓐ ⓑ ⓒ ⓓ
24.	ⓐ ⓑ ⓒ ⓓ		74.	ⓐ ⓑ ⓒ ⓓ		124.	ⓐ ⓑ ⓒ ⓓ
25.	ⓐ ⓑ ⓒ ⓓ		75.	ⓐ ⓑ ⓒ ⓓ		125.	ⓐ ⓑ ⓒ ⓓ
26.	ⓐ ⓑ ⓒ ⓓ		76.	ⓐ ⓑ ⓒ ⓓ		126.	ⓐ ⓑ ⓒ ⓓ
27.	ⓐ ⓑ ⓒ ⓓ		77.	ⓐ ⓑ ⓒ ⓓ		127.	ⓐ ⓑ ⓒ ⓓ
28.	ⓐ ⓑ ⓒ ⓓ		78.	ⓐ ⓑ ⓒ ⓓ		128.	ⓐ ⓑ ⓒ ⓓ
29.	ⓐ ⓑ ⓒ ⓓ		79.	ⓐ ⓑ ⓒ ⓓ		129.	ⓐ ⓑ ⓒ ⓓ
30.	ⓐ ⓑ ⓒ ⓓ		80.	ⓐ ⓑ ⓒ ⓓ		130.	ⓐ ⓑ ⓒ ⓓ
31.	ⓐ ⓑ ⓒ ⓓ		81.	ⓐ ⓑ ⓒ ⓓ		131.	ⓐ ⓑ ⓒ ⓓ
32.	ⓐ ⓑ ⓒ ⓓ		82.	ⓐ ⓑ ⓒ ⓓ		132.	ⓐ ⓑ ⓒ ⓓ
33.	ⓐ ⓑ ⓒ ⓓ		83.	ⓐ ⓑ ⓒ ⓓ		133.	ⓐ ⓑ ⓒ ⓓ
34.	ⓐ ⓑ ⓒ ⓓ		84.	ⓐ ⓑ ⓒ ⓓ		134.	ⓐ ⓑ ⓒ ⓓ
35.	ⓐ ⓑ ⓒ ⓓ		85.	ⓐ ⓑ ⓒ ⓓ		135.	ⓐ ⓑ ⓒ ⓓ
36.	ⓐ ⓑ ⓒ ⓓ		86.	ⓐ ⓑ ⓒ ⓓ		136.	ⓐ ⓑ ⓒ ⓓ
37.	ⓐ ⓑ ⓒ ⓓ		87.	ⓐ ⓑ ⓒ ⓓ		137.	ⓐ ⓑ ⓒ ⓓ
38.	ⓐ ⓑ ⓒ ⓓ		88.	ⓐ ⓑ ⓒ ⓓ		138.	ⓐ ⓑ ⓒ ⓓ
39.	ⓐ ⓑ ⓒ ⓓ		89.	ⓐ ⓑ ⓒ ⓓ		139.	ⓐ ⓑ ⓒ ⓓ
40.	ⓐ ⓑ ⓒ ⓓ		90.	ⓐ ⓑ ⓒ ⓓ		140.	ⓐ ⓑ ⓒ ⓓ
41.	ⓐ ⓑ ⓒ ⓓ		91.	ⓐ ⓑ ⓒ ⓓ		141.	ⓐ ⓑ ⓒ ⓓ
42.	ⓐ ⓑ ⓒ ⓓ		92.	ⓐ ⓑ ⓒ ⓓ		142.	ⓐ ⓑ ⓒ ⓓ
43.	ⓐ ⓑ ⓒ ⓓ		93.	ⓐ ⓑ ⓒ ⓓ		143.	ⓐ ⓑ ⓒ ⓓ
44.	ⓐ ⓑ ⓒ ⓓ		94.	ⓐ ⓑ ⓒ ⓓ		144.	ⓐ ⓑ ⓒ ⓓ
45.	ⓐ ⓑ ⓒ ⓓ		95.	ⓐ ⓑ ⓒ ⓓ		145.	ⓐ ⓑ ⓒ ⓓ
46.	ⓐ ⓑ ⓒ ⓓ		96.	ⓐ ⓑ ⓒ ⓓ		146.	ⓐ ⓑ ⓒ ⓓ
47.	ⓐ ⓑ ⓒ ⓓ		97.	ⓐ ⓑ ⓒ ⓓ		147.	ⓐ ⓑ ⓒ ⓓ
48.	ⓐ ⓑ ⓒ ⓓ		98.	ⓐ ⓑ ⓒ ⓓ		148.	ⓐ ⓑ ⓒ ⓓ
49.	ⓐ ⓑ ⓒ ⓓ		99.	ⓐ ⓑ ⓒ ⓓ		149.	ⓐ ⓑ ⓒ ⓓ
50.	ⓐ ⓑ ⓒ ⓓ		100.	ⓐ ⓑ ⓒ ⓓ		150.	ⓐ ⓑ ⓒ ⓓ

▶ California Real Estate Sales Exam 2

1. Who may legally withdraw funds from a trust account?
   a. a salesperson licensed to the broker if specifically authorized in writing by the broker
   b. the buyer if specifically authorized in writing by the broker
   c. the seller if specifically authorized in writing by the broker
   d. the selling agent if specifically authorized in writing by the listing agent

2. Which of the following is NOT real property?
   a. *fructus naturales*
   b. air rights
   c. easements
   d. trade fixtures

3. A subagency cannot be created without
   a. the principals' consent.
   b. a written contract.
   c. the buyer's permission.
   d. approval of the agent's broker.

4. Commingling of trust funds occurs when
   a. reasonably sufficient funds are deposited into a trust account, not to exceed $200, to pay service charges or fees levied or assessed against the account by the bank or financial institution where the account is maintained.
   b. funds are deposited into a trust fund account belonging in part to the broker's principal and in part to the broker when it is not reasonably practicable to separate such funds.

   c. funds are deposited into a trust fund account in connection with mortgage loan activities.
   d. commissions, fees, or other income earned by the broker and collectible from the account are left in the trust account for more than 25 days from the date they were earned.

5. A written summary of a property's documents that shows evidence of title is known as
   a. CLTA policy.
   b. ALTA policy.
   c. abstract of title.
   d. parcel survey.

6. Which best describes real estate?
   a. land only
   b. land and improvements
   c. the bundle of rights
   d. easements

7. In evaluating a borrower's income for loan purposes, the least weight would be given to
   a. overtime pay.
   b. investment earnings.
   c. part-time employment.
   d. co-borrower income.

8. A salesperson employed by a listing broker is an agent of the
   a. listing broker.
   b. any subsequent buyer.
   c. owner/seller.
   d. He has no agency responsibility under the listing agreement

9. Market value can be simply defined as
   a. value to anyone.
   b. any value arrived at by formal methods.
   c. the most likely selling price of the property.
   d. the most likely asking price of the property.

10. The elements of an enforceable contract are
    a. express, consideration, mutuality, and lawful object.
    b. communicated, written, competent parties, and lawful object.
    c. lawful object, expressed, written, and competent parties.
    d. competency, mutual consent, lawful object, and consideration.

11. A low loan to value (LTV) ratio would indicate
    a. government financing.
    b. a large down payment.
    c. low buyer equity.
    d. conventional financing.

12. Which of the following terms describes improvements that are part of the real estate?
    a. encumbrances and easements
    b. encumbrances and chattels
    c. fixtures and attachments
    d. emblements and amenities

13. The CLTA standard title insurance policy in California does not protect against
    a. lack of capacity.
    b. forgery.
    c. invalid deed delivery.
    d. unrecorded easements.

14. All of the following laws prohibit discrimination. Which law claims that everyone is entitled to full and equal accommodations, advantages, facilities, privileges, or services in all business establishments of every kind?
    a. Holden Act
    b. Unruh Civil Rights Act
    c. Fair Employment and Housing Act
    d. California Civil Code (Section 54-55.1)

15. What is the monetary remedy to anyone who has been discriminated against in violation of the Unruh Act?
    a. up to twice the amount of actual damages, but not less than $1,000
    b. up to three times the amount of actual damages, but not less than $1,000
    c. up to four times the amount of actual damages, but not less than $1,000
    d. up to five times the amount of actual damages, but not less than $1,000

16. An increase in retail sales at "Back-to-School" time is an example of which kind of economic trend?
    a. business
    b. seasonal
    c. cyclical
    d. long-term secular

17. All contracts require all of the following EXCEPT
    a. a proper writing.
    b. a legal purpose.
    c. consideration.
    d. an offer and acceptance.

18. The "bundle of rights" includes which of the following?
  a. right to enjoy
  b. right to encumber
  c. right to gift
  d. all of the above

19. An actual agency between the principal and agent is created by
  a. express contract.
  b. accident of circumstances.
  c. the actions or inactions of the principal.
  d. the actions or inactions of the agent.

20. If a listing is entered into on June 10, and expires at midnight on July 10, how many days have passed?
  a. 30 days
  b. 31 days
  c. 32 days
  d. 33 days

21. Which of the following would be considered the lender's best protection?
  a. credit score of the borrower(s)
  b. appraised value of the property
  c. sources of income from the borrower
  d. term insurance policy

22. Which of the following is an economic characteristic of personal property?
  a. age
  b. size
  c. utility
  d. weight

23. Real estate cycles seem to be related to the
  a. supply of real estate.
  b. availability of money.
  c. demand for real estate.
  d. all of the above

24. A person that transfers title to real property is know as the
  a. grantee.
  b. grantor.
  c. trustor.
  d. beneficiary.

25. Real property can be
  a. encumbered.
  b. exchanged.
  c. disposed by the use of a will.
  d. all of the above

26. All copies of the deposit receipt would most likely be signed by the
  a. buyer(s).
  b. seller(s).
  c. buyer(s) and seller(s).
  d. buyer(s), seller(s), and broker.

27. Lenders who advertise must meet Truth in Lending Act disclosure requirements with respect to the loan rate and terms. These include which of the following?

a. specific credit terms in the ad are not necessary

b. if an advertisement includes a rate, it must state the rate as an annual percentage rate (APR), using that term

c. if the annual percentage rate may be increased after the first year of the loan, the advertisement does not need to state that fact

d. no rate other than the APR may be mentioned in the ad

28. The owner of the property signs an open listing with many different brokers. Which of the following is true?

a. A time limit of no greater than 90 days must be placed on open listings.

b. The commission will be split according to the amount of brokers.

c. The full commission will be paid by the owner to each broker.

d. The first broker who finds a qualified buyer is entitled to the commission.

29. Seller Green entered into an Exclusive Agency listing with his broker. Two weeks later he agreed to sell his property to his brother-in-law. The broker would be entitled to

a. one-half his normal commission.

b. a full commission.

c. no commission.

d. may look to the buyer for the commission.

30. Economic principles that relate to the marketability of real estate help real estate professionals primarily in the

a. sales comparison and cost approaches.

b. income approach.

c. reconciliation process.

d. income and cost approaches.

31. If a broker wants to mention financing in an advertisement but does not want to disclose all terms, which of the following would not be acceptable under the Truth-in-Lending Act?

a. assumable loan

b. financing available

c. owner will carry with a 5% down payment

d. easy monthly payments

32. Non-financial encumbrances include

a. judgments.

b. attachments.

c. encroachments.

d. none of the above

33. A non-voluntary lien on real property includes

a. judgment lien.

b. construction lien.

c. special assessment.

d. all of the above

34. A valid deed contains all of the following elements EXCEPT

a. a legal description.

b. execution by the grantor.

c. a granting clause.

d. execution by the grantee.

35. An ostensible agency cannot be created by anyone other than the
  a. agent.
  b. principal.
  c. third parties.
  d. customer.

36. When a principal accepts the benefits of a transaction performed by a person who is not an agent of the principal, an agency is created by
  a. *caveat emptor.*
  b. ratification.
  c. avulsion.
  d. hypothecation.

37. Generally, the most popular mortgage loan is the
  a. 7-year fixed rate.
  b. 30-year fixed rate.
  c. interest only loan.
  d. adjustable rate mortgage.

38. Trust fund accounting records must include all of the following EXCEPT
  a. trust fund receipts and disbursements, presented in chronological sequence.
  b. the balance of the trust fund account, based on recorded transactions.
  c. the expenses of the brokerage.
  d. the balance owed to each beneficiary or for each transaction.

39. On an exclusive listing, a broker can be disciplined for
  a. not submitting property tax information.
  b. failure to give a copy of the listing agreement.
  c. failure to include a definite termination date.
  d. both **b** and **c**

40. What kind of trust funds are likely to be received and not placed in a broker's trust account?
  a. borrowers' payments forwarded to lenders
  b. earnest money checks made out to the broker
  c. rents from properties managed by the broker
  d. cash belonging to a buyer or seller during the negotiation of a transaction

41. Refinancing should be considered if
  a. interest rates drop by any amount.
  b. a mortgage banker or broker offers a no-closing-cost loan.
  c. the market rate drops by 2%.
  d. after refinancing, you are able to recover your cost of redoing your loan within less than two years.

42. An agent may disobey the instructions of his or her principal
  a. under no circumstances.
  b. when communication with the principal is not possible.
  c. when the agent does not intend to collect a commission.
  d. but will be subject to criminal prosecution.

43. An "easement in gross" is typically created for which of the following?
   a. the servient tenement
   b. the dominant tenement
   c. a utility company
   d. none of the above

44. A deed granted to the purchaser at a court ordered sale is a
   a. gift deed.
   b. tax deed.
   c. sheriffs deed.
   d. grant deed.

45. A broker must exercise reasonable supervision over which activities of his or her salespersons?
   a. number of hours worked per week
   b. handling of trust funds
   c. property preview activities
   d. community service activities

46. The majority of home loans fall under which area?
   a. VA
   b. FHA
   c. conventional
   d. state or local housing agencies

47. A real estate purchase contract is
   a. an agency.
   b. a unilateral contract.
   c. a bilateral contract.
   d. none of the above

48. Under California law a husband and wife each own
   a. equal interest in all of the real properties they own.
   b. a 50% interest in each other's property.
   c. an undivided one-half interest in all community property and the right of survivorship applies.
   d. none of the above

49. Seller financing of home purchases are an example of
   a. institutional lending.
   b. creative financing.
   c. land contracts.
   d. contract of sale.

50. Responsibility for insuring that all parties are notified of the termination of an agency agreement rests with
   a. the broker.
   b. the agent.
   c. the principal.
   d. legal counsel.

51. Reasonable supervision of salespersons includes the establishment of policies, rules, procedures, and systems to manage certain activities EXCEPT
   a. transactions requiring a real estate license.
   b. documents which may have a material effect upon the rights or obligations of a party to a transaction.
   c. advertising of any service for which a real estate license is required.
   d. prospecting activities.

52. An increase in the value of an inexpensive home in a neighborhood of high-priced homes would be an example of
 a. physical depreciation.
 b. highest and best use.
 c. regression.
 d. progression.

53. In general partnership where title to the property is vested as a tenancy in partnership which of the following does NOT apply?
 a. Partners cannot transfer their interests to another without the consent of the other partners.
 b. Partners interest are undivided and need not be equal.
 c. Partners have equal rights to use partnership property for partnership purposes.
 d. Spouses of partners have a direct community property interest in the partnership property.

54. An owner refuses to convey property after signing the acceptance on a purchase contract. Specific performance can be enforced by
 a. the purchaser.
 b. the broker.
 c. either **a** or **b**
 d. neither **a** or **b**

55. The laws regarding escrow may be found in the
 a. California Financial Code.
 b. Business and Professions Code.
 c. California Administrative Code.
 d. Uniform Commercial Code.

56. Intermediation refers to
 a. mortgage disclosures.
 b. withdrawal of money from savings accounts.
 c. increase in deposits.
 d. supply and demand.

57. A home on a street would probably not sell for $100,000 if similar homes nearby were available for $90,000. This illustrates the principle of
 a. conformity.
 b. substitution.
 c. consistent use.
 d. anticipation.

58. If a broker wants to delegate the responsibility and authority to supervise and control the activities of non-licensed persons to a broker acting in the capacity of a salesperson to the employing broker, the employing broker must
 a. require a bond from the designated broker.
 b. enter into a written agreement with respect to the delegation of responsibility.
 c. require five years experience as a salesperson.
 d. pay the designated broker a fee.

59. A signed lease for a period of six months only, is an example of
 a. an estate at will.
 b. an estate of years.
 c. a tenancy of entireties.
 d. an estate from period to periods.

60. The seller accepts the offer but make some changes. The broker notifies the buyer of the acceptance, thus
  a. a bilateral contract is made.
  b. a unilateral contract is made.
  c. no contract has been made.
  d. the buyer must submit a counteroffer.

61. The loan to value (LTV) is best described as a
  a. ratio of the loan to the sale price.
  b. ratio of the loan to the appraisal.
  c. ratio of the loan to the secondary market.
  d. ratio of the loan to the federal index.

62. A visual inspection of accessible areas of the property must be conducted by
  a. the listing broker.
  b. the buyer's broker.
  c. the buyer.
  d. the listing and buyer's broker.

63. The NW $\frac{1}{4}$ of the NW $\frac{1}{4}$ SW $\frac{1}{4}$ of Section 10 contains
  a. 1 square mile.
  b. 640 acres.
  c. 40 acres.
  d. 120 acres.

64. The seller sells the property "AS IS." The broker knew that the plumbing was in bad repair and did not inform the buyer. The buyer could sue
  a. no one, since the property was sold as is.
  b. As is implies that there are no problems.
  c. the broker.
  d. the seller.

65. An unlicensed sales assistant may
  a. solicit sellers.
  b. solicit buyers.
  c. negotiate sales.
  d. sell his or her own property.

66. Alex Parker listed his home for sale with a local broker in the area. After six months the listing agreement expired without a sale. To insure that his agent does not bind Mr. Parker to any sales contracts upon conclusion of the listing agreement Mr. Parker should
  a. execute a notice of termination.
  b. give notice to any third parties they may have had contact with.
  c. extend the agreement.
  d. advise the agent in writing upon expiration of the agency.

67. An independent escrow company must be licensed by the
  a. Department of Real Estate.
  b. FDIC.
  c. Department of Corporations.
  d. California Attorney Generals Office.

68. A square parcel has an area of 3,097,600 square yards. This is equivalent to
  a. 1 section.
  b. 640 acres.
  c. 1 square mile.
  d. all of the above

69. When a lender processes a loan, they consider red flags as
  a. company policy.
  b. zero tolerance.
  c. discrepancies.
  d. processing timeframe.

70. One of the jobs NOT assigned to the Real Estate Commissioner is to
   a. examine complaints against licensees.
   b. regulate specific aspects of the sale of subdivisions.
   c. settle commission disputes.
   d. investigate non-licensees alleged to be performing acts for which a license is required.

71. An offer based on a $90,000 loan assumption was made and accepted. During the escrow process it was found out the actual loan was $85,000, not $90,000. Which of the following is true?
   a. The buyer needs to come up with the difference in cash.
   b. The seller must carry a note for the difference.
   c. The buyer can void the contract.
   d. The seller can reduce the price by the difference.

72. When the broker represents the seller exclusively in a transaction, his or her obligation to the buyer is
   a. not an obligation of any sort.
   b. for an honest and truthful relationship.
   c. a fiduciary duty.
   d. the same duty as the selling broker.

73. The Real Estate Commissioner may investigate the actions of any person acting in the capacity of a real estate licensee and may suspend or revoke a real estate license where the licensee is guilty of all of the following EXCEPT
   a. acting as a dual agent.
   b. making any substantial misrepresentation.
   c. making continued misrepresentation.
   d. commingling with his own money or property the money or other property of others which is received and held by him.

74. Section 1 is found in which corner of the township?
   a. NE
   b. SE
   c. NW
   d. SW

75. Which of the following real estate transactions would legally require that an escrow be opened?
   a. sale of real property
   b. exchanges
   c. loans
   d. liquor license transfer

76. A person operating as a real estate agent under the supervision of a licensed broker must have earned a salesperson license by meeting all of the following requirements EXCEPT
   a. be at least 21 years of age.
   b. pass a qualifying examination as required.
   c. complete the real estate principles course.
   d. be honest and truthful.

77. Optionor best describes
   a. the broker.
   b. the owner.
   c. the buyer.
   d. the lender.

78. A lender is always concerned with fraud and will allow which of the following to report it?
   a. loan officers
   b. processors
   c. clients
   d. all of the above

79. Eminent domain may be delegated to which of the following?
   a. public utilities
   b. public schools
   c. public hospitals
   d. all of the above

80. Demand has no effect on value unless there is also
   a. purchasing power.
   b. an overabundant supply.
   c. scarcity.
   d. desire.

81. A person dies intestate and his or her representative is unable to locate an heir within two years of death and no heirs come forward to claim the property within five years of this person's death. This property will transfer in title to the State of California through the process of
   a. intestate succession.
   b. escheat.
   c. probate.
   d. none of the above

82. Rina Sands has employed an agent to bid on several parcels at an upcoming public auction and has requested that her identity not be revealed to any third parties to the transactions. Ms. Sands would be considered
   a. an ostensible agent.
   b. an undisclosed principal.
   c. a specific agent.
   d. a blind trust.

83. Federal Housing Administration (FHA) loans are
   a. insured.
   b. guaranteed.
   c. pre-payment loans.
   d. primary lenders.

84. A public report for the purchase of a home in a new subdivision would be issued by the
   a. Department of State Subdivisions.
   b. Department of Corporations.
   c. Department of Lands and Parks.
   d. Department of Real Estate.

85. After the first license renewal, subsequent license renewals require the licensee to complete 45 hours of continuing education; 12 hours of which must include
   a. ethics, agency, fair housing, and finance.
   b. ethics, agency, fair housing, and trust funds.
   c. ethics, fair housing, appraisal, and economics.
   d. legal aspects, home inspection, trust funds, and escrow.

86. An option set forth in a lease would be a(n)
   a. encumbrance.
   b. appurtenance.
   c. consideration.
   d. covenant.

87. Urban blight does NOT result from
   a. racial changes in a neighborhood.
   b. loss of employment.
   c. deteriorating structures.
   d. lower income and educational levels.

88. The Real Estate Recovery Fund is created through collection of a fixed amount from
   a. property taxes.
   b. the Federal government.
   c. the California Association of Realtors.
   d. each license fee.

89. A building inspector determined that some materials proposed in a construction project were not in accordance with the local building code. The inspector concluded that the use of these materials would not create any safety hazards and hence approved the plans. This is an example of a(n)
   a. conditional use permit.
   b. exception.
   c. infraction.
   d. variance.

90. A Preliminary Public Report would allow a subdivider to
   a. obtain reservations only.
   b. sell a limited number of parcels.
   c. pre-sell the entire subdivision.
   d. do nothing until the Final Report is issued.

91. During periods of low inflation,
   a. interest rates increase and property prices decrease.
   b. interest rates increase and property prices increase.
   c. interest rates decrease and property prices increase.
   d. interest rates decrease and property prices decrease.

92. Which loans are available for FHA and VA programs?
   a. 15-, 20-, 25-, and 30-year fixed rate
   b. adjustable rate mortgages
   c. graduated payment mortgages
   d. all of the above

93. The Real Estate Recovery Fund
   a. is a health care program for licensees.
   b. assures the recovery of catastrophic property losses from natural causes.
   c. assures the payment of otherwise non-collectable court judgments against licensees who have committed fraud, misrepresentation, deceit, or conversion of trust funds in a transaction.
   d. offers compensation to licensees who have been injured while practicing real estate.

94. Zoning ordinances typically do NOT include which of the following?
   a. building height
   b. lot coverage
   c. parking requirements
   d. electrical and insulation codes

95. When buying or selling property for his or her-self, a real estate licensee should disclose this fact
   a. at no time since it will weaken their bar-gaining advantage.
   b. upon close of escrow.
   c. in writing as soon as possible.
   d. upon the consummation of a sales contract.

96. Ethics are
   a. a set of principles or values by which an individual guides his or her own behavior and judges that of others.
   b. a religious belief.
   c. a mantra.
   d. an objective set of rules or laws that assure the well being of citizens.

97. Environmental impact reports may be required from which of the following entities?
   a. the federal government
   b. state governments
   c. local governments
   d. all of the above

98. The Code of Ethics and Professional Conduct, found in the Regulations of the Commissioner, considers which of the following to be unlaw-ful conduct for a licensee?
   a. showing property to a prospective buyer who is also working with another licensee
   b. representing the buyer and seller in a transac-tion with their full knowledge and approval
   c. stating or implying to a seller during a list-ing presentation that the licensee is not allowed to charge less than the commission quoted to the owner by the licensee
   d. making an offer to purchase the licensee's own listing after terminating the agency relationship established by the listing

99. A gross lease means the lessee pays
   a. a percentage of the gross.
   b. a percentage of the net.
   c. all the owner's costs plus rent.
   d. a flat rent.

100. Alienation clauses are found within the Deed of Trust and refer to
   a. getting upset with your neighbor.
   b. the transferring of an estate.
   c. giving up possession, but still keeping title.
   d. using the property as security.

101. Depreciating an investment property by $50,000 in one year would
   a. increase its market value by $50,000.
   b. decrease its market value by $50,000.
   c. increase its book value by $50,000.
   d. decrease its book value by $50,000.

102. A listing broker has just received three offers for the purchase of their seller's home. To insure that they receive favorable treatment, one of the selling agents has offered a $500 bonus to the listing agent if his offer is pre-sented first. The listing agent should
   a. accept the bonus without mention to the seller.
   b. advise the seller of the $500 bonus, and present all offers at the same time.
   c. ignore the bonus, and present all offers at the same time.
   d. only present the offer with the highest price.

103. Structural pest control certification reports must be given to
   a. the buyer of the property.
   b. the seller/owner of the property.
   c. the lender on the property.
   d. all of the above

104. Private controls do NOT include
   a. landscape standards.
   b. exterior paint colors.
   c. zoning changes.
   d. satellite dishes or antennae.

105. Which of the following would be considered fee simple?
   a. real property
   b. a lease
   c. a bequest
   d. tenancy at sufferance

106. An option means
   a. a fiduciary agreement.
   b. a lien.
   c. to enter into a contract.
   d. a contract to keep open.

107. After the Multiple Listing Service (MLS), the most popular technical applications used by top salespeople are
   a. home banking programs, tax preparation programs, and geographic information systems.
   b. farming programs, prospecting programs, and desktop publishing.
   c. email, mobile phones, and digital cameras.
   d. pagers, spreadsheets, and contract preparation programs.

108. Real property taxes are considered to be
   a. a progressive tax.
   b. an *ad valorem* tax.
   c. a sales tax.
   d. a form of income tax.

109. Changes in technology usage suggest an increased reliance by real estate agents on
   a. the internet.
   b. pagers.
   c. DVDs.
   d. hard-wired phones.

110. In regards to covenants, conditions, and restrictions (CC&Rs),
   a. CC&Rs must be recorded in the county where the property is located in order to become binding.
   b. agreement of a stated percentage of property owners is required for changes to existing CC&Rs or for new CC&Rs to be implemented.
   c. both **a** and **b**
   d. neither **a** nor **b**

111. A nearby broker takes a listing agreement from Hank Richardsen for the sale of his home. Two weeks after commencement of the agreement the home is destroyed in a fire. Under these circumstances
   a. the listing is terminated.
   b. the fire would have no effect on the listing.
   c. the agreement would continue in effect until the property is rebuilt.
   d. the agent is owed a commission.

112. When an earth dam suddenly gives way and fails is an example of
a. accretion.
b. avulsion.
c. reliction.
d. erosion.

113. California renters under month-to-month rental agreements who live in residential rentals for one year or more must be given
a. 20-day notice to move out.
b. 30-day notice to move out.
c. 40-day notice to move out.
d. 60-day notice to move out.

114. Sam Jones recently purchased a new home with cash and a new loan for the price of $300,000. What is the amount of the Documentary Transfer Tax owed by the buyer, Mr. Jones, on the sales price?
a. $110.10
b. $220.00
c. $303.00
d. $330.00

115. Tenants have the right to a "move-out" inspection of a rental unit no earlier than
a. one week prior to the termination of the tenancy.
b. two weeks prior to the termination of the tenancy.
c. three weeks prior to the termination of the tenancy.
d. four weeks prior to the termination of the tenancy.

116. Generally, for all real estate transactions which of the following would be required to be recorded?
a. an open listing
b. lead paint disclosures
c. an option
d. none of the above

117. Usury laws apply to
a. financial institutions.
b. all lenders.
c. non-institutional lenders.
d. private lenders.

118. The value of income properties is based on
a. its capacity to appreciate.
b. its capacity to continue producing an income.
c. its capacity to double its income.
d. its capacity to depreciate.

119. Each unit in a triplex rents for $1,000 per month. The property sold for $432,000. What is the annual gross income multiplier (GIM)?
a. 10
b. 8
c. 12
d. 15

120. Percolating water is
a. underground water.
b. runoff water from rain.
c. water on the earth's surface.
d. none of the above

121. Regulation Z (Truth in Lending Law) gives recession time to the borrower for how long?
a. 1 day
b. 3 days
c. 30 days
d. 45 days

122. The best method used to appraise a retail center would be to use
a. the market approach of price per square foot of building area.
b. the market approach of price per front foot.
c. a gross income multiplier and the gross annual income.
d. the capitalization of the market estimate of the net operating income.

123. If an agent's power is coupled with an interest, the principal
a. may cancel the agency upon 30-days notification.
b. may terminate per the terms of the agency agreement.
c. will be unable to terminate the agency.
d. may cancel the listing agreement at any time.

124. The right of the government to take private property for the public good is known as
a. severance damages.
b. eminent domain.
c. Writ of Execution.
d. variance.

125. The Subdivided Lands Act is administered by
a. local city governments.
b. local county governments.
c. the Department of Real Estate.
d. both a and b

126. Gross rent is
a. income less expenses.
b. income plus expenses.
c. income plus vacancy factor.
d. income received before any expenses are deducted.

127. Functional obsolescence for a home would NOT include
a. close proximity to a major highway.
b. small closets.
c. a poor floor plan.
d. an overbuilt kitchen.

128. To subordinate means
a. to subrogate.
b. to lease.
c. to buy.
d. to be secondary.

129. A deed of reconveyance moves the title from
a. the trustor to the trustee.
b. the trustee to the trustor.
c. the beneficiary to the trustor.
d. none of the above

130. Which method is typically used in estimating the replacement cost of a home?
a. index method
b. cubic foot method
c. quantity survey method
d. square foot method

131. What is NOT a requirement for a mobile home to become real property?
a. It must be set on a permanent foundation.
b. A certificate of occupancy is obtained.
c. registration with the Department of Motor Vehicles (DMV)
d. a building permit

132. Real estate commissions in California
   a. are set at 6%.
   b. are always negotiable between seller and broker.
   c. must provide a minimum of 3% commission to the selling broker.
   d. must provide a minimum of 3% commission to the listing broker.

133. Which of the following laws will be applied to the sale of a retail business?
   a. local zoning laws
   b. Bulk Transfer Act
   c. housing and community development laws
   d. environmental hazard disclosure laws

134. The zoning act designed to control the development near hazardous earthquake faults is known as
   a. Mello-Roos.
   b. Alquist-Priolo.
   c. Police power.
   d. Subdivision Map Act.

135. An example of a common interest subdivision is
   a. a timeshare.
   b. a community apartment project.
   c. both **a** and **b**
   d. neither **a** nor **b**

136. The obligation to prepare and deliver a Transfer Disclosure Statement lies with
   a. the seller alone.
   b. the buyer alone.
   c. the seller and his or her agent.
   d. the escrow holder.

137. When working for a broker, real estate law considers the salesperson as a/an
   a. independent contractor.
   b. employee.
   c. 1099 worker.
   d. assistant.

138. A Transfer Disclosure Statement is not required
   a. when the seller is a minor.
   b. when the sale is "as is."
   c. when the transfer is by an administrator of a decedent's estate.
   d. when the house is more than ten years old.

139. The Natural Hazard Disclosure Law requires
   a. all sellers to disclose if a property is in certain mapped natural hazard zones.
   b. all sellers to disclose if a property contains hazardous materials.
   c. all sellers to disclose if a property is near an ancient landslide.
   d. all sellers to disclose if a property is in a federal or state poor air quality zone.

140. The four broad forces that affect value are
   a. density, variety, human scale, and architecture.
   b. demand, utility, scarcity, and location.
   c. physical, social, economic, and political.
   d. cost, market, income, and reconciliation.

141. Which of the following is NOT a disclosure required by the Natural Hazard Disclosure Law?
   a. whether the property is located in an earthquake fault zone
   b. whether the property is located in a seismic hazard zone
   c. whether the property is located in a flood hazard area
   d. whether the property is located in a federal or state park

142. A broker who receives earnest money from clients can place these funds in
   a. trust accounts.
   b. company general accounts.
   c. client checking accounts.
   d. DRE general accounts.

143. There are many forces that influence the value of real property. Which of the following is NOT a material fact negatively affecting that value?
   a. property located in area where principle of progression is a major force
   b. recurring leaks in the basement
   c. defects in plumbing
   d. lot line boundary disputes

144. An apartment owner spent $2,000 last year to replace four dishwashers. In a 20-unit apartment house, what annual expense could be projected for dishwasher replacement, assuming all units had dishwashers? (Assume a useful life of ten years for a dishwasher.)
   a. $500
   b. $2,000
   c. $3,500
   d. $1,000

145. The commission paid to an agent in California is normally
   a. based on a flat fee.
   b. specified by Statute.
   c. not negotiable.
   d. based on a percentage of the sales price.

146. Sellers have an obligation to
   a. state any defects they are aware of.
   b. supply an assessment of the property's structural integrity.
   c. disclose any damage from flooding or the danger of future flooding.
   d. disclose any negative reason for selling the property that would affect the value to the buyer.

147. When must the appraiser adjust sale prices for the effects of seller financing?
   a. in every case
   b. in no case
   c. in appraising for eminent domain
   d. whenever financing has influenced the price

148. Public records can be checked to verify which of the following items about a property?
   a. any recorded easements, restrictions, or other reservations or interests affecting the property
   b. environmental hazards
   c. encroachments
   d. functional obsolescence

149. The subject property is very similar to one key recent sale, except that the sale property has an extra full-bath. The cost of installing a full bath in the den of the subject would be about $10,000. Analysis of sales indicates a market premium of about $5,000. The sale sold for $130,000. What is the indicated market value of the subject property?
   a. $120,000
   b. $130,000
   c. $125,000
   d. $135,000

150. The Truth in Lending Act (Regulation Z) applies to lender's practices
   a. if the loan is for $25,000 or more.
   b. if the loan is secured by a residence.
   c. if the loan is for commercial or agricultural loans.
   d. for all business loans.

▶ **Answers**

1. a. According to Commissioner's Regulation 2834, withdrawals from the trust account may be made only upon the signature of one or more of the following: the broker in whose name the account is maintained; the designated broker-officer if the account is in the name of a corporate broker; a salesperson licensed to the broker if specifically authorized in writing by the broker; an unlicensed employee of the broker covered by a fidelity bond at least equal to the maximum amount of trust funds to which the employee has access at any time if specifically authorized in writing by the broker who is a signatory of the trust account.

2. d. Trade fixtures are installed by a tenant in connection with a business on the leased property, hence they are personal property.

3. a. Subagents are those upon whom the powers of an agent have been conferred by the listing agent but can only be created with the principal's consent.

4. d. Commingling occurs in the following instances: Personal or company funds are deposited into the trust fund bank account. (This is a violation of the law even if separate records are kept.) Trust funds are deposited into the licensee's general or personal bank account rather than into the trust fund account; commissions, fees, or other income earned by the broker and collectible from the account are left in the trust account for more than 25 days from the date they were earned.

5. c. The recorded public history of a particular property establishes a "chain of title" and is know as an abstract of title.

6. b. Real estate consists of land and improvements only.

7. c. One of the criteria for determining the sources of income is the length or the stability of that income; generally part-time employment is not considered.

8. c. Under the listing agreement, the seller usually gives authority to delegate some authority to other brokers and salespersons but they have the same duties and responsibilities to the seller as the listing agent.

9. c. Market value is the most likely selling price.

10. d. The main ingredient missing in the other choices is *consideration*, the transfer of money or something of value.

11. b. The more that a person places as a down payment, the lower the loan to value is and the lender is more likely to make the loan possible.

12. c. *Fixtures and attachments* is another term that refers to manmade improvements that are attached to the land (part of the real estate).

13. d. Standard title insurance does not insure against unrecorded easements placed on a property by a grantor.

14. b. The Holden Act, or the Housing Financial Discrimination Act of 1977, prohibits discriminatory loan practices on the part of financial institutions; the Unruh Act gives everyone equal accommodations, advantages, facilities, privileges or services in all business establishments; the Fair Employment and Housing Act prohibits discrimination in the sale, rental or financing of practically all types of housing; Section 54-55.1 of the California Civil Code prohibits discrimination in the rental, lease, or sale of housing accommodations because of race, color, religion, sex, marital status, national origin, ancestry, age, familial status, or disability as well as precluding restrictions on seeing eye dogs and signal dogs from "no pet" clauses.

15. b. California Civil Code Section 52 provides monetary remedies to persons who have been discriminated against in violation of the Unruh Act. Whoever denies, aids, or makes any discrimination contrary to the law regarding business establishments is liable for each and every offense for the actual damages and any amount that may be determined by a jury or court up to a maximum of three times the amount of actual damage but not less than $1,000.

16. b. Increase in sales around "Back-to-School" time is an example of a seasonal trend. There are other retail seasonal trends that occur before and during summer, winter, and spring.

17. a. Not all contracts have to be in writing in order to be valid.

18. d. The "bundle of rights" includes all of the listed choices.

19. a. The actual agency is created by agreement in contrast to the ostensible agency, which is created by subsequent ratification of the principal.

20. c. All days are counted to include the day it starts and ends.

21. b. Actually, nothing is for sure and the lender will make a judgment call on the ability of the person and the property that he or she is using as a security, but out of all the choices the property is more of a sure thing than anything else.

22. c. Utility is an economic characteristic of personal property.

23. d. All of the choices apply. You need supply and demand for real estate and the availability of money for financing since most purchases are not all cash.

24. b. The grantor is the person that grants property or property rights, usually the seller in the transaction.

25. d. Real property can be encumbered, exchanged, and disposed by the use of a will.

26. a. The buyer(s) signs the deposit receipt for the earnest or deposit submitted and is given a copy for the money or something of value submitted. The seller does not sign this receipt, he or she just acknowledges that something was submitted. By doing this, it shows the seller that this buyer is interested in the property.

27. b. The annual percentage rate (APR) combines the interest rate with the other costs of the loan into a single figure that shows the true annual cost of borrowing, giving the borrower a standardized yardstick by which to compare financing from different sources.

28. d. When an open listing is given to more than one broker, it is the first broker who finds a qualified buyer (one who is ready, willing, and able to purchase) who is entitled to the commission.

29. c. In an exclusive agency listing, the owner has the right to independently sell the property without paying a commission to the broker.

30. a. The economic principals that relate to the marketability of real estate help real estate professionals in the sales comparison and cost approaches to value.

31. c. Under the Truth-in-Lending Law, if the amount of down payment, the amount of any payment, the number of payments, the period of repayment, the dollar amount of any finance charge, or the fact that there is no charge for credit is mentioned in an advertisement, the following disclosures must appear in the ad: the cash price or amount of the loan; the number, amount, and frequency of payments; the annual percentage (APR); and the deferred payment price in some cases.

32. c. An encroachment (an improvement, partially or wholly on or over another property) is an example of a non-financial encumbrance.

33. d. A judgment lien, a construction lien, and a special assessment are all non-voluntary liens.

34. d. A valid deed has five essential elements but does not require execution by the buyer or grantee.

35. b. This type of agency can only occur when the acts or omissions of the principal cause a third party to believe the agent is acting on behalf of the principal.

36. b. Ratification takes place when the principal accepts the benefits of a transaction done by a person.

37. b. Most homeowners want the stability of monthly loan payments and a fixed-rate loan will allow the borrower to properly account for the money needed on a monthly basis.

38. c. Trust funds are funds held for the benefit of others in the performance of acts for which a real estate license is required.

39. d. A termination date on all exclusive listings is required by Real Estate Law. Agents are required to give a copy of an exclusive listing to the seller. Failure to do so does not invalidate the listing, but it may result in disciplinary action against the agent. (California Real Estate Law, Business and Professions Code, Section 10142.)

40. a. Even though the broker is handling the funds, as long as he or she keeps a record of the funds, payments intended for a lender are not required to be placed in a trust account.

41. d. There are always costs related to any real estate transaction. However, if the borrower is refinancing based solely on interest rates, then as long as he or she can get his or her closing cost back within or fewer than two years it may make sense.

42. b. If there is no time to communicate with the principal for instructions, an agent may disobey the instructions of the principal.

43. c. An easement in gross does not benefit a specific real estate parcel. These easements benefit individuals or organizations such as a utility company.

44. c. A deed that derives out of a judicial action is known as a *sheriff's deed.*

45. b. Ultimately, the broker is responsible for the lawful accounting of brokerage trust funds and should oversee salespersons to make sure they are keeping records of all transaction funds. As independent contractors, salespersons are responsible for the results of their labor and the broker does not need to supervise their activities or time spent producing the results.

46. c. All lenders do conventional lending (conforming and jumbo), but not all do government loans.

47. c. The purchase contract is between the buyer and the seller.

48. c. Under California law a husband and wife each own an undivided one-half interest in all community property and the right of survivorship applies.

49. b. Sometimes when a seller sells their home, they offer to the buyer to carry a note to assist the buyer in the down payment of that home; this is called *creative financing.*

50. c. If the principal has concerns of being obligated by an agent at the conclusion of a contract they must give notice to any third parties.

51. d. Prospecting, or the process of acquiring new customers and clients, is an activity regulated by the salesperson, generally without the supervision of the broker.

52. d. The principal of progression is when the price of inexpensive homes increase as more expensive homes are built and sold in the neighborhood.

53. d. Spouses of partners *do not* have a direct community property interest in the partnership property.

54. a. The contract is really between the buyer and the seller, which gives the buyer the right to sue.

55. a. Escrow law is found in the California Financial Code.

56. c. When the market rebounds and individuals get a better return on their money, they pull from their equity and place the money within their savings accounts to increase liquidity. This is referred to as *intermediation.*

57. b. The principle of substitution implies that a person will not pay more for a property if another property is available with comparable utility and desirability for a lesser price.

58. b. A broker's responsibility must be delegated in writing.

59. b. An "estate of years" is a lease agreement for a definite period fixed in advance.

60. c. When the broker notifies the buyer of the changes, there is not any paperwork submitted. If acceptance by the buyer to the proposed changes is verbal, then generally the broker representing the seller will submit a counteroffer to the buyer's agent.

61. b. This answer is the ratio of the loan amount to the appraised value of the subject property.

62. d. Legally, the buyer's broker and the listing broker are required to conduct a diligent visual inspection of accessible areas.

63. c. The area is $\frac{1}{2} \times \frac{1}{2} \times \frac{1}{4} \times$ (1 square miles) = $\frac{1}{16}$ square mile; $\frac{1}{16} \times 640$ acres = 40 acres.

64. c. The agent will always have to inform known facts to all parties.

65. d. A real estate license is not necessary to sell one's own home.

66. b. The only way that a seller can insure they are not bound to a contract from a former agent is to notify all third parties of the termination.

67. c. An independent escrow corporation must be licensed by the Department of Corporations.

68. d. A square parcel has an area of 3,097,600 square yards and is equivalent to 640 acres = 1 section = 1 square mile. Solution: convert the square yards to square feet; $\frac{3,097,600}{9}$ (square feet in a square yard) = 27,878,400 square feet; $\frac{27,878,400 \text{ square feet}}{43,560 \text{ square feet in one acre}}$ = 640 acres = 1 section = 1 square mile.

69. c. Whenever a variance from the norm appears in a loan request, the underwriter takes note of the inconsistency: the red flag. By working with the agents involved or directly with the parties to the loan, they will seek a resolution to the discrepancy.

70. c. Commission disputes are settled in civil court.

71. c. The contract is agreed upon according to the terms and conditions set, if something changes then the buyer has the option to end the contract.

72. b. As an exclusive agent for the seller, an agent has a fiduciary duty. As to other parties including the buyer he must maintain truthful and honest dealings.

73. a. Dual agency is not a violation of real estate law. Failure to disclose the acting for more than one party in a transaction without the knowledge or consent of all parties is a violation of real estate law and subject to disciplinary action.

74. a. Section 1 is found in the NE corner of the township.

75. d. There are three occasions whereby in California law an escrow must be conducted. The three occasions are a transfer of liquor license, the sale of securities, and probate sales.

76. a. The minimum age for a real estate licensee is 18 years of age.

77. b. The owner is the person who gives the option.

78. d. Fraud is a major concern to lenders and all have the ability to report any concerns so that the lender will limit its exposure.

79. d. Eminent domain may be delegated to public schools, public utilities, and public hospitals.

80. **a.** Without purchasing power, demand cannot affect value.

81. **b.** Escheat is the legal process whereby the title of a property owned by a deceased person is reverted to the state for lack of heirs or want of legal ownership.

82. **b.** An undisclosed principal is one that does not reveal their identity to third parties to the transaction.

83. **a.** Most people think that FHA is a lender and makes loans, when in fact they do not make loans; they just insure the loss of a portion of the loan.

84. **d.** As provided in the Subdivided Lands Law, purchasers of a home in a new subdivision must receive a public report from the Real Estate Commissioners office.

85. **b.** Forty-five hours of continuing education are required every four years, including 33 hours of consumer education, ethics, agency, fair housing, and trust funds.

86. **d.** A covenant is a promise. In this case, the landlord promises to abide by the option when and if exercised at the discretion of the tenant and within the time constraints established within the option agreement.

87. **a.** Racial changes do not contribute to urban blight. All of the other choices listed do.

88. **d.** A portion of each license fee is set aside for the Recovery Fund.

89. **b.** The approval of these nonstandard materials by the building inspector was example of an *exception*.

90. **a.** The Preliminary Report allows subdividers to obtain reservations only. They cannot sell, and the deposit is fully refundable.

91. **c.** When inflation is low, interest rates are low as well. Lower interest rates allow buyers to pay higher prices and still maintain reasonable payments.

92. **d.** Government loan programs offer all of the given options to a qualified borrower in the purchase or the refinance of the subject property.

93. **c.** A fund of last resort is for consumers who have obtained a final judgment against a real estate licensee based on fraud or certain other grounds and has been unable to satisfy the judgment through the normal post-judgment proceedings. The applicant must file the application within one year of the final judgment and show that he or she has made all reasonable efforts to satisfy the judgment from the assets of not only the judgment debtor but also all other persons who may have been liable in the transaction.

94. **d.** Zoning ordinances typically do not include electrical and insulation codes. These items are typically controlled by the Building and Safety Departments.

95. **c.** The Real Estate Commissioner created a regulation requiring disclosure of license status, which has the effect of law.

96. **a.** This choice is a definition of ethics.

97. **d.** The federal government, state government, and local governments may require environmental impact reports.

98. **c.** Commissions are not set by law and must be negotiated between the listing broker and the seller.

99. **d.** The owner will access all costs and accordingly charge a flat rate.

100. b. If the borrower changes the terms of the original agreement of the loan, then this clause allows the lender to call the loan and request for the amount to be paid in full. An example of this would be adding other people to the title who are not on the loan.

101. d. Depreciation is applied to book value. When a property depreciates its book value decreases.

102. b. To make a secret profit is a breach of the fiduciary relationship. The agent has a duty to advise the seller (principal) of the bonus.

103. d. Structural pest control certification reports must be given to the buyer and seller of the property as well as to the lender on the property.

104. c. Private controls do not include zoning changes. Zoning changes fall under public land controls.

105. a. Almost all real property will have encumbrances affecting title and possession.

106. d. This clause allows options to be open and have the ability to change according to the party's mutual desires.

107. c. These results are according to NAR research.

108. b. An *ad valorem* tax is a tax that is charged in proportion to the value of the property and literally means "according to value."

109. a. These results are according to NAR research.

110. c. CC&Rs are private deed restrictions that are placed on property by a previous owner or the original developer. The Statute of Frauds requires that CC&Rs be in writing. They must be recorded. After they are recorded, they run with the land, and unless otherwise stated they have no time limitation. CC&Rs can be added to or modified by a stated per-

centage of affected property owners. If there is no stated percentage, then a unanimous agreement is required.

111. a. Civil code section 2355 provides that an agency is terminated by the extinction of the subject which, in this case, would be the home listed for sale.

112. b. When an earth dam suddenly gives away and fails is an example of *avulsion*.

113. d. This is a new California law as of January 2003.

114. d. The tax is computed at the rate of 55 cents for each $500 of consideration or new money borrowed. Therefore, $\frac{\$300,000}{\$500} \times .55 = \$330.00$. This can also be calculated at the rate of $1.10 for each $1,000. Therefore, $\frac{\$300,000}{\$1,000} \times 1.10 = \$330.00$.

115. b. This is a new California law as of January 2003.

116. d. Most counties will record anything with a fee attached; but in real estate, record documents like deed of trust, notes, and grant deeds are generally recorded with the county assessors.

117. b. The purpose of Usury Laws is to protect borrowers from being charged excessive interest. This includes extremely high closing costs charged by a real estate lender.

118. b. The income approach to value estimates the present worth of future benefits from ownership of an income producing property using the formula of net $\frac{income}{capitalization\ rate} =$ value of property.

119. c. The GIM $= \frac{(Sales\ Price)}{(Gross\ Annual\ Income)} = \frac{\$432,000}{\$36,000} = 12$.

120. a. Percolating water is underground water.

121. b. After a borrower refinances a home, they are given a three-day recession period to review the loan documents they just signed and see if they really do, in fact, want this loan. Recession periods are only on refinances, not purchases.

122. d. Retail centers are income-producing properties, hence the income approach to value is the most common method. The income approach to value typically uses the capitalization of the market estimate of the net operating income.

123. c. Section 2356 of the Civil Code states that if an agent's power is coupled with an interest the principal is unable to terminate the agency and the interest must be something more than compensation for services.

124. b. The involuntary conversion of a private citizen's property by the government is the *right of eminent domain* and the landowner must receive fair market value for the taking of their property.

125. c. The Subdivided Lands Act is administered by the Department of Real Estate.

126. d. Total income before expenses are deducted is gross rent. Gross rent less vacancy factor or rental loss is effective gross income. Net operating income is determined by subtracting certain expenses (taxes, insurance, management, maintenance, utilities, and reserves) from effective gross income.

127. a. Close proximity to a freeway is an economic obsolescence. It is a loss in value due to outside forces.

128. d. To be *subordinate* means that a document may be in a junior position to another document. For instance, suppose you have an existing first trust deed on your property that also has a subordination clause. If you wanted to pull some equity out of your property, the new lender may require that they be in a first trust deed position instead of a junior trust deed position. Because the existing first trust deed has a subordination clause it will become junior to the new trust deed as soon as the new loan is procured.

129. c. When a money encumbrance is paid it must be shown in the public records. For instance, when a $100,000 trust deed is recorded it indicates that there is a $100,000 money obligation against the property. When the debt is paid off, there is no way of removing the debt document from the public records. Consequently, a deed of reconveyance is recorded. It shows that the money encumbrance was paid off in full by the trustor.

130. d. The simplest way to determine the replacement cost of a home is to measure the outside of a home and determine its square footage. Take the total square footage and multiply it times the per-square-foot cost of construction. For instance, if the cost of construction per square foot is $100 and the home is 2,000 square feet, the value is $200,000.

131. c. A mobile home that has been placed on a foundation is registered with the county recorder as real property.

132. b. Commission rates are negotiable, and the listing agreement must contain this statement printed in Ten-Point Bold type.

133. b. Codes and laws involved in the sale of a business are: Uniform Commercial Code, Bulk Transfer Act, California Sales and Use Tax Law, and the Alcoholic Beverage Control Act.

134. b. The purpose of the act was to provide public safety and to assist government in prohibiting development in areas of high seismic hazard.

135. c. Common interest subdivisions include a time share and a community apartment project. Other examples are a condominium, a stock cooperative, and a planned unit development (PUD).

136. c. If more than one real estate agent is involved in the transaction, the agent obtaining the offer is required to deliver the disclosures to the prospective buyer before the execution of the offer to purchase. If delivered after the required time, the buyer has three days after delivery in person or five days after delivery by mail to deliver a termination of offer to the seller or seller's agent.

137. b. Under the DRE, a salesperson is considered an employee for supervision purposes only. The salesperson is supervised by the broker of record for the salesperson's agency.

138. c. A Transfer Disclosure Statement is not required when the transfer is by an administrator of a decedent's estate as defined by the California Civil Code Section 1102.3.

139. a. The Natural Hazard Disclosure Act requires all sellers to disclose if a property is in certain mapped natural hazard zones.

140. c. The four forces are physical, social, economic, and political.

141. d. The Natural Hazard Act does not require disclosure about whether or not the property is located in a federal or state park.

142. a. Under real estate law, when a salesperson or broker receives a check from the borrower for the purpose of purchasing a property, they then are required to place said funds into a neutral account called a *trust account.*

In brokerage commingling, the borrower's funds and the broker's funds go into the same account—a clear violation of real estate law.

143. a. The price paid for a property only reflects a subjective value based on what a buyer will pay and what a seller will take.

144. d. A typical dishwasher appears to cost $500 $(\frac{\$1,500}{3})$. It has an expected life of ten years hence a reserve of $50/year is needed for each dishwasher. There are 20 units in the building so the annual reserve needed is 20 × $50 = $1,000.

145. d. The fee paid to an agent for compensation of their services is usually a percentage of the sales price of the property.

146. a. The seller only needs to disclose matters of which he or she is aware.

147. d. When seller financing is below market rates as an incentive to buy, sales price is often above market value as a trade-off. An appraiser must adjust the sales price downward to use this sale as a comparable property.

148. a. Only easements, restrictions, or other reservations or interests affecting the property are likely to be recorded. None of the other items are matters of record.

149. c. This example illustrates that cost and value are two different concepts. Since the subject does not have the extra full bath, it is worth less than the comparable sale. Since the market reflects only a $5,000 premium for the extra bath, the comparable sale is adjusted downward by $5,000.

150. b. The Truth in Lending Act (Regulation Z) must be followed whenever a residence is pledged as security for a loan.

Scoring

Evaluate how you did on this second practice exam by again counting only the number of questions you answered correctly. Remember, questions you skipped or got wrong don't count. If you correctly answered at least 105 questions, you have scored 70%—the passing score in California. Remember that the number of questions on your exam may be different, and for insurance you should strive for the highest score possible.

Keep in mind that at this point how you did on each of the basic areas tested by the exam is more important than your score. Your percentage scores in conjunction with the LearningExpress Test Preparation System in Chapter 2 of this book will help you revise your study plan if need be. After your study plan is revised, turn again to the California Real Estate Refresher Course and the Real Estate Math Review in Chapters 4 and 5, and to the Real Estate Glossary in Chapter 6.

Use the table on this page to see where your strengths and weaknesses lie so that you can concentrate your efforts as you continue to prepare. After working more on your problem areas, take the third practice exam in Chapter 8 to see how much you have improved.

EXAM 2 FOR REVIEW

Subject Area	Question Numbers
Property Ownership and Land Use Controls and Regulation	2, 6, 12, 18, 22, 25, 32, 33, 43, 48, 53, 59, 63, 68, 74, 79, 81, 89, 94, 97, 103, 104, 110, 112, 120, 125, 135
Laws of Agency	3, 8, 19, 29, 35, 36, 42, 50, 62, 66, 72, 82, 95, 102, 111, 123, 132, 145
Valuation and Market Analysis	9, 16, 23, 30, 52, 57, 80, 87, 91, 101, 119, 122, 127, 130, 140, 144, 147, 149
Financing	7, 11, 21, 37, 41, 46, 49, 56, 61, 69, 78, 83, 92, 100, 105, 117, 121, 137, 142
Transfer of Property	5, 13, 24, 34, 44, 55, 67, 75, 84, 90, 108, 114, 124, 134
Practice of Real Estate and Mandatory Disclosures	1, 4, 14, 15, 27, 31, 38, 40, 45, 51, 58, 65, 70, 73, 76, 85, 88, 93, 96, 98, 107, 109, 113, 115, 118, 126, 131, 133, 136, 138, 139, 141, 143, 146, 148, 150
Contracts	10, 17, 20, 26, 28, 39, 47, 54, 60, 64, 71, 77, 86, 99, 106, 116, 128, 129

8 ▶ California Real Estate Sales Exam 3

CHAPTER SUMMARY

This is the third of the four practice tests in this book. Use this test to identify which types of questions are still giving you problems.

Y OU ARE NOW more familiar with the content and format of the California Real Estate Sales Exam and most likely you feel more confident than you did at first. However, your practice test-taking experience will help you most if you create a situation as close as possible to the real one.

For this exam, try to simulate real testing conditions. Find a quiet place where you will not be disturbed. Make sure you have two sharpened pencils and a good eraser. You should have plenty of time to answer all of the questions when you take the real exam, but you will want to practice working quickly without rushing. Be sure to leave enough time to complete the test in one sitting. Remember you will have 3 hours and 15 minutes for the actual exam. Use a timer or a stopwatch and see if you can work through all the test questions in the allotted time.

As before, the answer sheet you should use is on the next page. Following the exam you will find the answer key and explanations. These explanations, along with the table at the end of this chapter, will help you see where you need further study.

► California Real Estate Sales Exam 3 Answer Sheet

#					#					#				
1.	ⓐ	ⓑ	ⓒ	ⓓ	51.	ⓐ	ⓑ	ⓒ	ⓓ	101.	ⓐ	ⓑ	ⓒ	ⓓ
2.	ⓐ	ⓑ	ⓒ	ⓓ	52.	ⓐ	ⓑ	ⓒ	ⓓ	102.	ⓐ	ⓑ	ⓒ	ⓓ
3.	ⓐ	ⓑ	ⓒ	ⓓ	53.	ⓐ	ⓑ	ⓒ	ⓓ	103.	ⓐ	ⓑ	ⓒ	ⓓ
4.	ⓐ	ⓑ	ⓒ	ⓓ	54.	ⓐ	ⓑ	ⓒ	ⓓ	104.	ⓐ	ⓑ	ⓒ	ⓓ
5.	ⓐ	ⓑ	ⓒ	ⓓ	55.	ⓐ	ⓑ	ⓒ	ⓓ	105.	ⓐ	ⓑ	ⓒ	ⓓ
6.	ⓐ	ⓑ	ⓒ	ⓓ	56.	ⓐ	ⓑ	ⓒ	ⓓ	106.	ⓐ	ⓑ	ⓒ	ⓓ
7.	ⓐ	ⓑ	ⓒ	ⓓ	57.	ⓐ	ⓑ	ⓒ	ⓓ	107.	ⓐ	ⓑ	ⓒ	ⓓ
8.	ⓐ	ⓑ	ⓒ	ⓓ	58.	ⓐ	ⓑ	ⓒ	ⓓ	108.	ⓐ	ⓑ	ⓒ	ⓓ
9.	ⓐ	ⓑ	ⓒ	ⓓ	59.	ⓐ	ⓑ	ⓒ	ⓓ	109.	ⓐ	ⓑ	ⓒ	ⓓ
10.	ⓐ	ⓑ	ⓒ	ⓓ	60.	ⓐ	ⓑ	ⓒ	ⓓ	110.	ⓐ	ⓑ	ⓒ	ⓓ
11.	ⓐ	ⓑ	ⓒ	ⓓ	61.	ⓐ	ⓑ	ⓒ	ⓓ	111.	ⓐ	ⓑ	ⓒ	ⓓ
12.	ⓐ	ⓑ	ⓒ	ⓓ	62.	ⓐ	ⓑ	ⓒ	ⓓ	112.	ⓐ	ⓑ	ⓒ	ⓓ
13.	ⓐ	ⓑ	ⓒ	ⓓ	63.	ⓐ	ⓑ	ⓒ	ⓓ	113.	ⓐ	ⓑ	ⓒ	ⓓ
14.	ⓐ	ⓑ	ⓒ	ⓓ	64.	ⓐ	ⓑ	ⓒ	ⓓ	114.	ⓐ	ⓑ	ⓒ	ⓓ
15.	ⓐ	ⓑ	ⓒ	ⓓ	65.	ⓐ	ⓑ	ⓒ	ⓓ	115.	ⓐ	ⓑ	ⓒ	ⓓ
16.	ⓐ	ⓑ	ⓒ	ⓓ	66.	ⓐ	ⓑ	ⓒ	ⓓ	116.	ⓐ	ⓑ	ⓒ	ⓓ
17.	ⓐ	ⓑ	ⓒ	ⓓ	67.	ⓐ	ⓑ	ⓒ	ⓓ	117.	ⓐ	ⓑ	ⓒ	ⓓ
18.	ⓐ	ⓑ	ⓒ	ⓓ	68.	ⓐ	ⓑ	ⓒ	ⓓ	118.	ⓐ	ⓑ	ⓒ	ⓓ
19.	ⓐ	ⓑ	ⓒ	ⓓ	69.	ⓐ	ⓑ	ⓒ	ⓓ	119.	ⓐ	ⓑ	ⓒ	ⓓ
20.	ⓐ	ⓑ	ⓒ	ⓓ	70.	ⓐ	ⓑ	ⓒ	ⓓ	120.	ⓐ	ⓑ	ⓒ	ⓓ
21.	ⓐ	ⓑ	ⓒ	ⓓ	71.	ⓐ	ⓑ	ⓒ	ⓓ	121.	ⓐ	ⓑ	ⓒ	ⓓ
22.	ⓐ	ⓑ	ⓒ	ⓓ	72.	ⓐ	ⓑ	ⓒ	ⓓ	122.	ⓐ	ⓑ	ⓒ	ⓓ
23.	ⓐ	ⓑ	ⓒ	ⓓ	73.	ⓐ	ⓑ	ⓒ	ⓓ	123.	ⓐ	ⓑ	ⓒ	ⓓ
24.	ⓐ	ⓑ	ⓒ	ⓓ	74.	ⓐ	ⓑ	ⓒ	ⓓ	124.	ⓐ	ⓑ	ⓒ	ⓓ
25.	ⓐ	ⓑ	ⓒ	ⓓ	75.	ⓐ	ⓑ	ⓒ	ⓓ	125.	ⓐ	ⓑ	ⓒ	ⓓ
26.	ⓐ	ⓑ	ⓒ	ⓓ	76.	ⓐ	ⓑ	ⓒ	ⓓ	126.	ⓐ	ⓑ	ⓒ	ⓓ
27.	ⓐ	ⓑ	ⓒ	ⓓ	77.	ⓐ	ⓑ	ⓒ	ⓓ	127.	ⓐ	ⓑ	ⓒ	ⓓ
28.	ⓐ	ⓑ	ⓒ	ⓓ	78.	ⓐ	ⓑ	ⓒ	ⓓ	128.	ⓐ	ⓑ	ⓒ	ⓓ
29.	ⓐ	ⓑ	ⓒ	ⓓ	79.	ⓐ	ⓑ	ⓒ	ⓓ	129.	ⓐ	ⓑ	ⓒ	ⓓ
30.	ⓐ	ⓑ	ⓒ	ⓓ	80.	ⓐ	ⓑ	ⓒ	ⓓ	130.	ⓐ	ⓑ	ⓒ	ⓓ
31.	ⓐ	ⓑ	ⓒ	ⓓ	81.	ⓐ	ⓑ	ⓒ	ⓓ	131.	ⓐ	ⓑ	ⓒ	ⓓ
32.	ⓐ	ⓑ	ⓒ	ⓓ	82.	ⓐ	ⓑ	ⓒ	ⓓ	132.	ⓐ	ⓑ	ⓒ	ⓓ
33.	ⓐ	ⓑ	ⓒ	ⓓ	83.	ⓐ	ⓑ	ⓒ	ⓓ	133.	ⓐ	ⓑ	ⓒ	ⓓ
34.	ⓐ	ⓑ	ⓒ	ⓓ	84.	ⓐ	ⓑ	ⓒ	ⓓ	134.	ⓐ	ⓑ	ⓒ	ⓓ
35.	ⓐ	ⓑ	ⓒ	ⓓ	85.	ⓐ	ⓑ	ⓒ	ⓓ	135.	ⓐ	ⓑ	ⓒ	ⓓ
36.	ⓐ	ⓑ	ⓒ	ⓓ	86.	ⓐ	ⓑ	ⓒ	ⓓ	136.	ⓐ	ⓑ	ⓒ	ⓓ
37.	ⓐ	ⓑ	ⓒ	ⓓ	87.	ⓐ	ⓑ	ⓒ	ⓓ	137.	ⓐ	ⓑ	ⓒ	ⓓ
38.	ⓐ	ⓑ	ⓒ	ⓓ	88.	ⓐ	ⓑ	ⓒ	ⓓ	138.	ⓐ	ⓑ	ⓒ	ⓓ
39.	ⓐ	ⓑ	ⓒ	ⓓ	89.	ⓐ	ⓑ	ⓒ	ⓓ	139.	ⓐ	ⓑ	ⓒ	ⓓ
40.	ⓐ	ⓑ	ⓒ	ⓓ	90.	ⓐ	ⓑ	ⓒ	ⓓ	140.	ⓐ	ⓑ	ⓒ	ⓓ
41.	ⓐ	ⓑ	ⓒ	ⓓ	91.	ⓐ	ⓑ	ⓒ	ⓓ	141.	ⓐ	ⓑ	ⓒ	ⓓ
42.	ⓐ	ⓑ	ⓒ	ⓓ	92.	ⓐ	ⓑ	ⓒ	ⓓ	142.	ⓐ	ⓑ	ⓒ	ⓓ
43.	ⓐ	ⓑ	ⓒ	ⓓ	93.	ⓐ	ⓑ	ⓒ	ⓓ	143.	ⓐ	ⓑ	ⓒ	ⓓ
44.	ⓐ	ⓑ	ⓒ	ⓓ	94.	ⓐ	ⓑ	ⓒ	ⓓ	144.	ⓐ	ⓑ	ⓒ	ⓓ
45.	ⓐ	ⓑ	ⓒ	ⓓ	95.	ⓐ	ⓑ	ⓒ	ⓓ	145.	ⓐ	ⓑ	ⓒ	ⓓ
46.	ⓐ	ⓑ	ⓒ	ⓓ	96.	ⓐ	ⓑ	ⓒ	ⓓ	146.	ⓐ	ⓑ	ⓒ	ⓓ
47.	ⓐ	ⓑ	ⓒ	ⓓ	97.	ⓐ	ⓑ	ⓒ	ⓓ	147.	ⓐ	ⓑ	ⓒ	ⓓ
48.	ⓐ	ⓑ	ⓒ	ⓓ	98.	ⓐ	ⓑ	ⓒ	ⓓ	148.	ⓐ	ⓑ	ⓒ	ⓓ
49.	ⓐ	ⓑ	ⓒ	ⓓ	99.	ⓐ	ⓑ	ⓒ	ⓓ	149.	ⓐ	ⓑ	ⓒ	ⓓ
50.	ⓐ	ⓑ	ⓒ	ⓓ	100.	ⓐ	ⓑ	ⓒ	ⓓ	150.	ⓐ	ⓑ	ⓒ	ⓓ

► California Real Estate Sales Exam 3

1. Once a contract is valid, failure to perform as agreed is known as
   a. novation.
   b. an illegal act.
   c. breach.
   d. damages.

2. The legal process of making a real estate document a part of the public records is known as
   a. chain of title.
   b. recording.
   c. title insurance.
   d. acknowledgment.

3. Which of the following does NOT contribute to the stability of a neighborhood?
   a. homogeneous buildings
   b. residences in the path of urban directional growth
   c. many families that have children attending school
   d. a rapid turnover of population

4. Title insurance companies are regulated by the
   a. State Attorney General.
   b. Department of Real Estate.
   c. California Insurance Commissioner.
   d. Secretary of State.

5. Which of the following is not real property?
   a. an easement
   b. mineral rights
   c. lease
   d. growing of trees

6. The balance of the trust fund account must be equal to
   a. the broker's trust fund liability to all owners of the funds.
   b. the original amount deposited.
   c. twice the broker's trust fund liability to all owners of the funds.
   d. the amount owned by at least half of the owners of the funds.

7. How would you best describe a waiver?
   a. a bilateral agreement that returns the parties to the previous position
   b. a bilateral agreement that leaves the parties as they are
   c. a unilateral act that effects the position of both parties to the contract
   d. a revocable act

8. A verbal agreement to sell would be enforceable where
   a. the purchase price is less than $1,000.
   b. each party of the transaction agrees to the deal.
   c. the contract is voidable.
   d. the buyer takes possession, makes a down payment, and improves the property.

9. If threats or duress are applied during the creation of a contract, then the contract is
   a. void.
   b. voidable.
   c. illegal.
   d. unenforceable.

10. Real property is which of the following?
a. land only
b. improvements affixed to the land
c. land, improvements, and chattels
d. land, things affixed to the land, and appurtenances

11. When there is a trust fund shortage, and the disbursement of any of the funds will reduce the balance of the funds in the account to an amount less than the existing aggregate trust fund liability of the broker to all owners of the funds, the broker must
a. close the account.
b. notify all owners of the funds in the account that their funds will be unavailable to them until the account has recovered from the shortage.
c. ask all owners to deposit an equal amount to make up for the shortage.
d. obtain the written consent of every principal who is an owner of the funds in the account.

12. Federal and California laws prohibit discrimination in the sale, rental or use of real property based on all of the following EXCEPT
a. sex.
b. race.
c. religion.
d. smokers.

13. When one person represents another person in a business transaction which law applies?
a. California Criminal Code
b. Business and Professions Code
c. Law of Agency
d. Uniform Relocation Act

14. The test for a fixture includes
a. agreement, relationship, and intent of the parties.
b. method of attachment.
c. adaptability.
d. all of the above

15. The law provides for restrictions used for senior citizen housing developments. The term "senior citizen" is defined as
a. a person 60 years or older or one who is 55 years or older in a senior citizen housing development.
b. a person 62 years or older or one who is 50 years or older in a senior citizen housing development.
c. a person 65 years or older or one who is 50 years or older in a senior citizen housing development.
d. a person 67 years or older or one who is 50 years or older in a senior citizen housing development.

16. An appraiser would most likely use a depth table in appraising which of the following types of property?
a. an apartment building site
b. agricultural land
c. a commercial lot
d. an industrial lot

17. An investor should consider hedging against inflation through
a. insurance annuity.
b. demand deposit.
c. government bonds.
d. equity asset.

18. An advertisement that states "100% financing" must also disclose
- **a.** nothing more about the down payment.
- **b.** the amount of the down payment.
- **c.** the implied down payment.
- **d.** the requirements for 100% financing.

19. The distinguishing characteristic of real property versus personal property is
- **a.** the cost of acquisition.
- **b.** that it is a long term asset.
- **c.** that it is immoveable.
- **d.** all of the above.

20. If there is a transition from a seller's market to a buyer's market, which of the following would be the result?
- **a.** There would be no effect on price.
- **b.** Sale prices would decrease due to an increase in supply and a decrease in demand.
- **c.** Sale prices would increase due to a decrease in supply and an increase in demand.
- **d.** There would be an increase in new construction.

21. In a highest and best use analysis of a site which of the following does NOT apply?
- **a.** marginally productive
- **b.** financially feasible
- **c.** physically possible
- **d.** legally permissible, economically productive

22. If a real estate broker chooses to use any name other than his or her legal name on a card, stationery, or advertising,
- **a.** he or she may do so.
- **b.** he or she must get permission from the Real Estate Commissioner.
- **c.** he or she must file a fictitious business name license in that name.
- **d.** he or she must get a legal name change.

23. Security deposits on rentals owned by a broker are considered
- **a.** trust funds.
- **b.** real property.
- **c.** the personal property of the broker.
- **d.** the property of the tenant.

24. A fiduciary is a person that
- **a.** acts independently of any direction.
- **b.** is acting in a position of trust and confidence.
- **c.** has no obligations to other parties.
- **d.** need not disclose all of the facts if they are considered irrelevant.

25. Of the following industries, which one has the greatest affect on the rise or fall of an area's economy?
- **a.** steel factories
- **b.** American farms
- **c.** garment
- **d.** construction

26. Which of the following is not a physical characteristic of personal property?
- **a.** size
- **b.** shape
- **c.** condition
- **d.** scarcity

27. When a grantor of title to property keeps an easement in a deed for a specific purpose they have created an easement by
  a. necessity.
  b. prescription.
  c. reservation.
  d. voluntary dedication.

28. Swing loans are sometimes referred to as
  a. junior loans.
  b. leasehold loans.
  c. bridge loans.
  d. construction loans.

29. The agent in a real estate transaction may represent
  a. only the seller.
  b. only the buyer.
  c. the seller, the buyer, or both.
  d. only one party to the transaction.

30. Real property can be
  a. deeded.
  b. mortgaged.
  c. assessed.
  d. all of the above

31. A deposit receipt, signed by the buyer but rejected by the seller must be kept by a real estate broker for
  a. three years.
  b. four years.
  c. five years.
  d. six years.

32. An encumbrance that is also considered a lien on real estate can be created by
  a. easements.
  b. zoning regulations.
  c. deed restrictions.
  d. special assessments.

33. The seller agrees in writing to sell the property to the buyer and then the seller refuses to perform. The buyer wants the property, so the buyer needs to bring suit against the seller for
  a. the differences.
  b. compensatory damages.
  c. recision.
  d. specific performance.

34. Which of the following is NOT an acceptable method for describing property in a grant deed?
  a. government survey
  b. metes and bounds
  c. recorded map
  d. common address

35. A broker must exercise reasonable supervision over the activities of his or her salespersons. Reasonable supervision does not include
  a. the establishment of procedures to oversee transactions requiring a real estate license.
  b. the handling of trust funds.
  c. the establishment of procedures to oversee the licensee's time management.
  d. regular and consistent reports of licensed activities of salespersons.

36. As an agent you were told that a 17 year old person (un-emancipated) owns the property you are planning to sell. Your contract to sell is
   a. valid.
   b. enforceable.
   c. laches.
   d. unenforceable.

37. Which of the following statements is true?
   a. All liens are encumbrances.
   b. Judgments are specific liens.
   c. An encroachment is a lien.
   d. A chattel mortgage is a lien on real property.

38. Broker Argento cannot complete his obligation under his listing agreement and assigns the listing to another broker in the area. The listing contract
   a. would be cancelled.
   b. remains unchanged.
   c. continues in effect with the sellers consent.
   d. will terminate upon expiration of its term.

39. A real estate broker is responsible for
   a. familiarizing salespersons with the requirements of federal and state laws relating to the prohibition of discrimination.
   b. organizing regular office meetings to familiarize salespersons with office regulations.
   c. monitoring salespersons' telephone use.
   d. the regular renewal of all salespersons' licenses.

40. Two brokers agree verbally to split the commission on the sale of this property. The verbal agreement is
   a. enforceable.
   b. unenforceable.
   c. void because of the Statute of Fraud.
   d. voidable.

41. An easement created by adverse use is legally acquired by
   a. implication of law.
   b. reservation.
   c. prescription.
   d. express grant.

42. A real estate license is not required for
   a. a real estate assistant.
   b. a loan broker.
   c. a salesperson who makes no sales, but pursues buyers and sellers.
   d. a salesperson who sells only new homes.

43. If the listing agreement does not contain a beginning date the listing becomes effective
   a. upon ratification by the seller.
   b. on the date the listing is signed.
   c. upon execution by the listing broker.
   d. after thirty-days.

44. Tenancy in common directly relates to
   a. a form of ownership.
   b. a form of survivorship.
   c. probate.
   d. partition action.

45. An unlicensed sales assistant may **NOT**
   a. show rental units.
   b. provide information about rental rates and other terms and provisions of a lease or rental agreement, as set out in a schedule provided by the broker.
   c. accept signed leases and rental agreements from prospective tenants.
   d. solicit tenants for broker-owned rentals.

46. A broker sold a home under an oral listing and was paid a commission. Which of the following is true?
- **a.** The sale is voidable.
- **b.** The broker has placed his/her license in jeopardy.
- **c.** The commission must be returned.
- **d.** none of the above

47. The unity of time, title, interest, and possession applies to which form of ownership
- **a.** tenancy in common
- **b.** tenancy in severalty
- **c.** joint tenancy
- **d.** tenancy in partnership

48. Which of the following is NOT an essential element of a grant deed?
- **a.** consideration
- **b.** name of parties
- **c.** granting clause
- **d.** legal description

49. By which method of acquiring property does the community property law apply to a husband and wife during marriage in California?
- **a.** gift
- **b.** inheritance
- **c.** devise
- **d.** purchase

50. Any monetary penalty received by the Department of Real Estate in lieu of suspending a salesperson's license is credited to
- **a.** the Recovery Account of the Real Estate Fund.
- **b.** the Real Estate Commissioner.
- **c.** the broker of record.
- **d.** the License Renewal Fund.

51. The seller defaults on an executed purchase contract. The broker is
- **a.** not entitled to the agreed commission.
- **b.** entitled to the agreed commission on defaults.
- **c.** entitled only to the commission on the close of escrow.
- **d.** entitled to half of the deposits after any expenses are taken out.

52. Graduated payment mortgages (GPM)
- **a.** provide for lower initial payments.
- **b.** have a fixed interest rate.
- **c.** allow buyers to consider their own personal earnings for the future.
- **d.** all of the above

53. A township contains
- **a.** six sections.
- **b.** 18 sections.
- **c.** 25 sections.
- **d.** 36 sections.

54. An efficient market has which of the following characteristics?
- **a.** many governmental restrictions
- **b.** an organized exchange conduit
- **c.** unique products
- **d.** unbalanced supply and demand

55. The term *conventional* means
- **a.** conforming or jumbo loans.
- **b.** government loans.
- **c.** construction loans.
- **d.** adjustable loans.

56. If a licensee is found guilty of violating real estate law, the Real Estate Commissioner may fine the licensee instead of suspending his or her license. The amount of the monetary penalty payable may not exceed
   a. $250 for each day of suspension stayed.
   b. $300 for each day of suspension stayed.
   c. $350 for each day of suspension stayed.
   d. $400 for each day of suspension stayed.

57. A listing agreement between a seller and broker is a contract
   a. for personal services.
   b. that never creates long-term obligations.
   c. that is usually only binding upon the seller.
   d. that cannot be terminated prior to its expiration date.

58. The area of a section is
   a. 1 square mile.
   b. 36 square miles.
   c. 25 square miles.
   d. 100 square miles.

59. Who is exempt from continuing education requirements?
   a. no one
   b. a person who has been a real estate licensee for 30 continuous years in California and is 70 years of age or older
   c. a real estate licensee who is also an attorney
   d. a real estate broker

60. In the metes and bounds legal description, the "bounds" refer to which of the following?
   a. distances
   b. monuments
   c. compass direction
   d. measures

61. Functional obsolescence can result from which of the following?
   a. normal wear and tear from daily use
   b. external influences such as being near an airport
   c. changes in market tastes and demand
   d. none of the above

62. Lenders typically sell all or part of their portfolio, or loan inventory, to
   a. life insurance companies.
   b. secondary market investors.
   c. savings and loan companies.
   d. commercial banks.

63. Limitations or regulations of property under government rights do NOT include
   a. condemnation.
   b. taxation.
   c. escheat.
   d. subornation.

64. A broker receives a full-price offer on a house he/she has listed in accordance with the terms of the listing. Before presenting the offer, another offer is brought to the broker which is less than asking price, but with better terms. The broker should
   a. refuse to accept the offer.
   b. present both offers at the same time.
   c. tell the other broker the property is already sold.
   d. present both offers in the order received.

65. *Disintermedian* refers to
   a. a course in financing.
   b. a decision based on the available facts.
   c. an increase of people's savings within their accounts.
   d. withdrawal of savings.

66. If an applicant for a real estate license has submitted evidence of completion of continuing education but the commissioner finds that the evidence submitted does not qualify, the commissioner may extend the license for
   a. 45 days.
   b. 60 days.
   c. 90 days.
   d. 120 days.

67. A real estate commission is normally based on
   a. loan amount financed.
   b. selling price.
   c. equity within the property.
   d. down payment from the buyer.

68. The taking of private property for public use without compensation is authorized under the principal of
   a. police power.
   b. eminent domain.
   c. condemnation.
   d. escheat.

69. The Recovery Account is a fund of last resort for a consumer who has obtained a final judgment against
   a. an attorney.
   b. an escrow company.
   c. a real estate broker.
   d. a seller.

70. Which of the following does NOT terminate an offer?
   a. The offeree fails to accept the offer within a prescribed time period.
   b. The receiver of the offer fails to fulfill a condition.
   c. The offeror rejects the offer.
   d. The buyer or the seller dies.

71. A licensed broker or salesperson upon whom the power of an agent has been conferred by the listing agent with the principal's authorization is a
   a. client.
   b. fiduciary.
   c. subagent.
   d. trustor.

72. If payment is made by the Department of Real Estate to a creditor from the Recovery Account, the license of the judgment debtor is automatically suspended until he or she
   a. apologizes.
   b. pays a penalty of $250 per judgment.
   c. pays $10,000 per judgment.
   d. pays the amount paid to the creditor plus interest.

73. A buyer signs a real estate purchase contract. The contract states that it is good for three (3) days. One day later, the buyer wishes to revoke the unaccepted offer. Which of the following is true?
   a. The buyer may revoke but is liable for the commission.
   b. The offer is irrevocable and must stand until the seller makes a decision.
   c. The buyer may revoke and recover any deposit given.
   d. The buyer may revoke but will forfeit any deposit given.

74. A property owner wishes to develop an office building on a corner lot which is zoned strictly for residential use. The property owner needs to apply for which of the following?
   a. down zoning
   b. variance
   c. nonconforming use
   d. conditional use permit

75. "Condition and quality of neighboring properties" is an example of which of the five elements of comparison for a sale?
   a. social
   b. terms of sale
   c. location
   d. physical

76. Zoning ordinances usually cover such matters such as
   a. permitted uses of the property.
   b. deed restrictions.
   c. building codes.
   d. the amount of rent charged to tenants.

77. A lease whereby the lessee pays the property tax is probably a
   a. percentage lease.
   b. net lease.
   c. residential lease.
   d. sandwich lease.

78. As a violation of real estate law, false promise is
   a. a false statement about what someone is going to do in the future.
   b. a false statement of fact.
   c. a false statement about something in the past.
   d. a false sworn statement.

79. Units of comparison used in the valuation of residential income properties include which of the following?
   a. price per square foot
   b. price per unit
   c. gross income multiplier
   d. all of the above

80. Most of the money used today for real estate financing comes from
   a. government funding.
   b. mortgage bankers.
   c. accumulated deposits.
   d. treasury bills.

81. Which of the following is considered an environmental hazard?
   a. lead based paint
   b. asbestos
   c. radon
   d. all of the above

82. A real estate broker must obtain a written authorization to sell from a business owner
   a. before advertising the property.
   b. before securing the signature of a prospective buyer.
   c. before showing the property to a prospective buyer.
   d. before offering it for sale to anyone.

83. Subagents have only those powers as given to them by the
   a. fiduciary.
   b. principal.
   c. listing agent.
   d. selling agent.

84. The primary strength of the sales comparison approach to value is that
   a. comparable data is always readily available.
   b. market adjustments are easily calculated.
   c. it is easy to understand and it is a direct reflection of buyers and sellers in the market place.
   d. all of the above

85. Under California law, properties must have
   a. a smoke detector.
   b. all water heaters either anchored or strapped to resist falling.
   c. an energy efficiency calculation.
   d. a termite inspection.

86. When speed and efficiency is needed in order to expedite a home loan, which of the following is most significant?
   a. the loan officer
   b. completeness of the file
   c. the borrower
   d. work loan of the lender

87. Which of the following is NOT one of the three usual ways to terminate an escrow?
   a. complete escrow
   b. implied contract
   c. mutual agreement
   d. court action, interpleader

88. The courts will NOT enforce which of the following private restrictions?
   a. racial restrictions
   b. restrictions against public policy
   c. restrictions that require an illegal use
   d. none of the above

89. A credit report will show to the lender the individual's ability to
   a. handle credit and debt.
   b. determine how many accounts they have.
   c. see which debts have the greatest balance.
   d. determine the number of late payments.

90. As an agent, a real estate broker represents
   a. buyers only.
   b. sellers only.
   c. the interests of his customers.
   d. an interest other than their own.

91. Covenants, conditions and restrictions (CC&Rs) can cover all of the following EXCEPT
   a. signs.
   b. pets.
   c. morals.
   d. landscaping.

92. A real estate broker is most likely to use optical image storage media
  a. to retain and store copies of all listings, deposit receipts, canceled checks, and trust records.
  b. to store copies of trust records only.
  c. to store copies of salesperson's transactions only.
  d. to keep a record of salesperson's activities.

93. All funds handled by escrow agencies must be kept in a/an
  a. impound account.
  b. trust account.
  c. bonded account.
  d. interest bearing account.

94. The gradual buildup of soil by the actions of water is called
  a. avulsion.
  b. erosion.
  c. accretion.
  d. reliction.

95. The direct endorsement program allows the lender to
  a. submit loans to FHA or VA.
  b. obtain the mortgage insurance premium (MIP).
  c. underwrite the transaction without sending it to FHA or VA.
  d. receive insurance premiums if the borrower defaults.

96. For an agent to represent the buyer and seller in a transaction, the broker must gain the consent of
  a. only the owner of the property.
  b. all parties to the transaction.
  c. only the buyer.
  d. only the third party.

97. Most real estate appraisals assignments value which interest?
  a. life estate
  b. leased fee
  c. fee simple
  d. leasehold

98. Littoral rights refer to
  a. non-flowing water.
  b. the underground water table.
  c. water in a flowing river.
  d. irrigation.

99. According to Real Estate Law, an optical image storage must be
  a. kept for two years minimum.
  b. non-erasable "write once, read many" (WORM), and not allow changes.
  c. erasable.
  d. non-printable.

100. When the broker represents the buyer exclusively in a transaction, his obligation to the seller is
  a. not an obligation of any sort.
  b. for an honest and truthful relationship.
  c. a fiduciary duty.
  d. the same duty as the listing broker.

101. New land added to a property can be produced by the process of
   a. accretion.
   b. reliction.
   c. both **a** and **b**
   d. none of the above

102. To obtain a VA loan, veterans must
   a. use their VA form 4506.
   b. secure their DD form 214.
   c. obtain their certificate of eligibility.
   d. obtain their discharge.

103. An escrow is considered to be complete when
   a. all funds have been deposited.
   b. all documents have been executed.
   c. all contingencies have been removed.
   d. all of the terms of the escrow instructions have been met.

104. A deed transfers title at the time of
   a. signing.
   b. acknowledgment.
   c. recording.
   d. delivery.

105. A study of how a subdivision will affect the ecology of the developments' surroundings is known as a/an
   a. negative impact report.
   b. environmental impact report.
   c. preliminary report.
   d. public report.

106. Which of the following is NOT a type of property manager?
   a. individual property manager
   b. individual building manager
   c. portfolio manager
   d. resident manger

107. When a broker represents the buyer and seller as a "dual agent" his obligation to the buyer is
   a. a fiduciary relationship.
   b. that of honesty and fair dealings.
   c. a higher duty than to the seller.
   d. secondary to that owed the seller.

108. A Standard Subdivision contains
   a. five or more improved lots with some areas owned in common.
   b. five or more improved lots with no areas owned in common.
   c. five or more unimproved or improved lots with no areas owned in common.
   d. five or more unimproved or improved lots with some areas owned in common.

109. Property managers usually base their fees
   a. on a flat fee.
   b. on a percentage of the gross rents collected.
   c. on a percentage of the net income.
   d. on a graduated scale.

110. The most reliable method of estimating land value is
   a. sales comparison.
   b. land residual technique.
   c. extraction method.
   d. allocation method.

111. A lender would prefer a deed of trust over the mortgage, why?

    a. Foreclosure is accomplished easily and quickly.

    b. A deed of trust requires less paperwork.

    c. There are no redemption periods.

    d. A deed of trust does not require foreclosure.

112. One of the following is not a step in calculating value using the income approach.

    a. Determine the net annual income.

    b. Deduct from the potential gross income an annual allowance for vacancy factor and rent losses.

    c. Subtract the mortgage payment (debt service) from the gross annual income.

    d. Estimate the potential gross income the property is capable of producing.

113. A Preliminary Title Report normally contains all of the following elements EXCEPT

    a. the name of owner.

    b. a survey of the property.

    c. a list of taxes and bonds.

    d. a list of recorded liens and encumbrances.

114. The tax that allows cities and counties to collect fees for the conveyance of property is known as

    a. sales tax.

    b. property tax.

    c. Documentary Transfer Tax.

    d. Gross Receipts Tax.

115. A sub-lessee could be best described as a(n)

    a. tenant.

    b. assignee.

    c. owner.

    d. assignor.

116. Disclosure laws require a broker to inform a buyer that

    a. the seller has an active life.

    b. someone died within the property seven years ago.

    c. there are persons of color next door.

    d. none of the above

117. The process of calculating the present worth of a property on the basis of its capacity to continue to produce an income stream is called

    a. estimated valuation.

    b. capitalization.

    c. intermediation.

    d. adjusted present value.

118. A licensed broker working as a property manager

    a. must not profit from private contracts at the expense of their owner.

    b. may manage the property to his own advantage.

    c. may not collect rents.

    d. has no obligation to maintain trust funds.

119. What is the simplest form of a business opportunity?

    a. sole proprietorship

    b. corporation

    c. partnership

    d. Real Estate Investment Trust (REIT)

120. Capitalization rates can be derived from

    a. market data sales.

    b. mortgage and equity components and rates.

    c. land and building components and rates.

    d. all of the above

121. Personally, your credit rights fall under which protection?
   a. Equal Credit Opportunity Act
   b. Fair Credit Reporting Act of 1971
   c. The Housing Financing Discrimination Act of 1977
   d. none of the above

122. The seller, Gina, gives her broker Allan an exclusive-agency listing. The seller has a relative, who is another broker, who finds a buyer at a reduced commission. Which of the following is true?
   a. Gina owes Allan his commission.
   b. Gina does not have to pay Allan.
   c. Gina's relative, who is another broker, must split the commission with Allan.
   d. Gina's relative, who brought in the buyer, is required to be paid the commission.

123. The Sales and Use Tax Law is relevant to
   a. the sale of inventory to retail customers in a business.
   b. the sale of real property to someone who is not a citizen of the United States.
   c. the transfer of a retail business which sells tangible personal property.
   d. the transfer of personal property which is incidental to the sale of real property.

124. The capitalization of the net income and deducting the depreciated replacement costs of the improvements gives
   a. the value of the land.
   b. the appraised value of the property.
   c. the depreciation schedule.
   d. none of the above

125. The obligation to prepare and deliver the Transfer Disclosure Statement to the buyer is imposed upon
   a. only the seller.
   b. only the sellers broker.
   c. the seller and the sellers broker.
   d. only the buyers broker.

126. A detailed statement regarding the condition of the property that must be provided to any buyer of one-to-four units by the seller is
   a. the Real Estate Transfer Statement.
   b. the Seller Financing Statement.
   c. the Natural Hazard Disclosure Statement.
   d. the Mello-Roos Disclosure Statement.

127. If the Transfer Disclosure Statement is delivered after the required date, the buyer has how many days after delivery in person to terminate the offer?
   a. one
   b. two
   c. three
   d. four

128. All persons or firms selling personal property in California must secure a permit from the
   a. State Board of Equalization.
   b. Department of Real Estate.
   c. local county tax assessor.
   d. Department of Corporations.

129. Conventional lending for single-family dwellings (1–4 units) is dominated by
   a. banks.
   b. mortgage bankers and brokers.
   c. equity or lines of credit.
   d. seller financing.

130. The Natural Hazard Disclosure Law requires
   a. a seller to inform a buyer if the property is located in an area subject to flooding in a dam failure.
   b. a seller to inform a buyer if the property is located in an area subject to poor air quality.
   c. a seller to inform a buyer if the property is located near a nuclear power plant.
   d. a seller to inform a buyer if the property is located near an airport.

131. An owner dies one month after giving a six-month exclusive right to sell listing. The owner's administrator does not wish to sell the property. Which of the following is true?
   a. The administrator is liable for the commission.
   b. The owner's estate is liable for the commission.
   c. The heirs are liable for the commission.
   d. none of the above

132. When a seller conforms to the requirements of the Natural Hazard Disclosure Law, he or she may make the required disclosures
   a. orally.
   b. through a real estate broker.
   c. on the Transfer Disclosure Statement.
   d. on any disclosure form.

133. The worth of an improvement is what it adds to the entire property's market value, regardless of the actual cost of the improvement. This is an example of
   a. the principles of progression.
   b. the principles of regression.
   c. the principles of anticipation.
   d. the principles of contribution.

134. A real estate broker listed a home for sale. Unfortunately, the broker passed away two-weeks after the listing was signed. The listing agreement would
   a. be terminated.
   b. continue in effect with the heirs.
   c. would require consent of the probate court to be in effect.
   d. for all practical purposes never have existed.

135. There are only four elements of value, all of which must be considered in estimating the worth of a property. Which of the following is NOT one of those elements of value?
   a. price
   b. demand
   c. scarcity
   d. utility

136. The instrument or document used to certify the transfer of title to personal property is a
   a. deed of trust.
   b. bill of sale.
   c. land contract.
   d. quitclaim.

137. An income property sells for $2,000,000 and has an annual net income of $150,000. The overall rate is
  a. 5%.
  b. 13.33%.
  c. 7.5%.
  d. 8.%.

138. A band of investment methods is used to develop a capitalization rate. The first trust deed is for 60% of the purchase price at a rate of 12%. The equity rate is at 6%. What is the indicated rate?
  a. 6.6%
  b. 13.6 %
  c. 9%
  d. 9.6%

139. The Real Estate Settlement Procedures Act covers all of the following types of loans EXCEPT
  a. FHA or VA insured loans.
  b. FNMA eligible loans.
  c. loans from FDIC insured institutions.
  d. second mortgages and trust deeds.

140. Replacement cost estimates are preferred to reproduction cost estimates because they are
  a. more accurate.
  b. more related to the market.
  c. less accurate.
  d. none of the above

141. A broker has recently completed a listing agreement for a small apartment building on the north side of town. Due to her other obligations and lack of knowledge in this area, she decides she cannot adequately represent the parties and would like to cancel the listing. Which of the following is true?
  a. She cannot cancel the agreement as the agent.
  b. She has a fiduciary duty to complete the contract.
  c. She may assign this contract to someone else in her place.
  d. She can renounce the agreement but may be subject to damages.

142. The most widely used method of estimating cost is the
  a. unit-in-place method.
  b. index method.
  c. comparative square foot method.
  d. valuation method.

143. *Hypothecate* means
  a. to give a thing as security without giving up possession.
  b. to sell.
  c. to substitute.
  d. to accept.

144. A buyer's acceptance of a property's condition is
  a. acknowledged by the buyer's signing the offer to purchase.
  b. a contract provision.
  c. determined by his or her taking possession after the close of escrow.
  d. automatic after escrow is opened.

145. A salesperson may receive a commission
   a. anytime a sale is completed.
   b. only from their employing broker.
   c. directly from the seller.
   d. directly from either the buyer or seller.

146. The final indicated value in the sales comparison approach is influenced by
   a. the number and size of the adjustments required.
   b. how the sales data cluster or spread out between high and low extremes.
   c. the range of indicated values.
   d. all of the above

147. When a property is sold "as is"
   a. a seller is not compelled to disclose any adverse conditions of the property.
   b. the seller has a duty to disclose known defects.
   c. a buyer accepts the property in any condition the seller wishes to present it.
   d. a buyer has three years to bring a lawsuit for damages as a result of the seller's lack of disclosure.

148. Seller Kopinski entered into a valid listing agreement with his broker. The broker was able to produce a willing buyer ready to purchase the property under the exact terms of the original listing agreement. Kopinski changed his mind and decided not to sell his property after all. The broker would most likely
   a. be owed no commission.
   b. have earned a full commission.
   c. not be considered the procuring cause.
   d. have to split the commission with the seller.

149. A mortgage broker will handle all of the following EXCEPT
   a. origination.
   b. servicing.
   c. appraisal.
   d. credit checks.

150. A mortgage would be released by
   a. payment in full.
   b. a deed or reconveyence.
   c. satisfaction of the mortgage.
   d. any of the above

▶ Answers

1. **c.** Every contract has specific terms and conditions and required performances, if it is not performed according to the contract as agreed upon, then the contract is breached.
2. **b.** The act of filing documents providing constructive notice in the office of the County recorder is known as recording.
3. **d.** A rapid turnover of population is usually the result of undesirable conditions.
4. **c.** In California, title insurance companies are under the jurisdiction of the Insurance Commissioner.
5. **c.** A lease is moveable or transferable by law and is considered personal property. Easements and mineral rights are used with the land for its benefit. Trees are attached to the land and are thus part of the real estate.
6. **a.** There must be, on deposit, enough funds to pay all owners off at any given time.
7. **c.** A waiver is a voluntary relinquishment of a right. A client or agent can waive rights that are for his/her own benefit. It can be caused by unilateral action or lack of action by one of the parties to a contract, affecting the position of either party or both parties to the contract.
8. **d.** Estoppel is created. Taking possession, paying consideration, and doing the improvements of the property shows agreement and that the contract is valid.
9. **b.** If threats or duress are applied during the creation of a contract, then the contract is voidable. This is the option of the injured party.

10. **d.** Real property consists of the land, that which is attached to the land, and that which is appurtenant to the land (rights such as easements, minerals, oil and gas, etc).
11. **d.** If the broker needs to make a withdrawal from a trust fund and there is a shortage, the broker must have written permission from all owners of funds in the trust.
12. **d.** Smokers are not listed in the law as a protected group.
13. **c.** The representation of another would be considered an agency relationship and would be subject to the Law of Agency.
14. **d.** All choices apply. Remember the memory aid MARIA (method, adaptability, relationship, intent, and agreement).
15. **b.** This is defined by fair housing laws.
16. **c.** Depth tables are most common in commercial lots. Depth-to-width ratio of the lot effect the value of these types of parcels.
17. **d.** Most investors will diversify their portfolio in order to hedge inflation, but most of their assets will be in residential or commercial real estate.
18. **a.** An advertisement that states "100% financing" requires no further disclosures because no down payment is required.
19. **c.** Real property consists of that which is immoveable by law. Real and personal property can have similar acquisition costs and can be long-term assets.
20. **b.** A buyer's market implies a decrease in demand and an increase in supply.
21. **a.** One of the criteria for analyzing "highest and best use" is that the use must be *maximally productive*. Therefore, the answer option that does NOT apply to an analysis is answer choice **a.**

22. **c.** A fictitious business name license in the name of the brokerage is required by the Real Estate Commissioner's Regulations.

23. **c.** Money received by a broker as a security deposit on his or her own rental property is received as an owner, not as an agent, and should not be placed in a trust account.

24. **b.** This is the definition of fiduciary duty under an agency contract.

25. **d.** Building of homes within communities will create a work force and show to all that we are on the road to recovery through growth.

26. **d.** Scarcity is an economic concept, not a physical characteristic. It is part of the law of supply and demand. The other choices are all physical characteristics.

27. **c.** Easements may be created by express grant, prescription, or reservation in a deed.

28. **c.** Sometimes we will attempt to sell one property so that we will have the cash for a second one. But sometimes the original property does not sell, and we have to buy this other property. This is where a swing loan becomes an effect tool.

29. **c.** In California, a licensed real estate salesperson or broker may represent both parties to a transaction.

30. **d.** All of the choices apply to real property.

31. **a.** All real estate contracts must be kept for three years by the broker.

32. **d.** The failure to pay special assessment can result in a lien being placed on the property. Deed restrictions, easements, and zoning regulations are physical encumbrances on the real estate and its use.

33. **d.** The buyer has to force the performance.

34. **d.** A property address may not be exclusive to one particular location and therefore is not considered to be sufficient as a legal description of property.

35. **c.** Salespersons are independent contractors and therefore are responsible for results, not the time they put into producing those results.

36. **d.** The agent should always check the title reports to ensure who the actual owners are of any property. If the person is found to be under age and has not been deemed an adult through a court action (emancipated), then the contract is unenforceable

37. **a.** A lien is a claim or charge upon a property or the title is made a security for payment, hence is it an encumbrance. Judgments create general liens on all real property owned by the judgment debtor, an encroachment is an encumbrance or a form of trespassing on another property, a chattel mortgage is a lien on personal property.

38. **a.** The listing contract is not assignable since it is a personal service contract between the principal and their agent.

39. **a.** A broker must make sure all agents are familiar with fair housing and discrimination laws as required by the Real Estate Commissioner's Regulations.

40. **a.** Since both brokers are licensed, professional, and know the rules, they both get paid. This is the one exception to the Statute of Frauds.

41. **c.** Prescriptive easements are acquired in the same way as ownership of land is acquired by adverse possession, except that no property taxes need to be paid. Easements of necessity (implication of law) are granted by court, easements by express grant or reservations are conveyed by deeds from the owner of the servient tenement.

42. a. An assistant who only makes reservations and takes messages does not need a real estate license.

43. b. If the listing contract does not contain a starting date, it is considered to be effective on the date it was signed by the seller.

44. a. Tenancy in common is a form of ownership. Joint tenancy deals with the right of survivorship. Probate is the court process that provides the legal mechanism to transfer title from the decedent to the decedent's heirs. A partition action is when the courts have the responsibility of selling the property.

45. d. A real estate license is required to solicit rentals.

46. d. Under California law all real estate transactions have to be in written form, in order to be solved in the courts if it comes to this. If the seller pays the prescribed commission and everyone is happy then it stands.

47. c. Only for joint tenancy is the unity of time, title, interest, and possession required.

48. a. Although consideration is normally required for the sale of property to occur, it is not an essential element for a valid deed.

49. d. It applies only by purchase with community property funds. The other methods of acquisition of property allow for the property to remain separate property.

50. a. The Recovery Account is funded by penalty fees.

51. b. An executed contract means that the seller has accepted the terms and conditions and if the broker brings a buyer to meets those standards, and the seller refuses, then the broker is entitled to his/her commission.

52. d. Generally, the interest rate starts at a number of percentage lower than the prevail rate. Over time this will catch up to the current rate. This allows buyers to consider personal future earnings.

53. d. There are 36 sections in a township.

54. b. An efficient market has an organized exchange conduit.

55. a. The term *conventional* encompasses both conforming and jumbo loans. Sometimes a lender will call jumbo loans non-conforming loans.

56. a. The Real Estate Commissioner has the option of suspending a licensee's license or requiring a penalty in money to be paid by the licensee as found in the Business and Professions Code.

57. a. A listing agreement is first and foremost an agency agreement between the seller and agent for personal services.

58. a. A section measures one mile by one mile.

59. b. All licensees must renew their real estate license every four years with the exception of someone holding a real estate license 30 years and who is over the age of 70.

60. b. The bounds are either monuments or landmarks and return to the starting point. The metes and bounds description start at a well mark point for the start and follows boundaries of land by courses and metes (measures, distances, or a compass direction).

61. c. Functional obsolescence results when a component of a structure (floor plan, size, etc.) does not conform to current market tastes.

62. b. In order to keep money within the market place, lenders need to sell off the loans that they make, so they look toward secondary market investors.

63. **d.** A clause found in a Mortgage or Trust Deed allows it to be secondary to a later recorded mortgage or trust deed.

64. **b.** A real estate professional has a fiduciary responsibility to submit all offers at the same time.

65. **d.** Historically, when the stock market is not producing enough return for individuals, they pull their assets from their savings accounts and invest within real estate.

66. **c.** The Real Estate Commissioner may extend a real estate license for 90 days while the licensee appeals the suspension of the license as found in the Business and Professions Code.

67. **b.** It does not matter what the listing price is, it only matters what one is willing to pay for the particular property. The commission is based on the selling price.

68. **a.** In the case of an emergency such as a spreading fire, the government under police power could destroy private property and not be liable for any compensation. Eminent domain is the power of the government to take land for public use upon payment of just compensation. Condemnation is the notice given by the government for eminent domain. Escheat is the legal process where by the title of property owned by a deceased person is reverted to the state due to lack of heirs.

69. **c.** The Recovery Account is a separate account in the Real Estate Fund established for the purpose of carrying out the provisions of the Real Estate Law regarding awards to consumers based on fraud, misrepresentation, deceit, or conversion of trust funds by real estate brokers.

70. **c.** The offeror is the maker of the offer, whereas the offeree is the receiver of the offer. It is not likely that the offeror will make and reject their own offer. It is possible for the offeror to rescind their offer before delivery of the offeree's acceptance. All the other choices would terminate an offer.

71. **c.** This is the definition of a subagency under a standard listing agreement.

72. **d.** A judgment debtor who filed a timely response to the Department of Real Estate may file a writ of mandamus to challenge the suspension of his or her license.

73. **c.** The buyer may revoke an offer and recover any deposit given any time before the delivery of acceptance of the offer by the seller.

74. **c.** The office building is a commercial use, which is a nonconforming use since the lot is zoned only for residential uses. A conditional use permit could apply if some commercial uses were allowed in residential codes. Variances tend to apply to setbacks and height limitations while down zoning lowers the intensity of the permitted uses.

75. **c.** The location of a property is affected by the condition and quality of its neighbors.

76. **a.** Permitted uses of a property fall under the zoning code. Deed restrictions and subdivision covenants are private, not public, restrictions. The rent charged to tenants is between the landlord and the tenant.

77. **b.** The tenant agrees to share in the expenses of the rented property, which generally means the market rent is less than what is normal.

78. **a.** A false promise may be used to influence or persuade one to action. If the promise is untrue or false, then it is a violation of California Real Estate Law.

79. **d.** Price per square foot, price per unit, and gross income multiplier are all units of comparison used in residential income property.

80. **c.** As depositors accumulate savings, these funds are available by the deposit institution for mortgage and trust deed loans either directly, or indirectly.

81. **d.** All of the choices are environmental hazards and are listed in the Buyers Inspection Advisory of the BIA-11, Page 2, from the California Association of Realtors (CAR).

82. **b.** Brokers must obtain a written authorization to sell from a business owner before securing the signature of a prospective purchaser to any such agreement, according to section 10176j of the Real Estate Law.

83. **c.** The listing agent confers authority onto a subagent by virtue of the agreement entered into with the seller.

84. **c.** Comparable data is not always available, and market adjustments are sometimes very difficult to quantify.

85. **b.** As of January 1, 1996 California law required that water heaters be strapped or braced. Every single family home sold must have a smoke detector. Energy efficiency calculations are required for new construction. A termite inspection is required by a lender in the sale of a residential property.

86. **b.** The more complete the loan file is prior to getting to the underwriter, the quicker and more efficiently the underwriter can come to a decision of approval or not.

87. **b.** An implied contract is not a method for terminating an escrow, while the other three given choices are.

88. **d.** All of the choices are against the law or public policy, and so are not enforceable by the courts. In fact, the courts would declare these restrictions illegal.

89. **a.** Lenders need to determine if the individual has the ability or the capacity of pay his or her debts; a credit report is used to make this assessment.

90. **d.** The agent's primary duty and responsibility is to represent the interests of their principal.

91. **c.** Morals fall under police power, which is a government control. All of the other choices fall under CC&Rs.

92. **a.** Optical storage systems consist of hardware, software (to control and manage scanning, compression, storage, indexing, search, retrieval, display, and distribution), storage medium (eg. disk), and scanner and disk drives on which the storage medium can be mounted and read.

93. **b.** Along with an annual audit of their books, escrow holders must keep all funds in trust accounts.

94. **c.** Accretion is the gradual buildup of soil by the actions of water. Avulsion is the loss of land through erosion by water. Reliction is the taking of title to adjacent land created by the withdrawal of water from a lake, sea, or river.

95. **c.** Under the direct underwriting endorsement program, applications for loans can be underwritten by lenders who certify that the trust deed complies with FHA or VA standards. FHA or VA may still suffer from the risks of loss from a default, but they can also remove the lender from the program if they find them to be incompetent in their underwriting. The direct endorsement program allows lenders to directly place loans without having to go through the more formal bureaucracy.

96. b. Under a dual agency, a broker is required to obtain the consent of all parties to the transaction including any third parties that may be involved.

97. c. The fee simple interest is the most common interest valued.

98. a. Littoral rights are the rights of property owners bordering lakes, seas, or oceans (non-flowing water) to a reasonable use of the water. Surface water rights (underground water table) depend on whether the water is flowing in a defined channel. Irrigation is used for the watering of crops and plants.

99. b. An optical disk is the most common type of optical storage medium. There are several types of optical disks: WORM disks (Write Once, Read Many), erasable (or rewritable) disks, magneto disks, and CD-ROM. WORM disks are blank when purchased and allow the user to record information on them. Once the information has been recorded it cannot be removed or altered. Rewritable disks enable the user to record information on a disk, erase it, and then replace it with new data. CD-ROMs contain pre-recorded information that cannot be changed or appended by the user.

100. b. As an exclusive agent for the buyer, an agent has a fiduciary duty. As to other parties including the seller he must maintain truthful and honest dealings.

101. c. Accretion is the gradual buildup of soil deposited from water. Reliction is the taking of title to adjacent land created by the withdrawal of water from a lake, sea, or river.

102. c. When a veteran is honorably discharged from the military, he or she is entitled to military benefits. One of those benefits is buying a home, which the certificate of eligibility says that the veteran is approved to receive. Most veterans believe their DD 214 *is* their certificate of eligibility because they never see the rest of the process. The DD 214 is necessary to authorize issuance of the Certificate of Eligibility.

103. d. Although escrow does require all of the first three answers to be completed, the escrow instructions must be complied with before escrow is considered completed.

104. d. Historically, landowners would gather a handful of soil and hand it over to the new owner and this was the symbolic gesture, nowadays the deed is delivered in escrow.

105. b. An EIR is normally required by the local city or county where a new development is located.

106. c. A portfolio manager deals with financial investments.

107. a. When an agent is acting as a dual agent for the buyer and seller, a fiduciary duty is owed to both and must be revealed to all parties to the transaction.

108. c. A Standard Subdivision consists of five or more unimproved or improved lots with no areas owned in common.

109. b. Gross rent is the entire income earned by the property before expenses are paid.

110. a. The sales comparison approach is the most reliable method for valuing land.

111. a. When a lender takes back the deed of trust through foreclosure, the process takes three months and 21 days, after which the lender will be able to sell the foreclosed property to someone else. There is no redemption period after foreclosure, therefore title can be granted to the new buyer immediately.

112. c. The formula for calculating value using the income approach is to divide the net annual income by the capitalization rate. The debt service is not considered in calculating the value.

113. b. A preliminary title report does include a legal description of the property, however it does not normally include a survey of the property.

114. c. The Documentary Transfer Tax Act allows the county recorder to collect revenues from the recordation of real estate documents.

115. a. A tenant can be the tenant or the tenant could sub-lease the space to another person, but they are still called tenants.

116. d. As a licensed real estate person, we are required to disclose many things as they relate to the property in question, but we are not allowed to judge anyone's life style and most definitely should not communicate this to a prospected buyer.

117. b. Capitalization is the mathematical process of estimating the present value of income property based on the amount of anticipated annual net income it will produce.

118. a. As a property manager, the licensee is acting in the capacity as an agent and may not make a secret profit at the expense of the principal.

119. a. Sole proprietorship is ownership by a single person and therefore is the least complex form of business ownership.

120. d. Capitalization rates can be derived from market data sales, mortgage and equity components and rates, and land and building components and rates. The last two choices are used in band of investment calculations for capitalization rates.

121. b. You are protected by the use of treating everyone equally.

122. a. Under an exclusive agency listing, the seller may sell the property without paying a commission to the listing agent. However, because another broker sold the property, a commission is due to Allan. How Allan and the other broker split that commission is of no concern to the seller.

123. c. The Sales and Use Tax Law protects a buyer of a business from a successor's liability by confirming the payment of state and local sales taxes by the seller of the business; releases sales liens against the property or provides a subordination agreement regarding those liens; and describes the tax liability on that portion of the sale price allocated to the personal property to be used in the business.

124. a. The capitalization of the net income gives the value of the property. Subtracting the value of the improvements from this yields the land value.

125. c. There are some exceptions under the Civil Code, however, normally the responsibility is considered to be shared by the seller and their broker.

126. a. the Real Estate Transfer Statement is meant to disclose facts about a residential property that could materially affect its value and desirability; the Seller Financing Statement is used when the seller carries back a note and trust deed; the Natural Hazard Disclosure Statement deals with geological conditions that would affect the value of a property; the Mello-Roos Disclosure Statement discloses the existence of a community facilities district, the issuance of bonds, and the levying of special taxes which finance certain public facilities and services.

127. c. The Transfer Disclosure Statement (TDS) must be given to a prospective buyer before execution of the sales contract or offer to purchase. If it is not, then the buyer has three days if the TDS is delivered in person, or five days after delivery by deposit in the U.S. mail, to terminate the agreement to purchase.

128. a. The Board of Equalization issues the permits in California and a separate permit is required for each place of business.

129. b. Mortgage bankers and brokers hold a greater share of the residential, conventional lending market than the runner up—Savings and Loan Institutions, which do a greater share of non-conventional loans.

130. a. Six disclosures are required under the Natural Hazard Disclosure Law. Four of the six are already required by law; disclosures regarding earthquake fault zone, seismic hazard zone, flood hazard area, or state-responsibility fire area. The two newest disclosures regard flooding in a dam failure or a very high fire hazard severity zone.

131. d. A contract is with one person and if this person is not available because of death, then the contract is unenforceable.

132. c. Disclosures may be made on a Natural Hazard Disclosure Statement (NHDS) or the Transfer Disclosure Statement.

133. d. The principles of contribution should be kept in mind by homeowners who want to change the character of their house in such a way that it no longer fits in the neighborhood. The cost of the improvement may not add to the value if the house is overbuilt for the area.

134. a. Whenever one party to an agency contract is not mentally or physically able to complete the agency relationship (personal service contract), it is terminated.

135. a. The four elements of value are: demand, utility, scarcity, and transferability.

136. b. The bill of sale is to personal property as the deed is to real estate when transferring legal ownership.

137. c. Use the formula $V = \frac{I}{R}$ which implies $R = \frac{V}{I} = \frac{\$150,000}{\$2,000,000} = 0.075 = 7.5\%$.

138. d. The indicated rate is calculated from a weighted average of the two rates $(0.6 \times 0.12) + (0.4 \times 0.06) = 0.096 = 9.6\%$.

139. d. Under RESPA, junior mortgages, such as home improvement loans, are exempt from the consumer notification provisions of the act.

140. b. Replacement costs relate more to the market than reproduction costs for most properties.

141. d. The broker can refuse to fulfill her obligations under the listing agreement, but may be subject to damages for breach of contract.

142. c. The comparative square foot method is the most widely used method of estimating cost.

143. a. Sometimes we are able to lien the property without changing possession and we do this by using the term *hypothecate*.

144. b. A buyer and seller must agree in the original offer to purchase regarding the provisions of the buyer's acceptance of the condition of the property.

145. b. A salesperson may only receive compensation for real estate transactions from their employing broker and must hold a valid real estate license.

146. d. The range of indicated values, the number and size of the adjustments, and the cluster or spread of sales data between the low and high extremes are applicable in the sales comparison approach.

147. b. Selling property "as is" does not negate the buyer's right to disapprove the condition of the property after inspection, nor does it negate the seller's duty to disclose known defects or make other required disclosures.

148. b. If an offer meets the exact terms of the listing, the agent has normally earned a commission, even if the owner refuses to sell to the buyer.

149. b. Generally, mortgage brokers do not use their own funds, so they will not do the servicing of their own loans.

150. d. A mortgage would be released by payment in full, a deed or reconveyence, or satisfaction of the mortgage.

Scoring

Again, evaluate how you did on this practice exam by finding the number of questions you got right, disregarding, for the moment, the ones you got wrong or skipped. If you achieve a score of at least 105 questions correct, you will most likely pass the California Real Estate Sales Exam.

If you did not score as well as you would like, ask yourself the following: Did I run out of time before I could answer all the questions? Did I go back and change my answers from right to wrong? Did I get flustered and sit staring at a difficult question for what seemed like hours? If you had any of these problems, be sure to go over the LearningExpress Test Preparation System in Chapter 2 to review how best to avoid them.

You probably have seen improvement from your first two practice exam scores and this one; but if you didn't improve as much as you would like, following are some options:

If you scored below the passing scores on each section, you should seriously consider whether you are ready for the exam at this time. A good idea would be to take some brush-up courses in the areas you feel less sure of. If you don't have time for a course, you might try private tutoring.

If you score close to the minimum passing score, you need to work as hard as you can to improve your skills. Go back to your real estate license course textbooks to review the knowledge you need to do well on the exam. If math is your problem area, check out the LearningExpress book, *Practical Math Success in 20 Minutes a Day.* Also, re-read and pay close attention to the information in Chapter 4, California Real Estate Refresher Course; Chapter 5, Real Estate Math Review; and Chapter 6, Real Estate Glossary. It might be helpful, as well, to ask friends and family to make up mock test questions and quiz you on them.

If you scored well above the minimum passing scores on each section, that's great! You have an excellent chance of passing your exam. Don't lose your edge, though; keep studying right up to the day before the exam.

Now, revise your study schedule according to the time you have left, emphasizing those parts that gave you the most trouble this time. Use the table on the next page to see where you need more work, so that you can concentrate your preparation efforts. After working more on the subject areas that give you problems, take the fourth practice exam in Chapter 9 to see how much you have improved.

EXAM 3 FOR REVIEW

Subject Area	Question Numbers
Property Ownership and Land Use Controls and Regulation	5, 10, 14, 19, 26, 30, 32, 37, 41, 44, 47, 49, 53, 58, 60, 63, 68, 74, 76, 81, 85, 88, 91, 94, 98, 101, 108
Laws of Agency	13, 24, 29, 38, 43, 57, 71, 83, 90, 96, 100, 107, 118, 125, 134, 141, 145, 148
Valuation and Market Analysis	3, 16, 20, 21, 54, 61, 75, 79, 84, 97, 110, 120, 124, 137, 138, 140, 142, 146
Financing	7, 17, 25, 28, 52, 55, 62, 65, 80, 86, 89, 95, 102, 104, 111, 116, 121, 128, 149
Transfer of Property	2, 4, 27, 34, 48, 87, 93, 103, 105, 113, 114, 128, 136, 139
Practice of Real Estate and Mandatory Disclosures	6, 11, 12, 15, 18, 22, 23, 31, 35, 39, 42, 45, 50, 56, 59, 66, 69, 72, 78, 82, 92, 99, 106, 109, 112, 117, 119, 123, 126, 127, 130, 132, 133, 135, 144, 147
Contracts	1, 8, 9, 33, 36, 40, 46, 51, 64, 67, 70, 73, 77, 115, 122, 131, 143, 150

9 ▶ California Real Estate Sales Exam 4

CHAPTER SUMMARY

This is the last of the four practice tests in this book based on the California Real Estate Sales Exam. Using all of the experience and strategies that you gained from the other three exams, take this exam to see how far you have come.

THIS IS THE last practice exam in this book, but it is not designed to be any harder than the other three. It is simply another representation of what you might expect on the real test. Just as when you take the real test, there should not be anything here that surprises you. In fact, you probably already know what is in a lot of it! That will be the case with the real test, too.

For this exam, pull together all the tips you have been practicing since the first practice exam. Give yourself the time and the space to work. Since you won't be taking the real test in your living room, you might take this one in an unfamiliar location such as a library. Make sure you have plenty of time to complete the exam in one sitting. In addition, use what you have learned from reading the answer explanations on previous practice tests. Remember the types of questions that caused problems for you in the past, and when you are unsure, try to consider how those answers were explained.

After you have taken this written exam, you should try the computer-based test using the CD-ROM found at the back of this book. That way you will be familiar with taking exams on computer.

Once again, use the answer explanations at the end of the exam to understand questions you may have missed.

► California Real Estate Sales Exam 4 Answer Sheet

1.	ⓐ	ⓑ	ⓒ	ⓓ	51.	ⓐ	ⓑ	ⓒ	ⓓ	101.	ⓐ ⓑ ⓒ ⓓ
2.	ⓐ	ⓑ	ⓒ	ⓓ	52.	ⓐ	ⓑ	ⓒ	ⓓ	102.	ⓐ ⓑ ⓒ ⓓ
3.	ⓐ	ⓑ	ⓒ	ⓓ	53.	ⓐ	ⓑ	ⓒ	ⓓ	103.	ⓐ ⓑ ⓒ ⓓ
4.	ⓐ	ⓑ	ⓒ	ⓓ	54.	ⓐ	ⓑ	ⓒ	ⓓ	104.	ⓐ ⓑ ⓒ ⓓ
5.	ⓐ	ⓑ	ⓒ	ⓓ	55.	ⓐ	ⓑ	ⓒ	ⓓ	105.	ⓐ ⓑ ⓒ ⓓ
6.	ⓐ	ⓑ	ⓒ	ⓓ	56.	ⓐ	ⓑ	ⓒ	ⓓ	106.	ⓐ ⓑ ⓒ ⓓ
7.	ⓐ	ⓑ	ⓒ	ⓓ	57.	ⓐ	ⓑ	ⓒ	ⓓ	107.	ⓐ ⓑ ⓒ ⓓ
8.	ⓐ	ⓑ	ⓒ	ⓓ	58.	ⓐ	ⓑ	ⓒ	ⓓ	108.	ⓐ ⓑ ⓒ ⓓ
9.	ⓐ	ⓑ	ⓒ	ⓓ	59.	ⓐ	ⓑ	ⓒ	ⓓ	109.	ⓐ ⓑ ⓒ ⓓ
10.	ⓐ	ⓑ	ⓒ	ⓓ	60.	ⓐ	ⓑ	ⓒ	ⓓ	110.	ⓐ ⓑ ⓒ ⓓ
11.	ⓐ	ⓑ	ⓒ	ⓓ	61.	ⓐ	ⓑ	ⓒ	ⓓ	111.	ⓐ ⓑ ⓒ ⓓ
12.	ⓐ	ⓑ	ⓒ	ⓓ	62.	ⓐ	ⓑ	ⓒ	ⓓ	112.	ⓐ ⓑ ⓒ ⓓ
13.	ⓐ	ⓑ	ⓒ	ⓓ	63.	ⓐ	ⓑ	ⓒ	ⓓ	113.	ⓐ ⓑ ⓒ ⓓ
14.	ⓐ	ⓑ	ⓒ	ⓓ	64.	ⓐ	ⓑ	ⓒ	ⓓ	114.	ⓐ ⓑ ⓒ ⓓ
15.	ⓐ	ⓑ	ⓒ	ⓓ	65.	ⓐ	ⓑ	ⓒ	ⓓ	115.	ⓐ ⓑ ⓒ ⓓ
16.	ⓐ	ⓑ	ⓒ	ⓓ	66.	ⓐ	ⓑ	ⓒ	ⓓ	116.	ⓐ ⓑ ⓒ ⓓ
17.	ⓐ	ⓑ	ⓒ	ⓓ	67.	ⓐ	ⓑ	ⓒ	ⓓ	117.	ⓐ ⓑ ⓒ ⓓ
18.	ⓐ	ⓑ	ⓒ	ⓓ	68.	ⓐ	ⓑ	ⓒ	ⓓ	118.	ⓐ ⓑ ⓒ ⓓ
19.	ⓐ	ⓑ	ⓒ	ⓓ	69.	ⓐ	ⓑ	ⓒ	ⓓ	119.	ⓐ ⓑ ⓒ ⓓ
20.	ⓐ	ⓑ	ⓒ	ⓓ	70.	ⓐ	ⓑ	ⓒ	ⓓ	120.	ⓐ ⓑ ⓒ ⓓ
21.	ⓐ	ⓑ	ⓒ	ⓓ	71.	ⓐ	ⓑ	ⓒ	ⓓ	121.	ⓐ ⓑ ⓒ ⓓ
22.	ⓐ	ⓑ	ⓒ	ⓓ	72.	ⓐ	ⓑ	ⓒ	ⓓ	122.	ⓐ ⓑ ⓒ ⓓ
23.	ⓐ	ⓑ	ⓒ	ⓓ	73.	ⓐ	ⓑ	ⓒ	ⓓ	123.	ⓐ ⓑ ⓒ ⓓ
24.	ⓐ	ⓑ	ⓒ	ⓓ	74.	ⓐ	ⓑ	ⓒ	ⓓ	124.	ⓐ ⓑ ⓒ ⓓ
25.	ⓐ	ⓑ	ⓒ	ⓓ	75.	ⓐ	ⓑ	ⓒ	ⓓ	125.	ⓐ ⓑ ⓒ ⓓ
26.	ⓐ	ⓑ	ⓒ	ⓓ	76.	ⓐ	ⓑ	ⓒ	ⓓ	126.	ⓐ ⓑ ⓒ ⓓ
27.	ⓐ	ⓑ	ⓒ	ⓓ	77.	ⓐ	ⓑ	ⓒ	ⓓ	127.	ⓐ ⓑ ⓒ ⓓ
28.	ⓐ	ⓑ	ⓒ	ⓓ	78.	ⓐ	ⓑ	ⓒ	ⓓ	128.	ⓐ ⓑ ⓒ ⓓ
29.	ⓐ	ⓑ	ⓒ	ⓓ	79.	ⓐ	ⓑ	ⓒ	ⓓ	129.	ⓐ ⓑ ⓒ ⓓ
30.	ⓐ	ⓑ	ⓒ	ⓓ	80.	ⓐ	ⓑ	ⓒ	ⓓ	130.	ⓐ ⓑ ⓒ ⓓ
31.	ⓐ	ⓑ	ⓒ	ⓓ	81.	ⓐ	ⓑ	ⓒ	ⓓ	131.	ⓐ ⓑ ⓒ ⓓ
32.	ⓐ	ⓑ	ⓒ	ⓓ	82.	ⓐ	ⓑ	ⓒ	ⓓ	132.	ⓐ ⓑ ⓒ ⓓ
33.	ⓐ	ⓑ	ⓒ	ⓓ	83.	ⓐ	ⓑ	ⓒ	ⓓ	133.	ⓐ ⓑ ⓒ ⓓ
34.	ⓐ	ⓑ	ⓒ	ⓓ	84.	ⓐ	ⓑ	ⓒ	ⓓ	134.	ⓐ ⓑ ⓒ ⓓ
35.	ⓐ	ⓑ	ⓒ	ⓓ	85.	ⓐ	ⓑ	ⓒ	ⓓ	135.	ⓐ ⓑ ⓒ ⓓ
36.	ⓐ	ⓑ	ⓒ	ⓓ	86.	ⓐ	ⓑ	ⓒ	ⓓ	136.	ⓐ ⓑ ⓒ ⓓ
37.	ⓐ	ⓑ	ⓒ	ⓓ	87.	ⓐ	ⓑ	ⓒ	ⓓ	137.	ⓐ ⓑ ⓒ ⓓ
38.	ⓐ	ⓑ	ⓒ	ⓓ	88.	ⓐ	ⓑ	ⓒ	ⓓ	138.	ⓐ ⓑ ⓒ ⓓ
39.	ⓐ	ⓑ	ⓒ	ⓓ	89.	ⓐ	ⓑ	ⓒ	ⓓ	139.	ⓐ ⓑ ⓒ ⓓ
40.	ⓐ	ⓑ	ⓒ	ⓓ	90.	ⓐ	ⓑ	ⓒ	ⓓ	140.	ⓐ ⓑ ⓒ ⓓ
41.	ⓐ	ⓑ	ⓒ	ⓓ	91.	ⓐ	ⓑ	ⓒ	ⓓ	141.	ⓐ ⓑ ⓒ ⓓ
42.	ⓐ	ⓑ	ⓒ	ⓓ	92.	ⓐ	ⓑ	ⓒ	ⓓ	142.	ⓐ ⓑ ⓒ ⓓ
43.	ⓐ	ⓑ	ⓒ	ⓓ	93.	ⓐ	ⓑ	ⓒ	ⓓ	143.	ⓐ ⓑ ⓒ ⓓ
44.	ⓐ	ⓑ	ⓒ	ⓓ	94.	ⓐ	ⓑ	ⓒ	ⓓ	144.	ⓐ ⓑ ⓒ ⓓ
45.	ⓐ	ⓑ	ⓒ	ⓓ	95.	ⓐ	ⓑ	ⓒ	ⓓ	145.	ⓐ ⓑ ⓒ ⓓ
46.	ⓐ	ⓑ	ⓒ	ⓓ	96.	ⓐ	ⓑ	ⓒ	ⓓ	146.	ⓐ ⓑ ⓒ ⓓ
47.	ⓐ	ⓑ	ⓒ	ⓓ	97.	ⓐ	ⓑ	ⓒ	ⓓ	147.	ⓐ ⓑ ⓒ ⓓ
48.	ⓐ	ⓑ	ⓒ	ⓓ	98.	ⓐ	ⓑ	ⓒ	ⓓ	148.	ⓐ ⓑ ⓒ ⓓ
49.	ⓐ	ⓑ	ⓒ	ⓓ	99.	ⓐ	ⓑ	ⓒ	ⓓ	149.	ⓐ ⓑ ⓒ ⓓ
50.	ⓐ	ⓑ	ⓒ	ⓓ	100.	ⓐ	ⓑ	ⓒ	ⓓ	150.	ⓐ ⓑ ⓒ ⓓ

► California Real Estate Sales Exam 4

1. Which of the following would be considered trust funds?
   a. general operating funds
   b. funds held for the benefit of others in the performance of acts for which a real estate license is required
   c. real estate commissions
   d. rents from broker-owned real estate

2. Which of the following is NOT real property?
   a. shares in a mutual water company
   b. air rights
   c. mineral rights
   d. emblements

3. In a mortgage, the borrower is the
   a. mortgagor.
   b. mortgagee.
   c. endorser.
   d. holder in due clause.

4. An understanding or agreement to do or not to do certain things is called
   a. a contract.
   b. mutual consent.
   c. express agreement.
   d. ratified.

5. A title insurance company's search of the public records would normally include all of the following sources EXCEPT the
   a. Federal Lands Office.
   b. County Clerks Office.
   c. County Recorders Office.
   d. Department of Real Estate.

6. A unilateral contract is and example of a(n)
   a. offer to purchase.
   b. executory.
   c. option.
   d. forbearance.

7. The offeror's earnest money check may be given to the offeree and does not need to be placed in the broker's trust account
   a. only upon written authorization from the offeree.
   b. only upon written authorization from the offeror.
   c. only upon written authorization from both offeree and offeror.
   d. only upon written authorization from the escrow holder.

8. Real property includes which of the following?
   a. mobile homes on wheels
   b. trade fixtures
   c. *fructus naturales*
   d. *fructus industriales*

9. The fiduciary duty created by a listing agreement is most similar to that of
   a. trustee to beneficiary.
   b. trustor to beneficiary.
   c. assignee to assignor.
   d. lessor to lessee.

10. Most mortgage loan originators fall into which group?
    a. mortgage bankers and/or mortgage brokers
    b. mortgage bankers or saving and loans
    c. banks or credit unions
    d. realtors

11. The test for a fixture does NOT include which of the following?
  a. amount the fixture is worth
  b. method of attachment
  c. relationship between the parties
  d. agreement and intent of the parties

12. The laws regarding agency are found in the
  a. Business and Professions Code.
  b. California Civil Code.
  c. Uniform Commercial Code.
  d. California Administrative Code.

13. Three of the most important functions of title insurance include all of the following EXCEPT
  a. a search of the records.
  b. insurance against economic loss.
  c. disclosure of any physical problems with the property improvements.
  d. interpretation of the legality of the records.

14. Redlining, the practice of disapproving real estate loans in economically or physically blighted areas, is particularly prohibited by which of the following Fair Housing Laws?
  a. 1866 Civil Rights Act
  b. California Civil Code
  c. California Fair Employment and Housing Act
  d. Housing Financial Discrimination Act (Holden Act)

15. A person who sets up a business to run, generally will make the business entity a
  a. partnership.
  b. corporation.
  c. sole proprietor.
  d. limited partnership.

16. The security device normally used in California to pledge a property as collateral for a loan is a(n)
  a. judgment.
  b. attachment.
  c. mortgage.
  d. trust deed.

17. The Unruh Civil Right Act applies to which of the following?
  a. hotel rooms
  b. one- to four-unit residential apartment buildings
  c. commercial real estate
  d. mobile home developments

18. A person that employs or hires an agent is known as the
  a. third party.
  b. broker.
  c. principal.
  d. customer.

19. All of the following are ways to terminate a contract EXCEPT
  a. release.
  b. novation.
  c. verification.
  d. rescission.

20. The characteristics of real property include the
  a. right to sell.
  b. right to exclude.
  c. right to use.
  d. all of the above

21. It is unlawful to offer by mail, by telephone, in person, or by any other means, a prize or gift with the intent to offer a sales presentation
   a. without disclosing at the time of the offer of the prize or gift, the intent to offer that sales presentation.
   b. without disclosing at the time of the offer of the prize or gift, the name of the offeror.
   c. without disclosing at the time of the offer of the prize or gift, the time frame of the offer.
   d. without disclosing at the time of the offer of the prize or gift, the dollar value of the prize of gift.

22. Mortgage loan rates and costs are continually adjusting because lenders must
   a. handle understaffed peaks and demand periods.
   b. stay competitive.
   c. offer a variety of programs.
   d. keep the economy running.

23. Can an oral listing agreement be enforced, if it is the broker?
   a. yes, always
   b. no, never
   c. yes, but only if the Real Estate Commissioner approves this transaction
   d. yes, but only if the DRE approves this transaction

24. A developer who wishes to offer subdivision interests in California (other than in a time-share or Qualified Resort Vacation Club) located outside of California but within the United States must
   a. file a special public report with the Real Estate Commissioner.
   b. register the project with the Department of Real Estate and include certain disclaimers in advertising and sales contracts.
   c. be a California resident.
   d. advertise the project both in the state in which it is located and in California.

25. Mr. Blackacre delivers a grant deed to Mr. Smith upon completion of his purchase. Mr. Smith does not choose to record the deed with the county recorder's office. Under these circumstances, the deed would be considered
   a. valid.
   b. invalid.
   c. illegal.
   d. unrecordable after one year.

26. A real estate broker shall have a written agreement with each of his or her salespersons covering all of the following EXCEPT
   a. required hours of employment.
   b. material aspects of the relationship between the broker and salesperson.
   c. supervision of licensed activities.
   d. compensation.

27. The implied warranties regarding title and encumbrances that accompany a grant deed
   a. must be in writing.
   b. need not be in writing.
   c. do not exist until the deed is recorded.
   d. are only contained in a quitclaim deed.

28. Which of the following loans requires a schedule of payments including principle and interest?
   a. term loan
   b. straight loan
   c. amortized loan
   d. balloon loan

29. In order for a contract to be valid, it must be
   a. unilateral.
   b. bilateral.
   c. for a legal purpose.
   d. in writing.

30. Which of the following is a physical characteristic of personal property?
   a. demand
   b. scarcity
   c. condition
   d. utility

31. Personal property CANNOT be
   a. deeded.
   b. hypothecated.
   c. assessed.
   d. willed.

32. Which of the following is NOT a method for creating an agency relationship?
   a. estoppel
   b. novation
   c. ratification
   d. express agreement

33. A licensed real estate broker must retain copies of all listings, deposit receipts, canceled checks, trust records, and other documents executed or obtained by him or her in connection with any transactions for which a real estate broker license is required for
   a. three years.
   b. four years.
   c. five years.
   d. six years.

34. Private mortgage insurance covers what portion of the loan amount?
   a. the upper portion of the loan
   b. the lower portion of the loan
   c. the entire loan
   d. the unused portion of the loan

35. Seller Smith agrees to allow broker Jones to represent him in selling his home. The best method to use as evidence that an agency relationship has been created is by
   a. executed escrow instructions.
   b. acceptance of consideration.
   c. a written listing agreement.
   d. an oral commitment.

36. A real estate broker may delegate the responsibility to supervise the activities of non-licensed persons to a real estate salesperson who has accumulated at least
  a. one year full-time experience as a salesperson licensee during the preceding five-year period.
  b. two years full-time experience as a salesperson licensee during the preceding five-year period.
  c. three years full-time experience as a salesperson licensee during the preceding five-year period.
  d. four years full-time experience as a salesperson licensee during the preceding five-year period.

37. When a contract is approved, it is said that it is
  a. ratified.
  b. understood.
  c. rescinded.
  d. implied agreement.

38. First-time buyer programs sponsored by Fannie Mae or Freddie Mac require
  a. a work history of seven years.
  b. higher qualifying ratios.
  c. an educational seminar.
  d. a fixed rate interest.

39. The responsibility for supervision of salespersons licensed to a corporate broker may be assigned by making reference to
  a. groups of salespersons working for the corporate broker.
  b. the broker who will be assigned the supervision of salespersons.
  c. each salesperson requiring supervision.
  d. a specified business address or address of the corporate broker rather than by listing the names of individual salespersons subject to supervision of the broker officer of the corporation.

40. When the actions or inactions of a principal cause a third party to believe that someone is acting as their agent
  a. an actual agency is created.
  b. an ostensible agency is created.
  c. A principal is never responsible to third parties.
  d. An agency can never be created without a written agreement.

41. Failure to perform a contract is
  a. a novation.
  b. a breach.
  c. no problem.
  d. void.

42. Which of the following allows the liquidity in the real estate market?
  a. PMI
  b. ECOA
  c. CRA
  d. FNMA

43. A monetary encumbrance does NOT include
   a. general liens.
   b. specific liens.
   c. deed restrictions.
   d. special assessments.

44. A broker has just listed a home for sale. The broker receives three offers after the first weekend but does not want to bother the seller with the first two because both contain a very low purchase price. If the broker decides not to advise the seller of the first two offers it would be considered
   a. acceptable, since he does not want to waste the sellers time.
   b. a misstatement of fact.
   c. a violation of law.
   d. collusion.

45. Certain exemptions from licensing requirements are allowed. Which of the following requires a real estate license?
   a. an attorney at law buying and selling real property for his own account
   b. a builder who also markets and sells eight or more properties a year
   c. someone who is in the business of leasing real property and collecting advance fees for the rental of real properties
   d. a receptionist working at a real estate office

46. If the buyer defaults, what percentage of the earnest money deposit that is held in escrow can the seller have under the liquidated damages clause?
   a. 1%
   b. 5%
   c. 3%
   d. 10%

47. Which of the following is normally considered to be the closing date?
   a. the date the documents are recorded
   b. the date the grant deed is executed
   c. the date all contingencies have been removed
   d. the date final escrow instructions are signed and returned

48. A voluntary lien on real property includes a
   a. mortgage.
   b. trust deed.
   c. real estate sales contract.
   d. all of the above

49. A broker has just listed a home for sale with an option to purchase. The broker's first duty is as a/an
   a. principal.
   b. optionor.
   c. optionee.
   d. agent.

50. An unlicensed employee of a property management firm may
   a. negotiate the lease of real property.
   b. negotiate the sale of real property.
   c. accept signed rental agreements from prospective tenants.
   d. accept a commission from a tenant for procuring a rental.

51. In regard to their dealing with third parties, an agent has a duty
   a. equal to that owed their principal.
   b. of honesty and fair dealing.
   c. without obligations.
   d. the same as that of a fiduciary.

52. Real estate demand is predicated by studies of
   a. population.
   b. the national labor force.
   c. disposable income.
   d. all of the above

53. The punishment for an individual falsely claiming to be a broker or salesperson is a fine
   a. up to $10,000 or imprisonment up to six months.
   b. up to $15,000 or imprisonment up to six months.
   c. up to $20,000 or imprisonment up to six months.
   d. up to $25,000 or imprisonment up to six months.

54. Which of the following are considerations of a well-drafted purchase contract?
   a. the date the buyer will take possession of said property
   b. the terms of any financing
   c. the address of the property
   d. all of the above

55. An easement CANNOT be created by
   a. deed.
   b. necessity.
   c. prescription.
   d. adverse possession.

56. Mr. Gonzalez has just agreed to list his duplex for sale with his broker, Mike Smith. As the listing agent, Smith must provide the required disclosure form to the seller
   a. prior to completion of escrow.
   b. prior to entering into a listing agreement.
   c. upon presentation of an offer.
   d. upon completion of the sale.

57. What is the fine for paying a fee to an unlicensed person who performs an act requiring a real estate license?
   a. $50
   b. $100
   c. $150
   d. $200

58. What does CHFA stand for?
   a. California Housing Federal Agency
   b. California Housing Finance Agency
   c. California Housing Finance Association
   d. California Housing Finance Act

59. If rezoning to a different use takes place in a residential neighborhood, it is most often an example of the principle of
   a. change.
   b. highest and best use.
   c. conformity.
   d. substitution.

60. All real estate licenses, except for the initial, conditional salesperson license, are issued for a period of
   a. two years.
   b. three years.
   c. four years.
   d. five years.

61. While in a purchase contract, something beyond your control happens and you cannot perform the contract, what must you do?
   a. Ask that the contract be terminated.
   b. You are in contract, you do not have any other options.
   c. Tear up the contract.
   d. Call your attorney.

62. An escrow holder may be any of the following EXCEPT
  a. a corporation.
  b. a limited partnership.
  c. an attorney.
  d. a real estate broker, acting as an agent to the transaction.

63. Titles to city parks and playgrounds are held in which form?
  a. tenancy in common
  b. severalty
  c. joint tenancy
  d. none of the above

64. A selling agent must disclose to the seller and buyer whether they are acting as a dual agent
  a. as soon as practicable.
  b. prior to accepting a listing agreement.
  c. prior to execution of a sales contract.
  d. no later than the close of escrow.

65. When supply and demand are in balance, value tends to be equal to
  a. the cost of reproduction plus normal profit.
  b. the loan appraisal.
  c. value in use.
  d. the asking price.

66. The Department of Real Estate enforces a federal law which requires all applicants for an original or renewal real estate license to submit proof of
  a. college graduation.
  b. payment of income taxes.
  c. social security status.
  d. legal presence in the U.S.

67. One of the basic rules of the law of agency is that
  a. an agent must disclose all facts to a principal regarding their property.
  b. an agent's first duty is to his customer.
  c. an agent has no obligations to third parties.
  d. a principal is not responsible for the acts of his agent.

68. For payment to an injured party to be made through the Recovery Fund,
  a. the Real Estate Commissioner must decide whether or not the agent is guilty.
  b. the guilty party must have been properly licensed at the time the cause of the action arose and must have been performing acts requiring a real estate license.
  c. the guilty party must admit guilt.
  d. the guilty party must sign a promissory note in favor of the Recovery Fund in which he or she promises to repay the amount given to the injured party.

69. A mature person (age 62 or more) has the ability to access his or her equity through
  a. FNMA.
  b. FHLMC.
  c. RAM.
  d. HOPE.

70. An agent may not gain an interest in the property of their principal without
  a. prior disclosure to the buyer.
  b. an Exclusive Listing Agreement.
  c. signed instructions from escrow.
  d. the principal's prior consent.

71. There are certain time periods in order to file a lawsuit. These are set
  a. by the statute of fraud.
  b. by the statute of limitations.
  c. by probate court.
  d. when time permits.

72. In a joint tenancy form of ownership, the unities required include
  a. time.
  b. title.
  c. interest and possession.
  d. all of the above

73. A portion of real estate license fees is used to
  a. fund continuing education classes.
  b. fund the Recovery Account.
  c. fund the Real Estate Bulletin.
  d. fund the licensing exam.

74. The fiscal policy of government is concerned primarily with
  a. interest rates.
  b. gross national product.
  c. government spending and taxation.
  d. urban development.

75. A purchase and sales agreement was completed between buyer and seller and an escrow was opened. Escrow instructions were executed and returned by both parties. The escrow agent discovered a conflict between the Purchase and Sale agreement and the escrow instructions.
  Which of the following is correct regarding this situation?
  a. The escrow instructions supplement the sales agreement.
  b. The original contract always prevails in disputes.
  c. The escrow instructions are not drawn from information in the sales agreement.
  d. The instructions and sales agreement are never interpreted together.

76. A real estate licensee may represent all parties in the same transaction ONLY
  a. after full disclosure to and with informed consent of all parties.
  b. in transactions of one to four units.
  c. in transactions where the parties each pay a portion of the commission.
  d. if he or she does not disclose the fact to either party.

77. A broker is successful in arranging the sale of her seller's property and has agreed to take back a trust deed as her commission. Accepting a trust deed for the commission is
  a. illegal under the Law of Agency.
  b. acceptable with the seller's prior consent.
  c. outside the jurisdiction of the listing agreement.
  d. an infraction of the Business and Professions Code.

78. When monthly loan payments are late, charges are assessed, and record keeping is required. This illustrates
   a. processing.
   b. servicing.
   c. analysis.
   d. closing.

79. A tenancy in common interest does NOT include
   a. right of survivorship.
   b. equal rights of possession.
   c. right to sell one's interest.
   d. right to pass one's interest by either will or succession.

80. What is the rule for pre-printed contracts?
   a. Handwriting takes precedence over printing.
   b. Printing takes precedence over typing.
   c. Handwriting take precedence over typing and or printing.
   d. all of the above

81. A listing agent received three offers on a property at the same time. What is the ethical conduct regarding presenting the offers?
   a. if the listing agent wrote one of the offers, he or she can present only that offer.
   b. present all offers and let the seller decide which one to accept.
   c. decide which offer is the best one and present that one to the seller.
   d. present his or her own offer as a principal without disclosing the presence of the other offers.

82. The party which is holding bare legal title under a deed of trust is the
   a. title company.
   b. escrow company.
   c. trustee.
   d. trustor.

83. Records stored as optical image files must be retained at least
   a. one year.
   b. two years.
   c. three years.
   d. four years.

84. One of the most important requirements of an optical image storage system that is used in a real estate brokerage is that it is
   a. connected to the Internet.
   b. approved by the Real Estate Commissioner.
   c. non-erasable.
   d. not indexed.

85. Which of the following best describes disposable income?
   a. money spent on recreation
   b. percentage of income spent on housing
   c. income spent on food and shelter
   d. income after personal taxes

86. The NW $\frac{1}{4}$ of the NW $\frac{1}{4}$ of Section 1 contains
   a. 40 acres.
   b. 36 square miles.
   c. $\frac{1}{4}$ square mile.
   d. 120 acres.

87. An agency relationship may be terminated in all of the following manners EXCEPT
  a. agreement.
  b. revocation.
  c. endorsement.
  d. expiration.

88. A tenant may
  a. spend up to one month's rent for repairs, but only twice within twelve consecutive months.
  b. make needed repairs whenever necessary and deduct it from the rent.
  c. use the leased property as security for a personal property loan.
  d. legally occupy the leased property after the lease has expired and a three-day pay or quit notice has been served.

89. Unlawful acts by a landlord include
  a. suing for each installment of rent when it is due.
  b. shutting off utilities.
  c. filing a lawsuit against the tenant for damages.
  d. re-leasing the premises.

90. The ability of a borrower/investor to control a large investment with a small amount of his or her own equity capital and a large amount of other people's money is known as
  a. leverage.
  b. redlining.
  c. yield control.
  d. capitalization.

91. What is the area of a section?
  a. 160 acres
  b. 640 acres
  c. 36 square miles
  d. 43,560 square feet

92. The maximum points, or loan origination fee, that can be charged to the borrower under an FHA program is
  a. 1.0%.
  b. 1.5%.
  c. 2.0%.
  d. 9.5%.

93. Income received from rental units before any expenses are deducted is
  a. net income.
  b. capitalized income.
  c. gross income.
  d. contract income.

94. A person under the age of 18 may enter into a valid contract only if he or she
  a. has been granted permission by his or her parents.
  b. is living on his or her own.
  c. is emancipated.
  d. has a partner.

95. In California, any existing Pest Control Inspection Report is required to be delivered to the buyer by
  a. the escrow agent.
  b. the listing broker.
  c. the selling broker.
  d. the lender.

96. The formal methods of legal descriptions do NOT include
  a. metes and bounds.
  b. the United States Government Survey System.
  c. the lot and block system, or a recorded map.
  d. an assessors parcel number.

97. What agency registers and licenses mobile homes?
  a. Department of Motor Vehicles
  b. Department of Real Estate
  c. Department of Housing and Urban Development
  d. Department of Housing and Community Development

98. An irrevocable listing agreement is entered into between the seller and the broker. Which of the following is most nearly correct regarding the listing?
  a. A listing may not be terminated without mutual consent.
  b. A listing may be terminated at any time by the seller.
  c. A listing must expire by its terms.
  d. An irrevocable agreement is always illegal in California.

99. What law protects a buyer of a business opportunity from liability for unpaid sales tax owed by the seller?
  a. Bulk Transfer Act
  b. Uniform Commercial Code
  c. Civil Code
  d. Sales and Use Tax Law

100. Upon the sale of a condominium, the seller must provide to the buyer all of the following EXCEPT
  a. CC&Rs.
  b. a title insurance policy.
  c. bylaws.
  d. financial statements from the homeowners' association.

101. What transactions are exempt from the obligation of the seller to deliver a Transfer Disclosure Statement?
  a. the sale of one to four units
  b. a foreclosure sale
  c. a lease-option sale
  d. the sale of a single family residence

102. The compensation paid to an owner for "devalued remaining property" as the result of an eminent domain action is known as
  a. just compensation.
  b. liquidation damages.
  c. severance damage.
  d. all of the above

103. The conveyance of land for a public use under statutory or common law is known as
  a. dedication.
  b. eminent domain.
  c. condemnation.
  d. none of the above

104. The age, condition, and any defects or mal-functions of the structural components and/or plumbing, electrical, heating, or other mechanical systems of a structure are disclosed in
  a. the Transfer Disclosure Statement (TDS).
  b. the Structural Components Disclosure.
  c. the Deposit Receipt.
  d. the Mello-Roos Disclosure.

105. The United States Department of Veteran Affairs (referred to as the VA)
  a. guarantees loans made to qualified veteran by approved lenders.
  b. determines the max amount of interest rate to be charged.
  c. acts as the lender in support of the troops.
  d. all of the above

106. How many days does a buyer have to rescind an offer after receiving the Natural Hazard Disclosure Statement that has been hand delivered?
  a. three days
  b. four days
  c. five days
  d. six days

107. In a tax-free exchange (1031), the cash or mortgage relief given in addition to the property is known as
  a. boot.
  b. basis.
  c. hard money.
  d. depreciation.

108. Under the Natural Hazard Disclosure Law, the disclosures must be made
  a. prior to a buyer making an offer.
  b. in a listing.
  c. as soon as practicable before the transfer of title.
  d. upon presentation of an offer.

109. Which of the following is NOT a contract?
  a. an unenforceable contract
  b. an expressed contract
  c. a void contract
  d. a rescinded contract

110. Value that is directed toward a particular use is
  a. market value.
  b. utility value.
  c. commercial value.
  d. residential value.

111. Zoning laws and ordinances do NOT include
  a. permitted uses.
  b. set backs.
  c. height limitations.
  d. insulation requirements.

112. Agent Ling has just closed escrow on the sale of a property. However, a dispute regarding the payment of commissions has occurred. If Ling decides to seek resolution of the dispute the recovery of commissions would be under the jurisdiction of the
  a. Department of Real Estate.
  b. California Attorney General.
  c. Department of Consumer Affairs.
  d. Civil Court.

113. The yearly tax deduction for wear, tear, and obsolescence on real estate investments that may be deducted from the property's income is known as
   a. boot.
   b. property taxes.
   c. prepayment penalties.
   d. depreciation.

114. A lender selling a loan at a ten-point discount would quote a price of
   a. 106.
   b. 95.
   c. 90.
   d. It depends on the lender.

115. An older building has a lot coverage of 75% while the current zoning law allows for only 50% lot coverage. This is an example of a
   a. conditional use.
   b. variance.
   c. nonconforming use.
   d. none of the above

116. John and Paula are just about to close escrow on their new home and the property is demolished. This contract probably is
   a. cancelled because performance is impractical.
   b. fine because insurance will cover the rebuild.
   c. cancelled because performance is impossible.
   d. none of the above

117. Corner influence would most likely have the greatest increase in the value for a(n)
   a. apartment house.
   b. single family home.
   c. office building.
   d. retail building.

118. A property inspector would typically **NOT** detect
   a. encroachments.
   b. water damage.
   c. lead-based paint.
   d. mold.

119. The term secondary market
   a. describes junior liens.
   b. is where loans are made to the borrower.
   c. must involve FNMA, FHLMC, and GNMA.
   d. is the market place where existing loans are bought and sold.

120. When the seller and the buyer agree to cancel the contract, they effect a
   a. release.
   b. novation.
   c. rescission.
   d. verification.

121. The present or anticipated supply of a product in relation to the demand for it is
   a. utility.
   b. subjective value.
   c. objective value.
   d. scarcity.

122. Agreements between brokers regarding commissions may be
   a. written only.
   b. oral or written.
   c. against public policy.
   d. illegal under the Statue of Frauds.

123. Under a deed of trust when a default by the borrower occurs, the trustee records a notice of default on behalf of the
a. trustor.
b. beneficiary.
c. trustee.
d. Title Company.

124. The California Coastal Zone Conservation Act protects which of the following?
a. public access to the coast
b. the coastal zone
c. the marine environment
d. all of the above

125. Federal law keeps track of the lending practices of institutional lenders to insure fair treatment of borrowers, and is monitored by the
a. Home Fairness Act.
b. Department of the Government.
c. Department of Banking.
d. Borrowers and Clients Protection Act.

126. Which of the following is an unenforceable private deed restriction?
a. All lots must be landscaped within one year of occupancy.
b. No homes in the development can exceed two stories high.
c. "For Sale" signs in front of the property are not allowed.
d. All roofs must be made of red tile.

127. Which of the following values has the least relationship to market value?
a. exchange value
b. book value
c. assessed value
d. loan value

128. A comparable sale must be a competitive property. This means the sale location should be
a. one that a potential buyer of subject property would consider.
b. always in the same neighborhood as the subject property.
c. in a slightly lower priced but nearby neighborhood.
d. none of the above

129. Deposits in commercial banks and savings and loan institutions are insured by the
a. Office of Thrift Supervision.
b. Resolution Trust Act.
c. Housing Finance Board.
d. Federal Deposit Insurance Corporation.

130. Covenants, conditions and restrictions (CC&Rs) CANNOT
a. go on forever.
b. exceed public zoning codes.
c. require the performance of lawful acts.
d. be removed by the grantee.

131. When a promise is given by one party and an expectation of performance is expected by the other person, it is known as a(n)
a. bilateral contract.
b. unilateral contract.
c. ratified contract.
d. contract under duress.

132. Appropriation of water allows for the
a. building of dikes prior to a flood.
b. taking or diverting of flowing water on public domain for personal use.
c. taking of non-flowing water.
d. diverting of surface water to an adjoining owner.

133. In order to improve the reliability of the information about a sale, the appraiser should
a. make at least an exterior inspection.
b. identify changes made since the sales date.
c. verify the price and terms of sale.
d. all of the above

134. After a buyer communicates disapproval to the seller after an inspection of the property
a. the buyer must proceed with the transaction regardless of the seller's reaction.
b. the seller must correct the item or the buyer can cancel the transaction.
c. the seller can cancel the transaction.
d. the buyer must pay for any correction of the item or the seller can cancel the transaction.

135. To adjust the sale price of a comparable sale with a 10% better location than the subject property one should
a. add 10% to the sales price.
b. subtract 10% from the sales price.
c. multiply the price by 10%.
d. none of the above

136. The activity of loan brokers are governed by
a. Real Estate Law.
b. Mortgage Loan Disclosure Law.
c. Real Property Loan Law.
d. Real Estate Code.

137. If the site represents 60% of the total value in a particular neighborhood, how much improvement value would be allocated from a $180,000 sale of a single family home?
a. $108,000
b. $72,000
c. $120,000
d. $50,000

138. Riparian rights refer to water flowing in a
a. stream.
b. river.
c. watercourse.
d. all of the above

139. Of the following sales, which would likely be given the most weight in the reconciliation process, where adjustments are made by percentage?
a. location +10, size −10, view 0
b. location +5, size +5, view −5
c. location 0, size −5, view −5
d. location −5, size +5, view +5

140. When a borrower completes all of the payments owed on a real estate loan the trustee is usually requested to record a
a. promissory note.
b. quitclaim deed.
c. full reconveyance.
d. trust deed.

141. The Subdivision Map Act does NOT apply to which of the following?
a. time shares
b. undivided interest
c. whole parcels of fewer than five acres where each new parcel to be created from the division will abut to a publicly maintained road
d. all of the above

142. A house under appraisal is known to have cost $240,000 to build in 1990 and had a cost index of 1.2 in relation to the base year of 1980 (Cost Index = 1.0). The construction cost index in 2004 is 1.8 in relation to the base year. What is the indicated reproduction cost in 2004?
   a. $288,000
   b. $432,000
   c. $200,000
   d. $360,000

143. A buyer can verify a height restriction on a property located in a certain neighborhood by
   a. asking the neighbors.
   b. checking with the city building department.
   c. asking the seller.
   d. checking with the escrow holder.

144. Given a rate = R and an income = I, the value = V of the property is calculated from which formula?
   a. $V = I \times R$
   b. $V = \dfrac{I}{R}$
   c. $V = \dfrac{R}{I}$
   d. $V = R \times I$

145. An office building has an age of 20 years. An appraiser inspects the property and estimates an effective age of 10 years. The building has a life expectancy of 50 years. How much has the building depreciated?
   a. 20%
   b. 40%
   c. 60%
   d. 15%

146. In the income approach to value, one needs to determine the net operating income (NOI). Which of the following items is NOT considered in determining the NOI?
   a. vacancy factor
   b. management fees
   c. utilities
   d. debt service

147. Before a loan can be made, a loan broker must provide an applicant with
   a. a final closing statement.
   b. a deposit receipt.
   c. a mortgage loan disclosure statement.
   d. a short-term disclosure statement.

148. A property was valued at $400,000 with a 5% capitalization rate. An investor wants an 8% return on his money. What price should the investor pay to buy this property and get an 8% return?
   a. $270,000
   b. $187,500
   c. $250,000
   d. $640,000

149. Which of the following does NOT apply in condominium projects?
   a. If the condominium association carries liability insurance greater than the statutory amount, an owner can be held liable for tort injury relating to the common area.
   b. Owners own their own units or space.
   c. Common walls and public areas are owned in common with all of the owners.
   d. The condominium project contains five or more units.

150. The subject property is a ten-unit apartment building. The monthly rent for each unit is $1,000/month. A smaller apartment building sold recently for $480,000 and it had an annual gross income of $60,000. Using this as the only data, one would estimate that the value of the subject property to be approximately
   a. $96,000.
   b. $950,000.
   c. $1,000,000.
   d. $900,000.

▶ **Answers**

1. b. The definition of trust funds is money received by real estate brokers or salespersons on behalf of others.

2. d. *Emblements* are cultivated crops which the tenant can remove, hence they are personal property.

3. a. The lender is considered the mortgagee and the borrower is considered the mortgagor under the mortgage.

4. a. When two or more people come together and agree to do something, this constitutes a contract.

5. d. A normal review of the public records would not include the Department of Real Estate records, since they do not retain records regarding property interests.

6. c. A unilateral contract is simply a promise to perform if someone acts upon the offer. However, the second party may act or not as they choose. However, if the second party does act, then the party making the promise must now perform. For instance, in an option, the owner of a home may accept option money from a prospective buyer to make the property unavailable to anyone, other than the optionee, for a specific period of time. During the period the optionee may or may not exercise the option, at their discretion.

7. c. Before the seller (offeree) accepts an offer, the buyer (offeror) owns the funds, and they must be handled according to the buyer's instructions. After the seller accepts the offer, the funds must be handled according to instructions from both buyer and seller.

8. c. *Fructus naturales* are uncultivated. naturally growing trees or plants and are considered real property.

9. a. An agency relationship most nearly resembles the responsibilities of a trustee to the beneficiary under a Deed of Trust.

10. a. Mortgage bankers work for the actual institutional lender, where as the mortgage broker is an independent loan originator.

11. a. Personal property is made real by meeting all five elements described in the acronym MARIE. The items include the method of attachment, its adaptability to the property, the relationship between the parties (lender/borrower, tenant/landlord, etc), and the intent and agreement between the parties. The price or value of the fixture has nothing to do with its designation as real or personal.

12. b. The California Civil Code contains the laws and requirements regarding agency.

13. c. A title insurance company does not warrantee or guarantee the physical condition of the premises or improvements.

14. d. The 1866 Civil Rights Act prohibits discrimination based on race in all property transactions; the California Civil Code prohibits discrimination in the rental, leasing, or sale of housing accommodations to the blind, visually handicapped, deaf, or otherwise physically disabled; the California Fair Employment and Housing Act prohibits discrimination in the sale, rental or financing of practically all types of housing; the California Fair Employment and Housing Act (Holden Act) particularly prohibits all financial institutions from discriminating in real estate loan approvals based on geographic location, the neighborhood, or any other characteristic of the property.

15. c. When an individual starts a business, he or she generally will start as a sole proprietor, until the business grows, then he or she will look at other business entities.

16. d. A trust deed is used in California to hypothecate or pledge a property as security for a loan.

17. c. Under the Unruh Civil Rights Act, civil action may be brought against persons conducting *business establishments* based upon discrimination regarding sex, color, race, religion, ancestry, or national origin. The exception is mobile home developments.

18. c. This choice is the correct definition of a principal in an agency relationship.

19. c. All of the choices, except *verification*, are ways one can terminate a contract.

20. d. Real property characteristics include the right to sell, the right to exclude, and the right to use.

21. a. It is not necessary to disclose, in advertising, the name of the offeror, time frame, or dollar value of a gift or prize.

22. b. In order for any lender to make money in any market they must loan money out. To be able to remain in the marketplace requires one to become innovative and competitive.

23. b. Real estate law dedicates that all listings must be in writing, including a termination date of said listing agreement.

24. b. The Department of Real Estate requires registration of out-of-state projects in order to monitor the project (Subdivided Lands Law).

25. a. A grant deed does not need to be recorded to be valid. However; it is recommended in order to provide all parties with constructive notice of its existence.

26. **a.** A salesperson is held accountable for results only, not the number of hours it takes to obtain the results.

27. **b.** The implied warranties exist in a grant deed without being explicitly stated or put in writing.

28. **c.** Principal and interest payments are made on a monthly and systemic method, which in turn will pay off the entire debt owed.

29. **c.** In order for any contract to be valid, it must be for a legal purpose.

30. **c.** Condition is a physical characteristic of personal property.

31. **a.** Personal property is transferred by a bill of sales not by a deed.

32. **b.** A novation is the substitution of one agreement for another; all of the other choices are acceptable methods for forming an agency agreement.

33. **a.** All documents used in the brokerage must be kept for a minimum of three years.

34. **a.** The upper portion of the loan is the correct answer, as the insurance allows the lender the ability to recover losses if the borrower defaults. The great majority of loan defaults occur during the first two years of the loan term.

35. **c.** The best evidence, as with all contracts, is by written agreement.

36. **b.** A supervising salesperson must have been working as a licensee for a least two of the past five years and must have a written agreement with the broker with respect to the delegation of responsibility.

37. **a.** The contract is ratified after the seller accepts the terms and conditions of the buyer's offer, and when that acceptance is delivered to the buyer.

38. **c.** The first-time home buyer program, or the community home buyer program, is based on educating the borrower in his or her responsibility of home ownership.

39. **d.** Only the address of the corporate broker or business address need be mentioned when assigned supervision duties of individual licensees.

40. **b.** An ostensible agency is created by the actions or inactions of the principal, which cause a third party to rely on or believe that someone is acting as an agent.

41. **b.** If either party to the contract cannot perform what the contract calls for, then it will be breach, due to non-performance.

42. **d.** Within the secondary market, Fannie Mae is a place where lenders can buy or sell existing mortgage loans.

43. **c.** A deed restriction is a non-monetary encumbrance.

44. **c.** An agent may not gain any advantage over his principal in dealing with their property; so the failure of an agent to present all offers to the principal is presumed to be a violation of law.

45. **c.** An attorney, a builder (or anyone for that matter), may buy and sell without a real estate license. People performing clerical duties are not required to have a real estate license unless they also act as agents performing duties that require a license.

46. **c.** If both parties initialed the deposit receipts liquidated damages clause and the buyer breaches the contract, then the seller may be eligible for some or all of the deposit. The liquidated damages clause limits the amount the seller gets to 3% of the sales price or the deposit, whichever is less. Generally the damages collected are split between the seller and the agent.

47. a. The closing date is considered to be the date that documents are recorded including the grant deed and any trust deeds.

48. d. Mortgages, trust deeds, and real estate sales contracts are voluntary liens.

49. d. A listing agreement containing an option to purchase is first a contract to employ the broker to act as an agent.

50. c. A real estate license is required to negotiate the sale or lease of real property. Only a licensee can accept payment from a principal for performing an act requiring a real estate license.

51. b. An agent does not owe the same level of loyalty as to their principal however an agent does have the duty of honesty and fair dealing.

52. d. Population, the national labor force, and disposable income are demand factors for real estate.

53. a. A person impersonating a broker or salesperson may be fined up to $10,000 or imprisoned up to six months.

54. d. A well-drafted contract will take in all of the choices listed, plus others related to this transaction.

55. d. Adverse possession is a method where title to property is actually acquired. It is not an easement.

56. b. California Civil Code Section 2079 requires the agency disclosure form be presented prior to execution of a listing agreement.

57. b. It is a misdemeanor, punishable by a fine not exceeding one hundred dollars for each offense, for any person, whether obligor, escrow holder or otherwise, to pay or deliver to anyone a compensation for performing any of the acts requiring a real estate license.

58. b. This is an agency designed to offer special mortgage programs, providing the borrower fits within the income and other qualifications needed in order to get the loan.

59. a. The principle of change is the reason for a rezoning.

60. c. The original, conditional salesperson license is issued for eighteen months, during which the licensee must take two additional college-level courses to qualify for a permanent, four-year license. The first, four-year renewal requires only three hours each of ethics, agency, fair housing, and trust funds, with renewal every four years after that being 45 hours of continuing education classes.

61. a. If the buyer cannot perform the contract because of elements outside of their control (medical issues, loss of job, or reduction in workforce), these are examples that allow the buyer to terminate the current contract.

62. b. A limited partnership may not act as an escrow holder because an independent company is required to be licensed by the Department of Corporations.

63. b. Sole or separate ownership can be held by a person, a corporation, an unincorporated entity, or by a government entity (city, county, state).

64. a. California Civil Code Section 2079 requires the agency disclosure form be presented to both buyer and seller as soon as practicable.

65. a. The cost of reproduction plus normal profit follows the law of supply and demand.

66. d. An applicant for a real estate license must show proof of citizenship or of being a legal resident alien, along with a State Public Benefits Statement (RE205).

67. a. One of the three basic rules of agency is that of full disclosure to the principal or client.

68. b. The Recovery Account is a fund of last resort for consumers who have obtained a final judgment against a real estate licensee based on fraud or certain other grounds and who has been unable to satisfy the judgment through the normal post-judgment proceedings.

69. c. This allows a mature person the ability to use their existing equity within their residences to provide monthly income, so they can have quality of life for their remaining years.

70. d. Gaining an interest in the principal's property without prior consent is considered a violation of an agent's fiduciary duty.

71. b. When there is a breach of contract any civil action must be started within a reasonable period of time. The Statute of Limitations sets those time limits. If legal action is not taken within the stated time period then the right to sue is lost.

72. d. Time, title, and interest and possession are required for a joint tenancy to exist.

73. b. A portion of license fees are used to fund the Recovery Account.

74. c. The government fiscal policy is concerned with spending and taxation.

75. a. The last executed document in a transaction is usually the escrow instructions and will normally be used to supplement the original sales agreement to determine the intentions of the parties to the contract.

76. a. Dual agency, or representing all parties to a transaction, is not a violation of real estate law, but failure to disclose dual agency in all cases is a violation of real estate law.

77. b. As long as the seller gives the broker her prior consent there is no prohibition on accepting a trust deed in exchange for the commission.

78. b. A lender will send monthly invoices and expect payment to be made according the terms of the promissory note. This is considered to be servicing the loan.

79. a. The rights of survivorship are allowed under a joint tenancy interest. It is not allowed in a tenancy in common interest.

80. c. Handwriting on a printed or typed contract will always take precedence. As a rule of thumb, if something is handwritten over, the parties place their initials next to the entry.

81. b. All offers must be presented to the seller.

82. c. Under the terms and conditions of the deed of trust, the trustee will hold the bare legal title to the property in which they are considered a neutral third party.

83. c. Records copied and stored as optical image files must be retained for three years, the same as other broker's records.

84. c. The optical image storage shall be non-erasable, "write once, read many" (WORM), that does not allow changes to the stored document or record.

85. d. Disposable income is the income available after personal taxes are assessed.

86. a. A section is 640 acres. The NW $\frac{1}{4}$ of that section is 160 acres. The NW $\frac{1}{4}$ of 160 acres is 40 acres.

87. c. Endorsement is the execution of an agreement; all of the other choices are methods for terminating an agency relationship.

88. a. If the landlord will not repair items that are necessary for the safety or welfare of the tenant, the tenant may make the repairs. The tenant may spend up to one month's rent. The tenant cannot exceed one month's rent for repairs. Repairs may be made only twice in a consecutive twelve month period.

89. b. A landlord must use due process when dealing with a tenant and may not shut off utilities, lock the tenant out, take the tenants property, remove doors and windows, or trespass.

90. a. The more money borrowed in relation to the value of the property, the greater the leverage.

91. b. A section measures one mile by one mile, which contains 640 acres.

92. a. Most government loans are restricted in the amount a lender or a mortgage broker can charge in points or loan origination fee. This is 1%.

93. c. Gross income is the total of rents, laundry room income, parking fees, garage rental fees, or any other source of income produced by the property.

94. c. In order for any minor to be treated as an adult, which includes entering into valid contracts, he or she has to have a court order appointing him or her as an adult. This process is called *emancipation*.

95. c. If more than one broker is acting as an agent to a transaction, the broker that obtained the offer is responsible for delivering the inspection report to the buyer.

96. d. The assessor's parcel number is not a formal method of legal description.

97. d. If an owner wants to move a mobile home after it has become real property, anyone who has an interest in it must approve, and thirty days before moving it the owner must notify the Department of Housing and Community Development (HCD) as well as the local tax assessor.

98. b. The Law of Agency gives the principal the right to terminate the listing agreement at any time.

99. d. Sales tax is collected as a percentage of the retail sales of a product by a retailer. The owner of a retail business may obtain a seller's permit, which allows him or her to buy the product at wholesale prices without paying sales tax. The retailer must then collect the proper sales tax from customers and pay it to the State Board of Equalization. A copy of the seller's permit and a clearance receipt, stating that the business is current on sales taxes, from the State Board of Equalization, should be requested by a buyer before assuming the ownership of a business.

100. b. A buyer must receive all of the choices except a policy of title insurance from the seller.

101. b. The sale of a property against the will of the owner because of default on a loan is exempt from Transfer Disclosure Statement requirements.

102. c. The entity involved in the eminent domain action will have to pay the property owner "severance damage" for any devaluation of the remaining property not taken in this action.

103. a. A dedication is the conveyance of land for public use under statutory or common law.

104. a. The Transfer Disclosure Statement discloses any information that would be important to the buyer regarding the condition of the property.

105. a. VA will guarantee to the lender making the loan that if the veteran defaults in this transaction, then the VA will provide monies to insure that the lender become whole again.

106. a. The Natural Hazard Disclosure Statement allows a rescission period of three days if the disclosures are hand-delivered, or five days if the disclosures are sent by mail.

107. a. The boot is the amount received to balance the equities in the exchange.

108. c. It is in the seller's and listing agent's interest to disclose early because the buyer can rescind the purchase contract during a certain period after getting the information.

109. c. The term *void* means that the contract never existed.

110. b. Utility value is termed *subjective value* and includes valuation of amenities which attach to a property, or a determination of value for a specific purpose or person.

111. d. Insulation requirements fall under building codes.

112. d. In California, the recovery of commissions would fall under the jurisdiction of the Civil Court through the filing of a lawsuit.

113. d. The deduction for wear and tear on investment property is known as *depreciation* and may only be calculated on the improvements since the land does not depreciate or wear out.

114. c. The property is 100% of value and when discount fees are considered, then this is subtracted from the whole amount, which means 100 minus 10 will equal 90.

115. c. Non-conforming uses result when an established use on one lot conflicts with a new zoning classification. The local government may permit the use to continue, indefinitely, for a limited period of time or impose other restrictions.

116. c. The contract calls for the property to be transferred in ownership. If the property is no longer there or is damaged, then the contract cannot be performed as required in order to be valid.

117. d. Visibility from the street would be most important for a retail building.

118. a. Encroachments would be detected by a surveyor.

119. d. Existing mortgages are bought and sold within this environment, so that money is always moving in a circular motion.

120. c. Both parties can agree to cancel a contract through the process of recission. If the listing agent did his or her job, then even though the contract has been canceled, the seller may still be required to pay the commission as agreed upon.

121. d. There are only four elements of value, all of which are essential. These are *utility*, *scarcity*, *demand*, and *transferability*. None alone will create value.

122. b. Agreements may be written or oral for the division of commissions and are not illegal or considered against public policy.

123. b. The beneficiary is the lender and would instruct the trustee to commence default proceedings upon non-payment of the debt by the trustor.

124. d. Public access to the coast, the coastal zone, and the marine environment are covered on the California Coastal Zone Conservation Act.

125. c. The Department of Banking is the agency which tracks mortgage loan originations to ensure that fairness of lending is adhered to.

126. c. Prohibition against "For Sale" signs would be unreasonable since they restrain alienation (conveyance).

127. b. Book value is the acquisition price less depreciation that has been taken. The other value terms are closely related to market value.

128. a. A comparable sale is one that a potential buyer of subject property would consider.

129. d. The money that clients place into their financial institutions is insured up to $100,000 per account. This falls under the FDIC.

130. d. CC&Rs cannot be removed by the grantee. They can be removed only by agreement of all those who have the right to enforce them (i.e. the other owners in the subdivision).

131. b. An open listing is much like a unilateral contract. In the open listing, the seller promises to pay the broker if the broker procures a ready, willing, and able buyer. The broker, however, is not obligated to the seller in any way to perform. However, if the broker does find a buyer and presents an offer, the broker has accepted the seller's offer to contract. Under a bilateral contract the seller promises to pay a commission for the broker's promise to use diligence in finding a buyer. In a unilateral contract, the seller promises to pay a commission as long as the broker acts (there is no promise of diligence on the part of the broker).

132. b. Appropriation is the taking, impounding, or diverting of flowing water on public domain from its natural course for some personal and exclusive use.

133. d. In order to improve the reliability of the information about a sale, the appraiser should make at least an exterior inspection, identify changes made since the sales date, and verify the price and terms of sale.

134. b. Acceptance of the property's condition is a contract provision, subject to inspections conducted at the buyer's expense and the buyer must communicate disapproval within a stated period of time. If the seller refuses to correct the items, the buyer must either proceed with the transaction or cancel the contract.

135. a. One should subtract 10% from the comparable's sale price since the comparable sale has a superior location.

136. c. Real Property Loan Law exists for the sole purpose to protect the consumer from loan brokers who are not following industry laws.

137. b. The site value is 60% of the sales price of $180,000 = (60% × 180,000) = $108,000. Hence the improvement has a value of $72,000.

138. d. Riparian rights are the rights to water touching land and flowing in a fixed or defined channel such as a river, stream, or watercourse.

139. c. This sale has the smallest net adjustment (0) and the least gross adjustment (10).

140. c. Under California Civil Code, Section 2941, the lender must forward a deed of reconveyance within 90 days of receiving the request from the trustee.

141. d. The Subdivision Map Act does not apply to time shares, undivided interests, and to whole parcels of less than five acres where each new parcel to be created in the division will abut to a publicly maintained road.

142. d. The cost in 2004 is the cost in 1990 times the ratio of the $\frac{(2004 \text{ cost index})}{(1990 \text{ cost index})}$; $240,000 $\times \frac{(1.8)}{(1.2)}$ = $360,000.

143. b. The building department of a city would have records showing restrictions in certain neighborhoods.

144. b. The value of property is calculated by $V = \frac{I}{R}$.

145. a. The estimated depreciation would be the effective age divided by the life expectancy ($\frac{10}{50} = 0.2 = 20\%$).

146. d. Debt service (interest plus principal payment on a loan) is not considered in the determination of the NOI.

147. c. This disclosure allows the borrower to see an estimate of the closing costs, so that he/she will have the opportunity to shop around to get the best deal possible.

148. c. Remember $V = \frac{I}{R}$. At a 5% capitalization rate, the property has an $I = V \times R = \$400,000 \times (0.05) = \$20,000$. Using an 8% return indicates a sale price $= V = \frac{I}{R} = \frac{\$20,000}{(0.08)} = \$250,000$.

149. a. An owner cannot be held liable for injury that occurs in the common area if the condominium association carries liability insurance is greater than or equal to the statutory amount.

150. b. The comparable sales had a gross income multiplier (GIM) of 8 ($480,000/60,000). The gross annual income of the subject property is $120,000 (10 × $1,000/month × 12). The value $V = $ GIM × GAI $= 8 \times \$120,000 = \$960,000$. The closest choice is $950,000.

Scoring

Once again, in order to evaluate how you did on this last practice exam, find the number of questions you answered correctly. The passing score for this practice exam is 105 correct answers (70%), but just as on the real test, you should be aiming for something higher than that on these practice exams. If you haven't reached a passing score on both sections, look at the suggestions for improvement at the end of Chapter 8. Take a look at the table on the following page to see what problem areas remain.

The key to success in almost any pursuit is complete preparation. By taking the practice exams in this book, you have prepared more than many other people who may be taking the exam with you. You have diagnosed where your strengths and weaknesses lie and learned how to deal with the various kinds of questions that will appear on the test. So go into the exam with confidence, knowing that you are ready and equipped to do your best.

EXAM 4 FOR REVIEW

Subject Area	Question Numbers
Property Ownership	2, 8, 11, 20, 30, 31, 43, 48, 55, 63, 72, 79, 86, 91, 102, 103, 111, 115, 118, 124, 126, 130, 132, 138, 141, 149
Laws of Agency	9, 12, 18, 32, 35, 40, 44, 49, 51, 56, 64, 67, 70, 77, 87, 98, 112, 122
Valuation and Market Analysis	52, 59, 65, 74, 85, 117, 127, 128, 133, 135, 137, 139, 142, 144, 145, 146, 148, 150
Financing	3, 10, 22, 28, 34, 38, 42, 58, 69, 78, 82, 92, 105, 114, 119, 125, 129, 136, 147
Transfer of Property	5, 13, 16, 25, 27, 47, 62, 75, 95, 100, 107, 113, 123, 140
Practice of Real Estate and Mandatory Disclosures	1, 7, 14, 17, 21, 24, 26, 33, 36, 39, 45, 50, 53, 57, 60, 66, 68, 73, 76, 81, 83, 84, 88, 89, 90, 93, 97, 99, 101, 104, 106, 108, 110, 121, 134, 143
Contracts	4, 6, 15, 19, 23, 29, 37, 41, 46, 54, 61, 71, 80, 94, 109, 116, 120, 131

How to Use the CD-ROM

SO YOU THINK you are ready for your exam? Here's a great way to build confidence and *know* you are ready: using LearningExpress's Real Estate Licensing Tester AutoExam CD-ROM software developed by PEARSoft Corporation of Wellesley, Massachusetts. The disk, included inside the back cover of this book, can be used with any PC running Windows 95/98/ME/NT/2000/XP. (Sorry, it doesn't work with Macintosh.) The following description represents a typical "walk through" the software.

To install the program:

1. Insert the CD-ROM into your CD-ROM drive. The CD should run automatically. If it does not, proceed to Step 2.
2. From Windows, select **Start**, then choose **Run**.
3. Type D:\Setup
4. Click **OK**.

The screens that follow will walk you through the installation procedure.

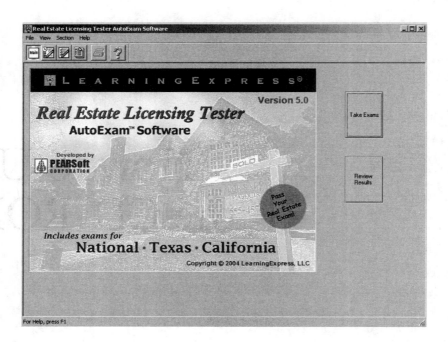

From the Main Menu, select **Take Exams**. (After you have taken at least one exam, use **Review Exam Results** to see your scores.)

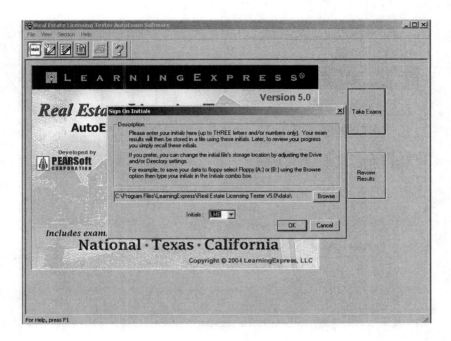

Now enter your initials. This allows you to record your progress and review your performance for as many simulated exams as you would like. Notice that you can also change the drive and/or folder where your exam results are stored. If you want to save to a floppy drive, for instance, click on the "Browse" button and then choose the letter of your floppy drive.

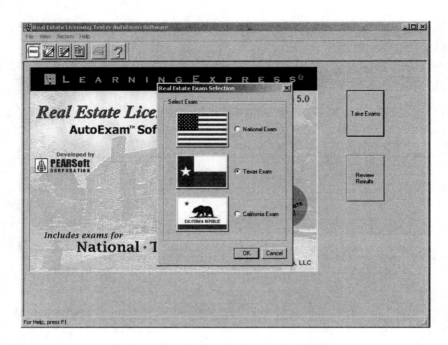

Now, since this CD-ROM supports three different real estate exams, you need to select your exam of interest. Let's try Texas, as shown above.

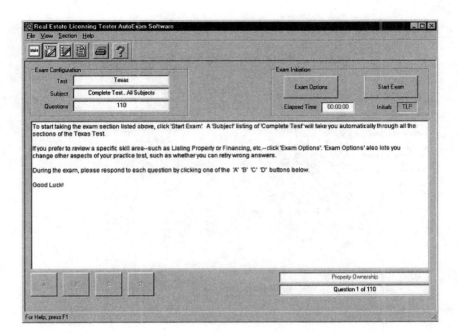

Now you are into the **Take Exams** section, as shown above. You can choose **Start Exam** to start taking your test, or **Exam Options**. The next screenshot shows you what your **Exam Options** are.

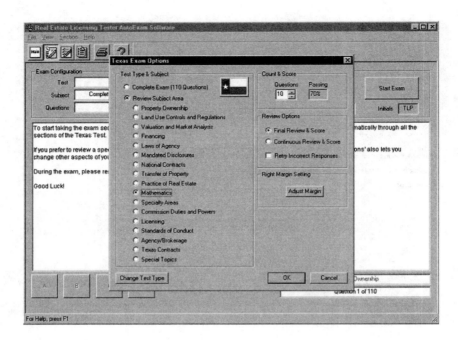

Choosing **Exam Options** gives you plenty of options to help you fine-tune your rough spots. How about a little math to warm up? Click **Review Subject Area**, and then the **Mathematics** option. Choose the number of questions you want to review right now. On the right you can choose whether to wait until you have finished to see how you did (**Final Review & Score**) or have the computer tell you after each questions whether your answer is right (**Continuous Review and Score**). Choose **Retry Incorrect Responses** to get a second chance at questions you answer wrong. (This option works best with **Review Subject Area** rather than **Complete Test**.) If you have chosen the wrong exam, you can click **Change Test Type** to go back and choose your exam. When you finish choosing your options, click **OK**. Then click the **Start Exam** button on the main exam screen. Your screen will look like the one shown next.

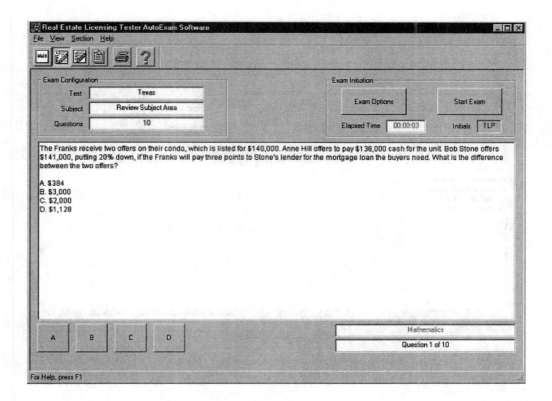

Questions come up one at a time, just as they will on the real exam, and you click on A, B, C, or D to answer.

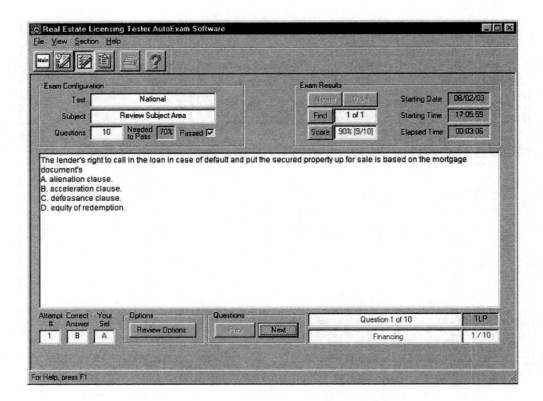

When you have finished your exam or subject area, you will have the option of switching to **Review Exams.** (If you don't want to review your results now, you can always do it later by clicking on the **Review Exams Section** button on the toolbar.) When you use **Review Results,** you will see your score and whether you passed. The questions come up one at a time. Under **Review Options,** you can choose whether to look at all the questions or just the ones you missed. You can also choose whether you want an explanation of the correct answer displayed automatically under the question.

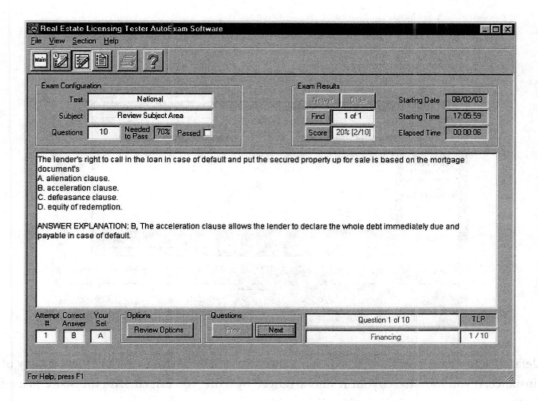

When you are in the **Review Results** section, click on the **Find** button to look at all the exams you have taken.

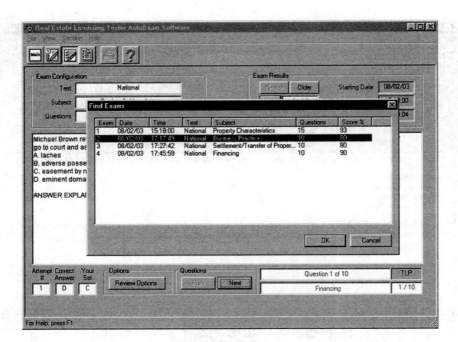

By default, your exam results are listed from newest to oldest, but you can sort them by any of the headings. For instance, if you want to see your results arranged by score, you can click on the **Score %** heading. To go to a particular exam you have taken, double click on it.

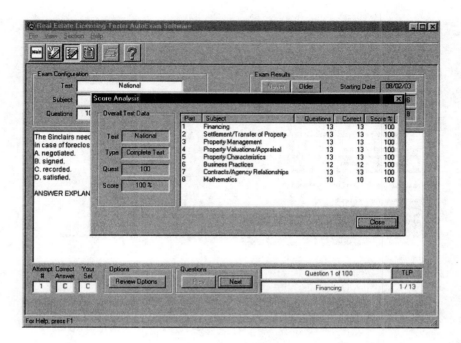

In the **Review Results** section, if you click on the **Score %** button, you will get a breakdown of your score on the exam you're currently reviewing. This section shows you how you did on each of the subject areas on the exam. Once again, you can sort the subject areas by any of the column headings. For instance, if you click on the **Score %** heading, the program will order the subject areas from your highest percentage score to your lowest. You can see which areas are your strong and weak points, so you will know what to review.

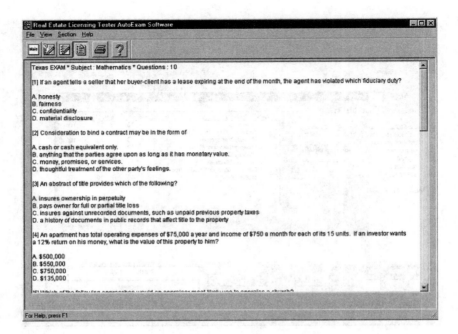

What's that? No time to work at the computer? Click the **Print Exams** menu bar button and you will have a full-screen review of an exam that you can print out, as shown above. Then take it with you.

For technical support, call 212-995-2566.

NOTES

NOTES

NOTES

NOTES

NOTES

NOTES